Michael Moorcock

VOYAGE OF DISCOVERIES

VOYAGE OF DISCOVERIES

by

JAMES PARKES
(JOHN HADHAM)

LONDON
VICTOR GOLLANCZ LTD
1969

575 00203 4

PRINTED IN GREAT BRITAIN
BY EBENEZER BAYLIS AND SON, LTD.
THE TRINITY PRESS, WORCESTER, AND LONDON

To
Dorothy
a Silver Wedding
Present

TABLE OF CONTENTS

BOYHOOD IN GUERNSEY

IN THE CENTRE of the island of Guernsey is the parish of St. Andrew. At its eastern end is the Manor of Rohais. My father was the falconer of the Manor, and I was born at Les Fauconnaires in December 1896. In actual fact, my father was an Englishman and a civil engineer, who had come to Guernsey to grow tomatoes and melons. But then, so had the Seigneur de Rohais. For the feudal system still covered the island, so that the one had become Lord of an ancient Manor, and the other his falconer. In principle Mr. Bainbrigge could ring us up and tell us he was going hawking that afternoon, and request us to provide the falcons. But we would undoubtedly have gone down on our knees at the front gate and raised the *Clameur de Haro*, did he come with his feudal levy to expel us from our farm for failing in our feudal obligations.

The pre-tourist Guernsey of my boyhood was a most gorgeous place in which to be young. Because we had a very rigid system of compulsory games at Elizabeth College, and I was much too frequently ill to fit into it, I was free to explore the island in my spare time, and I knew almost every field in it. I explored every cliff path and bay, every rock and cranny in its long coast line, knew it in summer calm and winter storm, revelled in all the colours of sea and land, discovered all its flowers, was familiar with all its butterflies, was passionately devoted to its fascinating and amusing history, and immensely admired the adventurous and pioneering spirit of the islanders. My one complaint against life was that I was not of full Guernsey descent. On the other hand, I had links with all the islands. My grandfather had built the naval harbour at Alderney—he was not responsible for its asinine design: that was forced on him by the Admiralty. My great-grandmother had for some time lived at Trinity Manor, Jersey; and two of my great-great-great aunts had lived in St. Peter Port during the Napoleonic war. I was the middle one of three children. David was eighteen months older than I; Molly was equally younger. Both were killed in the first war. We were a very united family, and I do not remember any serious quarrels. My mother died when I was a boy, after a long illness which left my father very poor.

He then took a courageous decision. In those days gentry always had at least one resident servant. My father had three children at school. He had a small inherited income and he decided that, rather than keep up public appearances and scrape for every penny behind the scenes, he would be comfortable. So, at the age of fifty, he learned cooking and housework, and we lived from then on without any outside help. He became a very good cook, but Molly and I used secretly to supplement his housework while he was doing the shopping. I did the garden, and David kept hens and provided all the eggs we needed, as well as selling some to neighbours. I was the financier of the three of us, for I used to supervise the prep. of the sons of a neighbour who also grew tomatoes. I worked for two hours six nights a week for half-a-crown a week. When I got a job six miles away teaching one man Latin for a shilling an hour, it seemed fabulous wealth. I also earned quite an amount as a book-binder. When it came to needing cash to spend, however, we all regarded what each had as part of a common fund. David might extract five shillings from me when he needed it one week, but I might just as well obtain help from Mollie when I needed it. These were not loans to be repaid, and we were so unpolitically minded that it never occurred to us we were practising communists!

As tomato growing at that time was in the doldrums, my father sold Les Fauconnaires, bought back a corner of one field (which we freed from all feudal obligations at considerable cost), and built a bungalow on it. It was on the top of a hill, very sunny and exposed to all the winds that blew. The most interesting thing about the bungalow—now burned down—is that it was haunted almost from the year we built it, though none of us had ever met a ghost in the old house where we could have been excused for finding one, since it was very ancient and very gloomy. Facing north, it was overshadowed by huge ilex trees and surrounded by ancient outbuildings. Its dry granite walls were nearly three feet thick, and during the winter we lay in bed listening to the rats collecting apples from the loft and rolling them bump, bump, down through the dry walls. The curious story of the haunting follows this chapter; here I would only say that ghosts and witchcraft were normal accompaniments of life in the Channel Islands.

There certainly were witches in the island, some of considerable power. It became amusing when they encountered modern law courts, either because they were frauds, or because they did something which could be tried in English. I remember one of the first kind appearing unexpectedly in the police court, before a magistrate who was new to the island background. He was gaily hearing evidence of illegal activities of which an old lady had certainly been guilty, when a jurat, who had come into the court on another case, spotted what was happening. He hastily sent the magistrate a note reminding him that the only statute dealing with witchcraft was that of Elizabeth I, and asking him whether he intended to have the old lady burned! The magistrate wisely adjourned for lunch.

The other case was extraordinary. Farmer A had bewitched the cattle of farmer B. He had then written threatening letters telling farmer B what he would do next. Farmer B felt that writing threatening letters was something that could be tried in English, so he sued farmer A. But neither was really interested in the letters. They were concerned with the witchcraft which could only be discussed and explained in *patois*—and the case was tried before a Bailiff who was indeed an islander, but did not know the *patois*.

At one point the Bailiff was trying to estimate the extent to which the plaintiff had been frightened.

"What did you feel like when you received the letters?" asked the Bailiff.

"I was troublesome."

"What do you mean by troublesome?"

"I was afraid of the wicked men in my house."

"But how many people were there in your house beside your family?"

"How was I to know?"

Good. Now we translate the key words into *patois*: 'trouble-some' is the English cover word for *ensorcellé*—bewitched; 'wicked men' is the cover word for *mauvais gens*—evil spirits. And how could the poor man tell how many evil spirits were infesting his house and tormenting and terrifying his cattle, as they certainly *were* doing? Like the magistrate, at this point the Bailiff wisely adjourned for lunch, where someone could explain to him what it was all about.

While my mother was alive we always spent three weeks of August in a cottage, first at Rocquaine, then at Vazon. We used to descend on the cottage with a van full of beds, tin baths, cooking pots and what not, while its regular occupants gave over to us their great canopied bed, their kitchen and their parlour. From the contemporary point of view, the amazing thing is that, during the three weeks involved, we regarded these now tumultuous bays as our private property, and hardly ever saw a stranger 'trespassing' in them. It was a wonderful time for us children; the farms, the fishermen, the little shops, and the French *patois* which all the country people then spoke, were as enchanting as the lovely bays, the rock pools and their varied life. Shrimp teas from our own nets, fish that had been caught by one of our fishermen friends the night before, and a three pound pot of apricot jam, were special treats associated with those joyful days.

My father was very skilful in building model yachts, and we all had one rigged to our choice. What's more, their steering could be so carefully adjusted that we could sail them right across the bay, or on a circular course half a mile out to sea. My father continued making model yachts until he was nearly eighty; and there came to be so many of them that there was a special class of 'Mr. Parkes' yachts' in the model yacht club races. He also built two boats—a smaller one called 'the punt' which was simply a box 7' 6" long, 21" wide and 9" deep with a sloping end in front; and a larger one rather like a contemporary dinghy. My sister and I used the small one, and we used to go right out to sea in it. I don't know why we were not drowned, considering the idiotic things we did. But my father, probably wisely, never told us how dangerous our antics were.

One year, I suppose when I was about twelve, I had been

more frequently ill than usual, so I missed a whole term, and was sent to spend the summer in Sark. I stayed with two delightful old ladies, Laura and Pattie Hale, at the head of Dixcart Valley. It was in the days of the old Seigneur who was, to put it very mildly, extremely eccentric. The year I was there the most surprising thing about the island was that every window sill on the ground floor was painted a brilliant yellow. There were granite houses and brick houses, stucco houses painted pink or white or blue, and wooden houses; but all alike had their downstairs window sills the same staring yellow. I naturally asked "Why?" "The Seigneur" was the answer.

Apparently an Englishman had bought a *quarantaine*—one of the forty farms into which Sark is divided—and had disputed the seigneurial rights with regard to the purchase. After careful consideration as to how he could impress the pestilent Englishman with the fact that he was the Seigneur, he had gone over to Guernsey, bought an immense pot of yellow paint, and walked round the island, his duck gun as usual under his arm, and had painted every window sill he could reach, daring anyone to stop him.

Sark was an island of passionate feuds, the two parties being usually led by the Seigneur and the Vicar. The Hales were staunch supporters of the former, and the latter led, I think, a rather difficult life. Like some of the Guernsey country clergy in those days, he was a French-speaking Calvinist who had accepted episcopal ordination; for many services were still in French, and this was the easiest way to provide them. It led at times to unexpected consequences. There was an occasion when the new Rector of Torteval was asked to preach in English at St. Peter's in the Wood. He explained that he could do so with a French manuscript before him, as he could not preach *ex tempore* in English. He mounted the pulpit and gave out the text: "The Ghost truly is wishful, but the meat is poorly." I hope the rest of the sermon kept up the standard!

Holidays on the bays ceased after my mother's death. She was deeply religious, and yet had a very independent mind. Though I was young when she died, she left a powerful influence on me, and I owed an enormous amount both to her regular lessons on Sundays and to her remarks at odd moments.

I was very fortunate after her death in that a friend of hers, Christine Ozanne, daughter of the Rector of St. Martin's, spotted me looking miserable at a party—I loathed parties— and invited me to the Rectory. I think that from that time onwards I spent as much time at St. Martin's Rectory as I did at home; and I certainly had many more serious discussions of everything under the sun there than I ever did with my father. It was not that there was enmity between my father and myself; but he was much more interested in my brother and sister, who played games, did not constantly go to bed with appalling headaches, did not write poetry or know where every flower that grew in the island was to be found.

My schooling began at a Dame School kept by several Miss Robins, but after a year I went to the Lower School of Elizabeth College. I left eleven years later as Senior Prefect. Elizabeth College was in an increasingly sorry state during those eleven years. The Headmaster, William Campbell Penney, had once been a brilliant pioneer; but he had stayed much too long, become much too lazy, and ended up as a complete hypochondriac, convinced he could not climb the vast flights of stairs in that pompous castellated building of 1826 which still dominates St. Peter Port. My first form master was Mr. Goodman, with whom I kept a lasting friendship, since he was an inveterate collector, and I spent many out-of-school hours arranging and classifying his varied collections.

We were horrible little snobs in the Elizabeth College of those days. We represented very much the English element on the island, as well as a few old Guernsey families, the Careys, De L'Isles, Ozannes, Doreys, and so on, but despised any unfortunate boy who spoke English with a good Guernsey accent —always exemplified by the solecism of asking "Where's he to?" instead of "Where is he?" Guernsey English is as quaint at times as Guernsey *patois*. I remember a little redhead standing on a ruined wall in the Cornet Street slum of St. Peter Port and screaming after her fleeing enemy: "I will smack her to the head, him."

The College was an interesting foundation. Its foundress was Elizabeth I, and its purpose was to educate Channel Islanders in English and in Anglican ways, lest they be sub-

verted by continental Protestantism. It was rich in scholarships
to Oxford, dating from the seventeenth century and devoted
to the same purpose. They had a special importance in that
our secular rulers had to go to Caen to study, since English
law did not apply in the islands. The College had decayed;
many of its endowments had been gently absorbed by island
families; and it had been refounded in a very advanced and
pioneering fashion by an intelligent Governor in 1826, with the
support of annual public grants from the States, but with the
status of an English Public School. Its most remarkable possession was an amazing library, rich in first editions, lovely
bindings, and a unique Erasmus. Happily they just survived
the German occupation from 1940 to 1944. One other master
with whom I formed a lasting friendship was the history master,
William Rolleston, who discovered me one Easter holiday
solemnly dusting and cleaning books, and repairing broken
bindings. He joined me, and between us we cleaned and
catalogued the whole library.

I was the last boy to receive a full Victorian education in the
classics. From the age of thirteen I had only one period a week
each of English, Scripture, Essay and History. The whole of the
rest of the week was spent in learning Latin and Greek, both of
which languages I had, of course, begun well before I was
thirteen. When I left I could write Latin and Greek as fluently
as I could English, and I could produce a beautiful example of
quite a selection of different styles. My favourites were either
Cicero's letters or Tacitus. I remember the moments when the
two languages came alive to me as vividly as a Salvationist
remembers the moment of his conversion. I was reading Cicero's
De Deorum Natura when I suddenly noticed that the Latin words
no longer represented to me their English equivalents. I was
thinking about them in Latin, turning them over in my mind in
Latin. The effect was that I became for some weeks entirely
unable to translate. If I was asked to do so, I began to give a
resumé or analysis of the passage in Latin. In Greek the same
thing happened during the reading of Aeschylus's *Prometheus
Vinctus*. Alas, neither talent survived four years of war, and an
Oxford where I was rarely fit enough to do a full day's work.

Had you asked me in 1913 to say Boo! to a goose, I think I

would have been uncertain of my ability to do so. In any case, I would have preferred not to. I was extremely shy, thoroughly timid, played no games, though I was (fortunately as it turned out) an inoffensive lance-corporal in the O.T.C., and I was a complete little 'swot'. Had you made the request in 1915, I would have had no difficulty in making the goose perfectly aware of my intentions, and perfectly amenable to them, without having to take the trouble to say Boo!

The reason for the change is that, when the school reassembled in September 1914, I found myself the Senior Prefect, because all the older boys had left to join the army. The period which followed up to December 1915, when I myself left, was unquestionably the most formative in my life.

I became Senior Prefect of a School visibly disintegrating under a thoroughly lazy and hypochondriacal Headmaster. He disliked me, and made no secret of it, because I did not play games. I loathed him and made no secret of my contempt for him. Many of the masters as well as the older boys had left to join the Forces, and we had a curious staff. The prefects were young and inexperienced, and, on the whole, timid in exercising their authority. I felt that everything depended on me. I was serious as only an adolescent can be, and determined that I would uphold all the standards of Kipling's *If*. My classical and literary scholarship came to my aid, and I modelled myself on all the forgotten heroes of literature and antiquity. Taking as my mottoes two Latin tags, *Oderint dum metuant*—let them hate me so long as they fear me—and *populus vult decipi, decipiatur*—the vulgar like to be deceived, deceive them—I sailed into battle with a stern front and a panic inside I was determined not to show.

Then it was that my one stable foundation of authority was the knowledge of the island I had gained when my compeers were spending their time on the playing field. The O.T.C. came to be the most important out-of-class activity, and in the O.T.C. scouting, signalling and manoeuvres came to be much more important than drill. I became the senior sergeant in the Corps, and I never lost a field day. My scouts and signallers were mostly country boys like myself. We could throw a network of intelligence over the island which could watch unseen the slightest movement of 'the enemy' by day or night. A dozen of us could ambush a battalion and then scatter unseen, to reassemble a mile away. If war could be conducted with umpires and dummies, it would be the most entrancing activity! Even when I was most unpopular in the school, I could still get as many volunteers as I wanted for any field day.

I did go through a period of violent unpopularity, and I was determined to make no concession to make myself more popular. I refused to overlook any breach of discipline. My punishments were severe. I was unapproachable. This latter was, in fact, because I constantly had such splitting headaches that I could hardly see; but I cultivated an attitude of remoteness. It all sounds very exaggerated now, and rather like a Desmond Coke story or *Stalky and Co.*—and indeed there were incidents that could have come straight out of one of those classics—but I doubt if I was wrong to believe that such discipline as was maintained in the school depended much more on me than it did on the Headmaster.

I had two friends on whom I could depend absolutely, Archie Campbell, now a Canon of the Episcopal Church of Scotland, and William Spiller, of whom I have lost sight. Both were good athletes and much more popular than I was. They constituted a body-guard when I needed one, not because I might be attacked, but because I had to have quiet when I had a splitting headache. Though none of us had ever heard of the word telepathy, we used to meet where we wanted, and when we wanted, and took it as perfectly natural that we should do so. In fact, I do not remember that we ever commented on the fact that it was very convenient that we did not have to fix up appointments with each other.

I spent the first term establishing the fact that, when I gave an order, it had to be obeyed. The crisis in that department came at our first O.T.C. camp. Two boys—privates so far as the corps was concerned, but both in the sixth form—deliberately and flagrantly disobeyed some order I had given. They were both considerably larger than I was. I sent for them. They came, full of bounce. I asked them whether they knew I had given an order, and had said that any boy who disobeyed it would be beaten? They replied that as they were also sixth formers they were uninterested in my orders, and that, anyhow, I could not beat a sixth former. Hoping that they did not see that my knees were shaking, I told them to follow me, took them to my room, and gave each of them a sound beating. I think they were more surprised that I did it, than I was that they took it from me. Anyhow, it solved the problem of my orders being obeyed, and the camp viewed me with a kind of mystic awe—but without any increase of affection! Henceforth if they *oderint*, there was less question that they *metuant*.

All this time I was also working with a scholarship in view; and I did not intend to collect a Channel Island scholarship, which would have been quite easy. In fact there were often more scholarships than candidates. David had collected one the previous year; but I intended to try for an Open one, and I wanted to get one at Hertford College. This was not only because it was one of the best to be got—it was £100 a year for four years—but because Mr. Penney was always boasting that he was a scholar of Hertford College. It was foolish of him to deny that I had brains; for it would have been more sensible to have told me that brains were not everything. But, as he did deny it, I intended to place him before the dilemma of either stopping to boast of his Open Scholarship, or of admitting my intelligence.

When he reminded me in the spring of 1915 that it was time to enter my name for a Channel Island Scholarship, and I told him that I was going for an Open one, he was so furious that he tried to persuade my father to refuse to allow me to do so. Knowing we were poor, he used the argument that it would be a wicked waste of money for me to go and sit for a scholarship in Oxford. When my father would not agree, he went so far as to refuse to allow the classics master, Mr. E. W. Hickie, to teach me either Latin or Greek verses, which Mr. Hickie had rightly said were essential for a candidate for an open classical scholarship to an Oxford or Cambridge College. Hickie at that time was perfectly aware of the relations between me and Penney, and came to me white with rage from his interview with the Headmaster. He asked me to come to him in the evenings twice a week to do verse, as the Headmaster had absolutely forbidden him to teach me verses in time the School paid for.

Life really was uncomfortably like an improbable school story!

Actually, I duly got the scholarship—thanks to Hickie's excellent tuition—and Penney did not even say or write a single word of congratulation, though it was the first Open Scholarship the school had collected for twenty-five years. When my marriage was recorded in *The Times* in 1942 I received a letter from an octogenarian Penney telling me he felt it was time the hatchet was buried, and sending us his good wishes. Naturally I accepted the peace offering. In fact, though I am sure it was not his intention, his hostility probably did more to allow my character to develop than his friendship would have done. But I think the cost was excessive. For in the middle of 1915 I had a serious collapse. Hickie had set me a Greek prose of scholarship level as a test. Five minutes after he had given it me, I walked up to him and asked him what I was supposed to do with it. He looked somewhat astonished, and said: "Turn it into Greek." I looked blankly at him and said: "What is Greek?" He quickly realised I was not trying to be impertinent, and told me not to worry, but to take a few days off and go home. But, what was very wise of him, he then went straight to the telephone and told Christine Ozanne what had happened; for I think he rightly guessed that my father would have had no idea what to do.

Guernsey is a small island, where everyone knows all about everyone else, and, fortunately, it had already been established that I spent so much time at St. Martin's because I was a cousin of the Ozanne's. In fact I always called Christine Ozanne 'Cousin'. So she could sail in and collect me with my father's willing agreement. She then borrowed a lovely old farmhouse above Petit Bot, installed herself in it, and put me to bed. My memory of what followed is a little vague, and I think I had quite a long time before I was able to get up again; but I spent a very happy convalescence on the cliffs and in the lovely garden of the farm. It belonged to the Baronne de Coudenhove, who, as Elsie Henderson, was a noted painter of animals. She was also the victim of my earliest recorded remark. At a party, earlier than that at which I was rescued by the Cousin, I was being bullied by a damsel of eight or nine. The

Baronne, then about seventeen, rescued me, whereon I told her confidentially that I thought the girls of the last generation were much nicer than the girls of this one! Fair, fat and fifty, the Baronne told me of her indignation at seventeen at being thought one of the girls of the last generation. However, she rescued me!

Recovered, I had to go back to the battle. By that time I was in control of the situation so far as life outside the class rooms was concerned. But I had the very difficult problem that 4B were making life hell for their temporary master, that they were spreading license throughout the school, and that I had absolutely no authority to punish them for their behaviour in class. Their form room was high up in the building and never visited by the headmaster. However, I saw a way round the difficulty. 4B were so thoroughly *exalté* that they felt it was their right to make life intolerable for everybody, and I warned them that I would not have them cheeking and disobeying me and the prefects. When they continued their evil ways, I solemnly summoned the whole form before the sixth, and gave them a week to reform their ways—which of course they didn't. The matter then developed in the best traditions of *Stalky and Co.* Two junior prefects, born Tribunes of the Plebs, announced that I was a tyrant (which I was) and sided with 4B. When the week elapsed with no sign of reformation from 4B, I called another prefects' meeting, told 4B that I would no longer tolerate their evil ways, and the Prefects caned the whole lot.

When there was a prefects' meeting, I had to enter it fully in the senior prefect's book, which was open to inspection by the headmaster. I had to give a full statement of the offence and of the punishment. This I did, making, of course, no reference whatever to their behaviour in form, but recounting in detail their evil deeds *vis-à-vis* the prefects.

Now it so happened that I, the son of an English immigrant, had whacked the heirs of all the Careys. One needs to be a Guernseyman to realise the enormity of the offence. Most of the Carey clan fumed with rage, while Edith Carey, the island historian, passionately defended me. To complicate the issue, 4B knew perfectly well that I had really whacked them for their abominable behaviour in form, though such a matter was never mentioned. Not unnaturally, however, the youthful Careys reported to their parents that they had been punished for their behaviour in form, and the matter was reported in this way to the headmaster by Carey parents who demanded my instant expulsion.

I was working alone in the sixth form-room when Penney descended on me breathing threatenings and slaughter.

"Have you whacked 4B?"

"Yes, Sir."

"What right had you to interfere in relations between a form and their form master?"

But I was not going to be caught by that. I blandly professed complete ignorance as to such relations, which were no concern of mine.

Then came the demand for which I was waiting, and which I had foreseen.

"Bring me the Book."

I brought it him, and there was, naturally, not the slightest mention of the form's behaviour in class; but a proper account of the warning given, the offences against the prefects committed, and the punishment awarded.

But Penney had another trump—as he thought—up his sleeve. "Did you give the boys the option of being reported to the headmaster?"

"Yes, Sir."

"When?"

"When I had whacked them, Sir."

"What use did you think that was?"

"I didn't consider it my place to decide on whether it was any use or not. I was merely conforming to the rules."

The result was a foreseeable explosion. Penney demanded the rule book; explained that he had written the rules himself, and knew what they contained. Triumphantly he pointed to the rule which said:

Any boy who is whacked by the Prefects must be allowed to appeal to the Headmaster.

I agreed that this was the rule, and insisted that I had obeyed it.

"What do you mean by such impertinence?"

"I am not being impertinent, Sir. The rule appears to me to be perfectly clear. It says that any boy who is whacked by the Prefects must be allowed to appeal to the Headmaster. Until we had whacked them, Sir, they were not whacked by the prefects, and so the appeal did not apply."

I had spotted the logical error of wording some time previously. I knew it could be made use of only once; and I intended, did I not have to use it, to pass it on as a strict secret to my successor. For a moment my fate hung in the balance. But Penney had a school-boyish and completely undignified sense of humour. I waited while he became more and more purple, and I was afraid he was going to have a stroke. Then he collapsed into gargantuan laughter, told me I would undoubtedly be hanged in the course of time, and that meanwhile I had provided him with perfect material for belabouring the Careys for interference in the just punishment of their wicked offspring.

Meanwhile, true to Kipling to the end, 4B sent an official deputation to the two Tribunes of the Plebs to thank them for their fruitless intervention on 4B's behalf. They offered, if the Tribunes would lead them, that the whole form would come and scrag me while I was working alone after school on the school records of the war, and was building up a register of O.E.'s serving in the Forces, with the aid of the Cousin, who took it over when I left. The assembly place for such illegal conspiracies was 'behind the gym'; so, on the afternoon of the intended attack (which I had learned of by devious ways), I went up to a class room overlooking the conspiratorial area, saw 4B assembling, seized a boy who happened to be passing, and sent him with a message to 4B that I would be leaving a little earlier than usual that afternoon, but that I still had an adequate supply of canes in the cupboard. That was the end of that. And from then on I ruled the school unchallenged till I left to sit for my scholarship and join the army.

I don't think that I learned much religion at Elizabeth College, but I did acquire a great deal from my mother and from the Cousin. It was, in fact, a common interest in religious enquiry that had originally brought them together. My father was agnostic, and my ancestors had been unitarians. We

children were left free to go to Church or not from our early
teens. All three of us did, though often not together. For David
was somewhat attracted to St. Stephen's, which was High
Church; and I loved the country parishes.

I had no thought at that time of being ordained. My ambition was to get into the Coin Department of the British Museum.
I was an enthusiastic coin collector, had even some the British
Museum had not got, and had admirable opportunities for
collecting in the island of Guernsey. For we had the most
wonderful monetary system until 1919, though all we islanders
took it as perfectly natural, and worked it quite easily.

We were the only British members of the Decimal Union.
We minted our own copper, and the unit was a *double*, though
I have no idea what medieval coin it 'doubled'. Its value was
a half farthing, and we always called eight doubles a 'penny'.
We had had paper pound notes ever since the famous Guernsey
Market notes which are still debated by economists. For silver
we used that of all the members of the Decimal Union. So we
had French, Belgian and Swiss francs, Italian liras and Greek
drachmas. Their value was ten 'pennies'; but we did not think
or pay in francs, but in shillings, a value not represented by
any actual coin.

To make it more complicated, the shilling (British) was
worth 100 doubles, but twelve pennies—a Guernsey shilling—
was only 96 doubles. In consequence, one had to check whether
a price had 'British' attached to it. If it did, then we just added
a halfpenny for every shilling of the price—and paid in francs!

Guernsey bought five franc pieces from the French Government when they were withdrawn from circulation in France.
My father had paid his men and his bills in such pieces, and
still brought home a bag of them every Friday. I was allowed
to go through them and pick out rarities, substituting ordinary
ones. In this way I had a perfect collection of all the issues
from l'An l of the First Republic to the *Liberté, Egalité, Fraternité*
figures of the Third.

I should add that the *official* coinage of the Island was neither
the shilling nor the franc, but the *livre Tournois*. This was a
mythical coin based on the value of corn in the market of—
I always forget whether it is Tournai or Tours—in the 14th

century. It was generally valued at one shilling and two pence.
This was the coinage in which was calculated a twentieth
century fine on a twentieth century motorist.

The Middles Ages affected our lives in other ways also. We
made, I think, no money payment to the Seigneur of Rohais;
but the Manor itself was on the *Fief le Comte*, and the Count of
the Isles was the Duke of Normandy—that is, the King of
England. Him we owed five chickens and two sacks of corn,
but he refused to receive it in kind, so that my father had to
argue annually with the appropriate official as to the values of
corn and poultry. We also owed annual *rentes* to a curiously
vague collection of people, all of whom could claim an annual
sum as heirs of the original Vavaseur de Jersaï, who had been
awarded the farm after the battle of Creçy in 1345. Land in
Guernsey could not be left by will. It was inherited jointly by
all the direct heirs. It was occupied and cultivated by one, but
he paid *rente* for their share to any brother or sister; and that
share descended in perpetuity, and was added to by the brothers
and sisters of every heir who occupied the property. So in the
end one owed *rentes* to a vast and curious assortment. I remember once opening the door to a complete stranger who told me
she had come to collect her *rente*.

"But I did not know we owed you *rente*."

"You would not know, you are too young. I only collect once
in fifty years."

I was terrified. I imagined we owed her hundreds of pounds.
I stammered:

"How much do we owe you?"

"Twenty *doubles*."

Twopence halfpenny every fifty years was her share of the
inheritance, but it gave her a number of rights over the purchase
or sale of the property. When we bought half a *vergée* to build
the bungalow, the thought that all our previous *rente* collectors
would come again to claim from us one fortieth of the original
rente on the twenty *vergées* of Les Fauconnaires was more than
my father could bear!

The British Museum was not my first choice of a career.
About the age of eight I decided to become an architect.
Nothing better illustrates the change from that day to this,

when architecture can be the most mature and exciting of the arts, than that the choice so infuriated my father, the Victorian civil engineer, that it clearly had to be abandoned. From his point of view an architect was an aesthetic sissy who added an imitation 'period' front to a building, designed by an engineer, whose construction he did not understand. However, I continued my interest in architecture by starting a collection of architectural photographs which still continues to grow.

During the whole period that I was senior prefect my father and I were living alone in the bungalow. David had joined up immediately war was declared. He had become a private in the Artists' Rifles (28th London) and soon after was given a commission in the South Staffordshire Regiment. He went to France in the first months of the war, reached a captaincy, and was killed in the winter of 1917 at Paschendael. Molly went to Cheltenham, I think in 1913, and was there until 1918 when she was lost in the torpedoing of S.S. *Leinster* in the Irish Sea. She had had measles and, as by that time we had no home, a school friend who had also had measles invited her to convalesce with her family in Ireland. I stayed in Guernsey till the winter of 1915, took my scholarship in December, and joined the army in January. As soon as I had gone, my father shut up the bungalow, and came over to London to put his experience as an engineer at the service of the Government. He became a draughtsman and factory designer. I don't think he ever recovered from being given half-a-crown and told to buy himself a drink by an officer who was junior to both his sons!

THE BUNGALOW GHOST

I AM RECALLING events of forty to fifty years ago, which we never wrote down at the time. But I must in fairness to us all add that we viewed any manifestation of the ghost with the utmost scepticism, cross-questioned the member of the family who had heard or seen it, and tried the most far-fetched explanation to discount it. Only if the incident survived this scrutiny did we put it down to the ghost. But we were all, every one of us, involved in its visitations. All of us either saw or heard it. And we knew that friends and neighbours also encountered it, though we never let on to them that what they had seen or heard was not—as they thought—one of us or an intruder.

For the ghost was 'an impersonating elemental'. It was an 'elemental' in the sense that it was not a departed human being. It had a mind, but it was definitely primitive, though fortunately not malicious. I do not think it could understand speech. It was an 'impersonator' in the sense that it manifested itself as someone, member of the family or other, who was constantly about the place. I took the name from *Ghostly Phenomena* by Elliot O'Donnell. He classified many kinds of ghost, and indicated where particular types were most likely to be experienced.

The ghost normally impersonated one member of the family to another, sometimes to two others in succession. Two of us might hear it at the same time, but I don't remember two of us seeing it simultaneously. I cannot now remember the order of the experiences which follow, but they all belong to the period 1910–1915 or 1919–1928. I went abroad in that year and my father sold the bungalow. Only once did it make our hair stand on end, and that was at tea time on a sunny summer afternoon. It had successfully deceived all of us, one after another; and our realisation that we 'had had the ghost again'

was greeted with peal after peal of very unpleasant laughter
from the empty field outside the window. Otherwise we encountered it by day or by night without a qualm.

I remember three early experiences. The bungalow was a
long building, with a passage down the middle and rooms on
both sides. At each end was a glass door. At the back the rooms
projected each side of the door, making a kind of hollow
square, and you could only see the back door itself from right
in front of it. You could not see it from the back gate. One day,
as I came in at the gate, I saw my father come out of this
hollow square with a milk-can, going to Mr. Naftel to fetch
the milk. I dropped my bicycle and called out "all right Dad,
I'll fetch the milk," but he didn't hear me and disappeared
round the end of the house. I ran after him, but the path along
the long side of the house was empty, though he would have
had to traverse a much longer distance to get out of sight than
I had to, to reach the corner. So I returned to the house, but
the back door, out of which he had just come, was locked; and
the bungalow was empty.

Another time it was my brother who had just come back from
school, and wanted to see my sister about something urgent.
As he came into the garden he realised with relief that she was
at home, as the piano was playing and she was the only one
who played it. But as he opened the door of the room the piano
stopped. The room was empty. Yet a third appearance of this
kind. I was acting in the school play and, when I came home
at night, my father used to make me a cup of cocoa. At the
time he was building a boat down at the front end of the
passage. He saw me come in with my bicycle by the back door,
put out the oil lamp, and go into the dining room. He came
down past the bicycle, went into the kitchen, and made the
cocoa. He brought it into the dining room, but I was not there,
nor anywhere else in the house. I came home, put my bicycle
in the passage, and went into the dining room, half an hour
later.

There were other incidents, which I have probably forgotten; but they explain how the ghost was always able to get
away with it. Every time you see your father or your brother,
you cannot heave a brick at him, 999 times he is actually there.

It is only the 1,000th that he isn't. The ghost always managed to have a normal exit nearer than we could be, so that it could pass out of sight without having to vanish through walls or anything silly like that. Its exit also allowed it to disappear without having to speak, and that is why I think it had a mind, but could not master the complexity of speech. When my father with the milk-can did not hear me, I was not surprised nor thought it unnatural, for my father was slightly deaf. I think that if it could have managed speech it would have done so, for it spent long periods watching us, so that it might then project into our minds exactly the right image. I used to look after the garden, and was often aware of the watching, and could have told you which window it was studying me from. Did I become convinced that somebody 'real' was there, and go in and search the bungalow, then, a short time after my fruitless search, footsteps would return down the passage and it would start watching me again from another window.

The fruit of this careful study appeared in due course. I met Mr. and Mrs. Lancashire, the pioneer carnation growers and near friends and neighbours of ours, one day in Smith Street. Mr. Lancashire took me to task, saying: "You're a rude young man. We passed the bungalow yesterday afternoon and you were working in the garden; but when we called to you, you just walked round the corner." I asked them what time that was, and carefully refrained from saying that at that time I was on my bicycle near Lancresse Common, and the bungalow was empty. So I just made the excuse that I was—fortunately— known to be very absent-minded and apologised for not hearing them. We had other cases where we were seen, or were heard, by neighbours, but we always managed to wriggle out of it without admitting that we had an active ghost on the premises.

During 1914 and 1915, when the post came very irregularly and very late, one of its favourite activities was impersonating the postman. One heard him come up the wooden-floored porch, one saw his light through the glass door, one heard and saw letters and newspapers fall on the mat, then there were the footsteps again, and the light disappeared round the corner. The letters and paper lay there until one stooped down to pick them up! I was working then for my scholarship, and my father was out most evenings drilling with the 'Gorgeous Wrecks'—so-called from their G.R. armbands—and I had a number of these harmless though irritating appearances. I did not tell my father as there were evenings when I was out and he was at home, and I wanted to see if it happened to him also. Sure enough, in due course I was greeted on my return one evening with: "The ghost has been again." So I said to my father: "I will tell you what it did." My father had had just the same experience as I had had. The letters were there as he walked down the half dark passage to collect them. They vanished as he prepared to pick them up, while the postman's footsteps could be heard on the gravel path outside.

One day in the early twenties I was having tea with Edith Carey, and she was then making a map of all the prehistoric sites she could find evidence for. Knowing my love of exploring every corner of the island she asked me whether I could add anything—unusual stones turned into field gateposts and so on. I told her of one or two I had noticed, and then added: "I can tell you another, if you will take the evidence."

"What," said Miss Carey "is the evidence?"

"A ghost," I replied, and told her that Elliott O'Donnell had noted that he had always found 'impersonating elementals' associated with cromlechs or similar sites. "I am sure", I added, "we have accidentally built our bungalow on the site of a cromlech, though there is not the slightest trace of its existence."

I added an experience which I had had several times, and which seemed to reflect memories of some ancient ritual.

As I remarked before, I looked after the garden. We were separated from the rest of the field only by a veronica hedge, and there were frequently cows in the field. Naturally I was on the look-out that they did not get into the garden. Once or twice I had been wakened at night by what I thought was the movement of cows, but had always found the field empty when I got up and looked out. Only slowly did I realise that it was odd that I could always see that the field was empty, because, in fact, it was always at the full moon that this happened. What I heard was cows (as I thought) swishing through the long grass towards the bungalow. I noted the wind, wondered whether it was the veronica, and told my father next morning that we might be having the ghost again. We treated it with our usual scepticism, looked into every possible source of the sound of movement in the wind, and decided it was probably the long grass near the veronica, though we could never get it to sound really like footsteps. So for some time it remained unproven.

Then I was awakened again one night—it was some months later—and lay in bed listening. I had spent the whole day in the garden, and cows would definitely have done a great deal of harm. But it was cold, and I did not want to get out of bed. I said to myself: "If that's the ghost, it can go on as long as it likes, but it will not get me out of bed." I listened for some time, but the more I listened the more convinced I became that it was undoubtedly cows. The footsteps swishing through the long grass were unmistakeable, and they were very near the hedge. I hopped out of bed and went to the window. Only when I looked out in the bright moonlight did I take in the fact I had forgotten—that the field had been ploughed. There was no long grass, or anything to produce any sound at all, as I looked straight out into the ploughed field. But across it, from all sides, footsteps came swishing through the long grass towards the bungalow.

"What is the name of your field?" asked Edith Carey.

"Le Jaonnêt," I replied. "The vineries were called Gorse-lands after it."

"Le Jaonnêt is a very common name," said Miss Carey reflectively. "Did it not have any further name—Le Jaonnêt de something?"

"No," I said. "I have never heard it called anything else."

Miss Carey possessed an amazing collection of old island records. She went and dug into this, and came back with a *terrier* of the Manor of Rohais at the time of Elizabeth I.

"You had five fields," she said when she had identified the farm of the falconer of the manor.

"Yes," I answered, "but I have forgotten the names of the others."

"There is one of them called Le Jaonnêt," she went on, "but in the sixteenth century it was called *Le Jaonnêt du Trépied*— the Gorseland of the Cromlech."

II

STUDIES IN BLACK AND WHITE:
SOLDIERING IN THE FIRST WORLD WAR

I STAYED IN England after my scholarship exam until I heard the result. Then I was asked to come and discuss matters with the Senior Tutor, Mr. Burroughs, later Bishop of Ripon. What he told me made me realise how completely I owed my success to the courage of Hickie in fighting Penney on my behalf. The College expected me to join the army, and told me my scholarship would be kept for me. I also intended to join the army, as all my contemporaries were doing. In actual fact, I do not think that I had ever heard of pacifism or conscientious objection, and had, in consequence, not given the idea any thought.

In the beginning of January 1916 I joined the Artists' Rifles, as David had done in 1914. It was one of the regiments which most attracted public schoolboys and men in the professions. In March I began what was to be characteristic of my military career, an astonishing series of alternatives of extreme black and white. Three hundred of us, all privates, for we were accompanied by no officers or n.c.o.s of our own, went by a Clyde river steamer in a March gale from Southampton to Rouen. Being accustomed to being sea-sick, I spent twenty-four hours looking after those who were not so accustomed, with the result that I was one of only four who were not sea-sick on the voyage! We arrived, more dead than alive, at the quayside at Rouen, and had several miles to march in the snow with full equipment to our camp. We were met by the adjutant on our arrival with approximately these words: "You think you are a lot of bloody gentlemen, and I'm a bloody ranker. Well, now you're a lot of bloody privates and I'm your bloody adjutant, and we'll see how you like it."

We were then made to stand naked for two hours in an almost unheated hut, waiting for a medical inspection. The rest of our treatment was on a par during the seventeen days we remained in Rouen. It was not surprising that we, who had been 300 on arrival, were only 146 when we entrained for Saint Omer, the H.Q. where the Artists were doing guard duty. Five were dead and the rest were in hospital.

So much for the black. Now for the white!

As the crow flies, Rouen is about 100 miles from Saint Omer. The journey took us thirty-eight hours. On arrival in a somewhat jaded condition we were immediately given a hot meal. We were then divided into four groups for the four companies. The O.C. of the company to which I had been allotted then came and welcomed us, and explained to us that we would live in an old French barracks with rooms of all different sizes. He had sent his Sergeant Major to go round and find out how many men each room wanted; and he suggested that, while that was being done, we should sort ourselves out, as doubtless we had fallen into groups of friends during our period in the army. They would then try to fit the groups into the needs of the rooms—which they did with infinite patience and kindness.

I joined three others, two my contemporaries, one an older man who was a choirman of Salisbury Cathedral. He had regaled us on the long journey by singing entire Gilbert and Sullivan operas. When we got to our room, the corporal in charge explained that, when they had themselves arrived, it had taken the quartermaster's department a fortnight to get their rations, so that they had had to eat out in the town or go without. So, as soon as they heard that a new draft was coming, they had begun to lay in stores as they could spare them. He then opened a cupboard and said "All this is yours". "All this" was a generous supply of bread, butter, cheese, tinned meats and jam, quite enough to last us till our rations came along.

If after these two experiences I did not know how to treat men when I myself became an officer, I could have no one but myself to blame!

Life at Saint Omer was delightful. David had been in the Battalion Scouts in 1914, and consequently I was invited to join them, which I did. They were a picked lot; we paraded quite separately from the rest of the men; did long route marches; became fit enough to do several miles at a double with full packs; trained in map reading, sketching and other special competences—and, alas, became expert navigators of the canals round Saint Omer in the heavy canal boats of the region. We had a special café on a canal where we used to rendezvous, and where the water was boiled so that we could safely drink it. But too many scouts turned up one day and, short of boiled water, I was given my *citron au vin blanc* with water straight out of the canal.

The poisoning that resulted was extremely complicated, because I had just been inoculated against typhus, and it had half taken. All the glands of my neck and head swelled up until I could not open my mouth. For three weeks I more or less lived on aspirin and three daily doses of medicine. I remarked to the sister that it was fortunate the medicine was so pleasant, as I could eat practically nothing. She laughed and told me it was just port wine! Such is the consequence of being brought up a complete teetotaller! One would have thought I would be put on a milk and liquid diet. But army regulations interposed. No special diet could be prescribed until the illness was diagnosed. About three doctors visited me daily, but they could not decide what was the matter with me. So no eatable diet! On the whole I was much more nearly killed by the R.A.M.C. than I ever was by the Germans.

I spent three months in hospital, ending up at Halloughton Hall, a country house in Warwickshire, where I saw my first English Spring. In Guernsey Spring comes early on the ground, but late on the trees. Here I revelled in a unified beauty in all the happy laziness of convalescence. Also I made the acquaintance of Maxstoke Castle and its tenant, the Rev. David Lee-Elliott. I was his guest for most of my subsequent army leaves, since the house in Guernsey was shut up, and in any case Guernsey was too far off for short leaves. I did manage to get there once or twice during the war, staying with the Cousin, and enjoying the devious ways in which the mail boat slipped across the Channel to avoid submarines. Going through the Race of Alderney in a gale was quite an experience.

Maxstoke was an enchanting place, a red sandstone square in a wide moat, built in the fourteenth century, and with a house of

2

many periods within the walls. When in full use it had the charm of sixteen staircases to nineteen bedrooms. Its entrance hall was on the first floor, and the butler had to go up the back stairs and come down the front stairs to answer the front door! For most of the war it was a V.A.D. hospital, like the neighbouring manor house in which I convalesced.

When I returned to duty in the summer of 1916 I was sent almost immediately to an Officer Cadet Battalion at Denham. For some reason, Denham was closed, and we were sent to what had been the Staff College at Camberley to complete our training. It was next to Sandhurst, and it amused us that we were 'officer cadets' while they were 'gentlemen cadets'. I was somewhat alarmed on reading battalion orders the day after my arrival to find myself down for Company Orders. Wondering what on earth I had done wrong, I reported next morning, and was marched into the presence of the Company Commander, Captain Jameson. When my name was announced by the Sergeant Major, he said to me: "You're a cousin of my wife's. She wants you to come to tea on Sunday." I stammered my thanks, and asked what offence I had committed. "Oh, none," he replied, "but to put you down for Company Orders was the quickest way to identify you among the several hundred who have just arrived."

In December I duly got my commission, and was attached to the Queen's, Royal West Surrey Regiment. I was sent down to the 3rd Queen's at Gore Court outside Sittingbourne, but almost immediately crossed to France, and arrived in the abominable 'Bull Ring' at Etaples. After a short stay I moved up to a village just behind the line on the south side of the Ypres Salient where the 10th Queen's were stationed. There was an even number of officers in the company to which I was sent, and each had half a batman. They all—the Company Commander included—refused to allow me to reduce one of the rations to a third. I was told to get one from my platoon. Nobody noticed that thus the junior officer had a batman to himself!

I was told of various ex-batmen that I might acquire, but I had no intention of living in a constant atmosphere of "Mr. X used to do this or that", or, worse still, "Mr. Y never did that".

So I asked my platoon sergeant to consider what member of the platoon, not being in his first youth, could reasonably be chosen for a lighter job. My sergeant chose well, and Johnson, a man about twice my age, became so kindly and efficient a batman that everyone from the second in command downwards tried unsuccessfully to steal him from me. To my great regret I lost touch with him when I was invalided home. I gave Johnson a list of the supplies I wanted always to be in my kit when we went up the line. Thereafter I did not have to worry. They were always there. When we first met, I gave him only one instruction. I said to him: "My job is to look after the platoon. Your job is to look after me." I hope I did my job as well as he did his. I had an admirable platoon sergeant, a postman, Sergeant King. In my early days I got him to give me character sketches of my n.c.o.'s. One of them was a very inefficient and untidy individual, whom Sergeant King completely described in the sentence: "Corporal X, Sir? Corporal X! He finds 'em in 'is watch." 'Them' was, of course, bugs!

The life of an infantry subaltern in the Ypres Salient has been described so often that I have nothing fresh to add to it. In my last period in the line I was in command of the Company for the simple reason that I was the only officer still alive. But I had, without knowing it, collected a dose of mustard gas. It was realised only when I suddenly went blind on parade some days after we had got out of the line. By various gradations I moved from hospital to hospital and ended up in London during the zeppelin raids of the autumn of 1917. I never got out to France again. Instead, I had another dose of black and white.

When I was finally deemed fit, I was posted back to our Third Battalion at Sittingbourne. It was a huge battalion, mostly composed of officers and men in training for the front, or returned men like myself. But it had an utterly detestable upper crust of individuals who played bridge and billiards with the colonel, few of whom had been to France, and who monopolised all the extra-pay positions in the battalion without either the will or the competence to do any of the work for which the extra pay was intended. All the training work of the battalion was done by temporary officers like myself; none of us ever got promotion, and, even when we were offered staff jobs (as we were, for we were an efficient lot), 'they' usually managed to have them cancelled.

The usual procedure was for a returned officer to be sent on a training or refresher course; and, in accordance with this policy, I was sent off to the Northern Command Gas School. It dealt, of course, entirely with anti-gas training, not with making or using gas. I found that the only way to remember all the gasses with which I had to deal was to turn them into the sad poem of an officer who died from a surfeit of long names:

> And, as he died, he whispered faint
> Like Mary Tudor's last complaint:
> Upon my heart will be descried
> 'Long names o'ercame him and he died.'
> With dichlorethylsulphide there
> Is diphenylchlorarsine rare,
> And on the other side of it
> Trinitroluol is writ . . .

I did so well at the Northern Course that I was attached to the Brigade Gas School, presided over by a brilliant officer, Captain Trend. The Gas School, though it served the whole brigade, was part of the 3rd Queen's, and was entirely staffed by them and taken on their strength.

Shortly afterwards I went on an advanced course to the Southern Command Gas School, and was summoned one day to the C.O.'s office. He asked me if I would like to join his staff. When I said I would, he told me to go back to my battalion and collect my kit, that I was now under his orders, and that he would arrange my transfer direct with the War Office. When I returned to Sittingbourne I was threatened with arrest if I tried to leave, or to hold any communication whatever with the C.O. of the Gas School. The colonel managed to get my transfer cancelled, and I was never able to explain to the C.O. what had happened. I was not the only temporary officer dealt with in that way.

However, in the winter of 1917–18 Trend was made adjutant —which meant one decent man in Headquarters—and I was appointed to succeed him. It was a curious situation, as I was the youngest in age, and the junior in rank, of my own staff, which consisted of two assistant gas officers, and four to six trained n.c.o.'s, as well as store men. Thanks to Trend's admirable work we were a very competent group. As we had in our control the whole training, together with the equipment with gas masks, of three to four thousand men, we needed to be good at our job. Trend had done the basic work so well that I was free to add frills which greatly improved our training capacities. They also took a great deal of the fear out of anti-gas training.

The ordinary man understood that, if he stopped a shell, it would damage him. But he was frightened of the invisible assault of gas. I found that one of my n.c.o.'s was a very good modeller, and we created a whole landscape along one side of my lecture room—which was an old greenhouse with raised beds along the sides. The whole of one side was a model of a typical Flander's landscape, from the town behind the line right up to the front line trenches, properly equipped at each stage for gas detection and protection. On the other side of the room was a model of the whole system of gas protection in the trenches themselves. When I gave a lecture I would appoint one man, sitting appropriately close, as gas sentry. He was very apt to take it as a joke. But we had laid on a model gas attack which could be set off by one of my n.c.o.'s from outside. Suddenly the sentry would find gas shells exploding all round the trenches.

In addition I started special courses for officers, the first of their kind anywhere. The result was that our School was constantly visited by red-hats and green-hats—i.e. members of the special anti-gas services. I was myself entitled by my job to a captaincy and the coveted green tabs which, of course, brought a specialist's pay. In fact I remained a second lieutenant, while a totally inefficient and unqualified captain played bridge and billiards with the colonel, wore the green tabs, and enjoyed the extra pay.

I had my revenge in the spring of 1918, at the time of the breakthrough which brought the Germans almost to the coast. I was working fourteen hours a day, often training and fitting men by moonlight, when I succumbed to the influenza epidemic.

There was nobody available to take my place, for I alone of my staff was entitled to certify that a man was fully trained and properly fitted with a tested mask. I sometimes had to lecture three hours on end with a temperature of 104. When I was not lecturing, I was carried out to my parade ground where I would have anything up to twenty squads doing different training. The n.c.o. who took me out would also take out a chair, and I directed all operations sitting down, until I was carried back.

This preposterous situation continued for a number of days without the colonel making the slightest attempt to find a substitute for me. The M.O., Captain Mortimer, was a very nice chap, who came to see me every day, but told me he could not give me any treatment until he could put me to bed properly. Meanwhile I was much safer not being doped. By the second week I was in a lovely mental condition. The gas officer remained 100% efficient. The personal 'me' was completely delirious. When I recovered I was astonished to find my complicated records were all in perfect order, without gaps or errors. But the gallivantings of the personal 'me', when I learned of them afterwards, astonished me still more! Apparently the M.O. had warned the colonel that under no circumstances was I to be contradicted or challenged; if I was, I would probably go straight off my head. I did not know this, but, at the same time, I had a wonderful time with all the 'high ups'. As I had no inhibitions I told them publicly what I thought of them. I ordered them off my parade ground, and they had to go. The miserable creature who wore my rank and drew my pay was rash enough to appear at one of my parades. I gave him a lecture on his conduct in front of the troops, and then told him to go away as I was busy. And all the time the admirable M.O. was watching me unbeknownst.

Finally so many of the high ups complained to the colonel about me that he carpeted me. Fortunately one of my friends was there when the message came to report immediately to the colonel in the orderly room; and he rushed to the M.O., who promptly arrived to assist at the ceremony. The result on the colonel was delicious. My 'reprimand' went something like this: "Major X tells me that you ordered him off the parade

ground—I am quite sure he had got on to the parade ground
by mistake, but don't you think you ought to have told him his
mistake privately? Then Captain X says that you rebuked him
in front of the troops. I am sure he was in the wrong, but don't
you think you could have told him about it afterwards?" And
so on all down the line, with the M.O. watching him with an
eagle eye. In the end the colonel said: "Don't you think you
have been working too hard? Wouldn't it be a good thing if
you took some leave from tomorrow?" To which, as I am told,
I replied that, if I was going on leave, I would do so now,
saluted and walked out!

Some time during my period at Sittingbourne I went into
hospital at Fort Pitt, Chatham. During my time in the Ypres
Salient I had once spent a week in water without taking my
boots off. When I took them off at last, I took most of the skin
of the soles of my feet with them. I suppose to protect what lay
beneath the skin I developed what became an unusual Dupuytren's contraction of the *planta fascia* of one foot, which they
decided to fillet. The anaesthetist put me under without looking at my medical history, and I promptly 'died'. I refused to
come round with artificial respiration; and, as a last resort,
he dipped towels in boiling water and flicked me all over the
body with them. This finally brought me round. But, when I
recovered consciousness, I felt myself all swathed in bandages,
and I knew I had gone for an operation on my foot. A sister
passed the foot of my bed just at that moment, so I called to her
feebly: "Sister, sister, they've operated on the wrong man." In
the next bed to me was the brigade musketry officer, Captain
Plater. One day his brother came to see him, Father Plater
S. J. of Campion Hall, Oxford. As I was going up to Oxford
after the war, Captain Plater introduced me. So I met probably the most canonisable saint I have ever known.

The average career of a gas officer lasted four months. When
I had been a gas officer for nine months, I went down with a
violent attack of dry pleurisy. Inevitably, as I was constantly
in the gas testing chamber, my working clothes were saturated
with chlorine. I had survived so long largely because I was
responsible for the gas training and inspection of all the anti-
aircraft stations between Chatham and Canterbury; and all

through the spring and summer of 1918 this gave me week-
ends in the gorgeous Kentish countryside, often ending up with
a Sunday in Canterbury Cathedral. But after the pleurisy the
M.O. told me I had to resign my post, and made me promise
to tell him of any offer or posting that came to me.

There followed the most disappointing day of my life. When
I told my boss on the telephone that I had to quit the brigade
school, he offered me the command of gas training in Sheppey,
which meant escape from Sittingbourne, a house and car,
officer's training courses (which were my speciality) and ten
thousand troops to supervise the training of. Excited, I went
straight to the M.O.

"There's the telephone," he said.

"What for?"

"Refuse it."

"Why should I?"

"My dear boy, don't you realise that in the damp climate
of Sheppey you would not be alive in a month?"

So I telephoned a refusal. An immediate answer came. I was
offered the Thames and Medway Garrison—the job to which
the Sheppey job was subordinate. I asked where I would live.

"You would live at the top of Chatham Hill," said my boss.

Triumphant I went to the M.O.

"Where would you work?"

"I would have a motorboat on the Medway, and a car, and
I would work right up to Maidstone."

"The telephone is still there," was all he would say.

So again I refused it, but my Boss was out. In the evening he
rang me up: "You're a difficult man to please," he told me.
"I've only one job left, and that is O.C. of the Command Gas
School." It would have meant the rank of major and I was still
a second lieutenant; and it would have meant that my whole
job would have been occupied with the courses for officers and
training staff which I had developed most. But that also I was
made to turn down—quite rightly, I suppose, as I would have
had a good deal of demonstration work to do in the gas
chamber.

So ended my gas career. I had accepted it in the first place
because, like a good many men in the army, by 1917 I was half

way to becoming a pacifist. But I felt that I was not sufficiently detached to be able to take so momentous a decision as it would have been to become a conscientious objector after more than two years in the army. To find a job in which I was concerned with saving life and not with destroying it seemed the right path to follow, and I had had experience of most kinds of gases while at the front. I still looked so young, and I had no wound stripes, that it was quite an important factor in getting the control of men who had come back from France and were much older than myself, that I could discuss with them personal experiences of gas attacks and their effects.

I was then sent, with two or three other officers, down to Lowestoft where the 19th Queens was stationed. In my case it was because of the M.O.'s insistence that I was moved to the bracing climate of the East Coast. We arrived at the station late in the evening. As I had a bike, I suggested that I should find the H.Q. and report our arrival. I made the suggestion with great misgiving. I was very tired, very unfit, and the reception given to a new arrival at Sittingbourne who appeared when the adjutant's office was closed filled me with apprehension. I expected very hostile treatment, if I was accorded any reception at all. I found the office, and actually found Captain E. S. Hall, the adjutant, still at work in it. When I came in he got to his feet, and came forward to shake hands—a thing I had no experience of an adjutant doing before! I had again passed from a black to a white.

He refused to let me go back to the station, saying that he would send down to collect the other officers and our luggage, while he took me along to the pleasant house on the front, facing the Denes, where the mess was, and where the unmarried officers lived. He got hold of the mess president, saw that all of us had a meal prepared for us, and then went home to where his family lived a few doors off. Later he came back to meet the other officers, and to see that we had everything we needed. He gave the other officers their companies, told them when and where to report, and told me, whom he had discovered to be still on the sick list, to come along to his office some time after nine.

In civilian life Hall was a distinguished architect, and was

2*

later President of the R.I.B.A. When I came in the morning, he asked what I could do. I replied that, so far as I could see, I was at the moment useless. I was not fit enough for the parade ground, I could not march because of the operation on my foot, and I was not allowed to go near gas. He then explained that his assistant adjutant was just going to command a company, and asked me whether I would like the job of assistant adjutant. I accepted at once.

My first week I did not know whether I was standing on my head or my heels. Business was conducted in a way to which I was totally unaccustomed. I sat across from the adjutant at a large table, and it was my task to answer the telephone—usually from the orderly room sergeant, Courtnay Sinkins, in the office below. Sinkins would ring up to know whether the adjutant was engaged as Private X had an insurance problem on which he felt unable to advise him. I delivered the message to Hall, and expected Hall to blast the telephone from its fittings at being expected to deal with a private's personal insurance. Instead there would follow a long discussion, probably ending with, "You'd better send him up. I can't see what his difficulty is." Hall would then stand up, lean against the mantelpiece, light his pipe, and discuss the whole business with Private X, until he was sure that Private X had got it all straight and knew what to do. If I went downstairs I would very likely find Sinkins doing the same kind of thing. Even if I went into the small office of that most dreaded warrant officer, the Regimental Sergeant Major, I would as likely as not find him solving some problem for somebody. My first Sunday morning, when I went to the 8 o'clock service in the great parish church of Lowestoft, I discovered part of the answer. The Second in Command, the Adjutant, most of the Battalion Orderly Room, several of the Company Commanders, and a fair sprinkling of n.c.o.'s and privates were all regular communicants.

One very pleasant duty fell to me. Just as I could not walk, so the adjutant could not ride. When the colonel wanted a mounted officer, I always accompanied him. I had learned riding in France—learned it the hard way. When I first went to the transport field I had beginner's luck. But, as I didn't fall off during various manoeuvres, the transport officer was convinced

I had lied in saying I had never been on a horse before. The next time I went for a lesson, he mounted me on an enormous creature with a mouth of iron that even the transport corporal would not ride, and which was employed to drag equipment too heavy to be run away with.

Needless to say, as soon as the transport officer cracked his whip, it lit out for Berlin, Copenhagen, or wherever the elephantine creature thought it would make for. I jumped hedges, leaped ditches, and, miraculously, always arrived back at the transport field some time later in the day, still on the back of my mount. In the 10th Queen's many of my men had been yeomanry, and knew much more about a horse than I did. One day, like a good platoon officer, I had managed to get a sizeable batch of tickets for the divisional cinema. I went into the platoon at dinner to pass them out. To my question as to who would like to go to the cinema that afternoon the reply was complete silence. A good platoon always has a licensed jester, who can tell the platoon commander what a situation really is. So I turned to Russell and asked him what the matter was. "Are you going riding this afternoon, sir?" he asked.

"Yes, I am, but what has that to do with it?"

"If you're going riding, sir, none of us want to go to a cinema."

Sure enough, some days later, when I jumped a very unpleasant hedge, I soared over most of my platoon carefully concealed behind it.

So I thoroughly enjoyed my very pleasant mare at Lowestoft. The second in command was a keen rider, and we had charcoal burners in a wood on an estate about ten miles off. On a fine afternoon that provided us with an excuse for a delightful ride, only about half a mile of which was on a metalled road.

In addition to the normal job of an assistant adjutant, I was also put in charge of the complicated business of disbanding the battalion, even before the war was completely over. This meant sending men, not into civil life, but into other army units. When demobilisation was added after the fighting was over, the complications were fantastic. The government was apt to surrender to any influence powerful enough to command votes, with the result that regulations became more and more unjust to the type of men we had, mostly countrymen, little shop-keepers, and men who had no powerful employer or trade union to demand their release. Actually I was myself entitled to my demobilisation among the first, for I was a scholar of Oxford, and students had a very high priority. But, as I had the whole matter in hand, the colonel begged me to stay on and complete my job. Naturally I did so.

When after the end of the war Hall was released from the army I succeeded him as adjutant. The regiment was not accustomed to having officers in their early twenties, since most of them were elderly territorials, and the consequences were sometimes amusing. Shortly after I succeeded Hall, several company commanders came to me and asked whether I had been changing the order that, as we were all crocks of one kind or another, not more than three days' light duty should ever be given together. It was a sensible rule for, if a man was not fit for our duties, it was clearly wise for the doctor to see him pretty frequently. I said I had certainly not changed the rule, but would go along and see the M.O. I was, by the way, still only a lieutenant. The captaincy which goes with the adjutancy took a long time to be gazetted. When the M.O. had finished with the man he was examining, I asked him if he would spare me a minute:

"M.O.," I said, "I understand you have been giving various men two and three weeks' light duty."

"What the hell's that got to do with you?"

"There's a battalion order that not more than three days' light duty shall be given at once."

"Well, what the hell's *that* got to do with you?"

"Company commanders are not prepared to accept the responsibility for their sick not seeing you for several weeks."

"If company commanders have a complaint they can bloody well come and tell me themselves, not send some damned whipper-snapper."

"Not at all; if company commanders are uncertain on a point of battalion orders their correct procedure is to check with the adjutant."

"And if the adjutant's got a complaint, the same applies. He can damned well come and see me himself."

"He has. I am the adjutant!"

The M.O. gave me one startled look to see if I was furious at my importance not being recognised. He saw I had been delaying the announcement as long as possible, and invited me out to dinner!

I had another wonderful encounter with him at a time when I was in the curious position of being my own superior officer. As one of the H.Q. I was on the strength of A company. Its O.C. had succeeded in getting a month's leave on urgent private affairs, and begged me to take command of the company, as I was the only officer in it of the required seniority. If I had it, I could delegate the actual daily routine to whom I liked. I consented, with the result that I received one morning, as adjutant, a complaint from the M.O., accusing O.C. A company of gross brutality, callous neglect of his men, and every other military offence he could think of. I wrote at once to myself, requesting 'an instant explanation to this Office' in exactly the same terms as I would have written to any other offending company commander. I then took the letter along to my sergeant major, and asked him how he would like to write a letter like that to himself. He read it and exclaimed: "Good Lord, Sir, what 'ave you done?" I gave him the M.O.'s letter.

What had happened was that Private X, a crock like the rest of us—I used sometimes to have to add in battalion orders: 'N.B. All men for this parade should have two sound legs'— had gone out for a walk before breakfast and fainted, whereas he knew he should not have taken exercise before he had taken food. Private X was a man of forty, and it had been a fine winter morning. Moreover, it had not been a parade, but an entirely voluntary walk.

Having ascertained the facts, I wrote a very aggrieved letter to myself as adjutant, regretting Private X having fainted, but protesting that I could not be held responsible. I then returned to the orderly room, wrote to myself and accepted my explanation. That done I replied to the M.O. requesting him 'before he made such serious complaints against my officers, to pay more attention to the facts'. The M.O., I might add, was old enough to be my grandfather! I then called my orderly room sergeant, whose name alas, I cannot remember, showed him the series of letters, and told him to take them to the M.O., and see if he spotted that all the signatures were the same. He did. But fortunately my facts were accurate.

The 19th Queen's was the most human battalion I encountered in my military career. We could do and ignore things in that battalion without any loss of essential discipline, which was unique in my experience. In the end, it became a question whether I was demobilised before I was court-martialled for ignoring some order or convention, and the same applied to the orderly room sergeant, who was my partner in most of my 'misdeeds'. Part of our trouble was the Colonel, who was an admirable antique but slow in intelligence.

On one occasion I had two men up before him for overstaying their leaves. I always went through the cases he would have to judge with the regimental sergeant major, so that I knew my facts. One of the men was a middle-aged man who always overstayed his leave, with the flimsiest excuses; and I told the colonel it was time he gave him a heavy sentence and a real tongue-lashing. The other was a boy of nineteen, living in the wilds of Yorkshire, eighteen miles from the bus which was to take him to the branch line whence he had to catch the only train of the day. He caught the bus, but floods had destroyed a bridge and the bus was halted. The boy ran several miles to the station and just missed the train. He telegraphed me at once, and sat for twenty four hours at the station so as to catch the train next day. All this I told the colonel, and added that regulations required me to bring him up, but that he clearly had earned no punishment.

The Colonel mixed the two up! He smiled sweetly at the obvious scrounger and hoped another accident would not happen to him, and tongue-lashed the boy till he wept. He then gave him twenty-eight days, the heaviest sentence he could give! That could not be allowed to pass, so I signalled to the R.S.M. to take him up to my office. After Orders, I went upstairs to where the boy was waiting. I explained everything to him quite frankly; and said that, while I could not impose on the other chap the punishment he deserved, I certainly was not going to allow him to serve his sentence, and to have a permanent black mark against his name. For any sentence by the colonel was automatically made part of his permanent military history on a particular Army Form— I forget its number.

I swore the boy to secrecy, and explained that we would have to forge a new record form for him, which I proceeded to do in his presence.

My colleagues and I became increasingly fed up with the general situation, and felt that our real loyalty was to the men serving with us, not to the 'high ups'. They had become impossible to respect. As I have said, the government had yielded to every kind of pressure from powerful bodies, which made demobilisation regulations completely unjust to the little man; and the army's attitude can be gauged from a top secret, very confidential visit I received one day from the Provost Marshall's Department—the army's department of justice—in which it was explained that I could be much quicker with courts-martial than was reasonable while the war was on; since a conviction would mean a considerable economy to the country. For the man concerned forfeited his gratuity! I was only concerned with one court-martial and was there delighted to ensure the officer's acquittal on a ridiculous charge.

Early in the spring of 1919 large numbers of prisoners of war began to arrive in England, and were sent to different units for the rest of their service, and for their demobilisation. All of the units around us had a quota; we had a couple of hundred. These men quickly became very dissatisfied, and added to the number of mutinies—never, I think, revealed to the public—which took place in the early months of 1919. In one neighbouring unit where the men had mutinied, I found out that *three weeks after they had arrived* they had no mess kit, no blankets, no explanations of their position with regard to pay and allowances, and these facts were unknown to the Colonel, the adjutant and the quartermaster!

The day our quota arrived I summoned all the company commanders to the orderly room, and gave them a list of things to find out whether the men knew—such as pay and allowances, the course of the war, the plans for their demobilisation and so on; while the quartermaster, who was with me, likewise told them what he wanted to know about their equipment. They were to report back to us at the end of the morning. Armed with this information I visited each company in turn, answered general questions, and then gave them an hour for their individual problems. By and large both the R.S.M. and myself were fairly sure there was not much danger of a mutiny from our own men. But we had one company away from the rest of us, lent for demolition work to a battalion with a bad reputation.

One Thursday evening, while I was working in the orderly room, the R.S.M. came in, and I could see at once by his face that something really bad had happened. This company, he told me, had decided to mutiny at the Adjutant's Parade on Monday morning. Incidentally, though it was called my parade, I never attended. I told the R.S.M. not to worry, and that I would deal with it. I sent him off cheered, and then sat down, wondering how on earth I *was* going to deal with it. At that moment the locked 'brigade bag' came in. I opened it, sorted out the stuff, and found a Special Message to the Army from the Prime Minister. Ah, I thought, this is just what I want. I read it, and it was the usual double-faced politician's twaddle. There had been some very public mutinies, and it was meant to be a warning—but one that wouldn't lose votes in an election.

I tossed it on one side, and then reflected. After all, Lloyd George was a name to conjure with: and he *might have* faced facts and talked sense. From that it was a short passage to the decision that he *would* talk sense—to the 19th Queen's at any rate! I called in my confidential clerk, an admirable man called Judd who died, alas, in the influenza epidemic shortly afterwards. I explained to him that I wanted this document exactly copied, with all its references but not its text. He would have to put several sheets on top of it, as it was clearly not a top copy. I then dictated a very firm and clear message from the Prime Minister, that he had been very patient so far, but that he had now given instructions that any further disorder should be firmly and immediately dealt with, as it only delayed general demobilisation and the restarting of normal life. I put the new text in battalion orders, instructing that it should be read aloud to every company on the first parade of the day.

I then had the problem of whether I should tell the colonel—
I have already given a specimen of his ability to cope with any
special problem. I didn't want to; on the other hand, I had no
intention of staying in the army, and it would have little effect
on me if I was sacked. But it would break the old man's heart
if his army career ended in disgrace. So I told him, assured
him that I and the R.S.M. had the situation completely in
hand, but that he, at sixty, could do what I at twenty-two could
not. He could go and be fatherly, and tell them that if they were
all good boys they would soon be home. I begged him not
to make the slightest reference to any possibility of trouble,
or to appeal to their loyalty and discipline. I told him when to
do it, where to do it, and for how long to do it! When I was as
sure as I could be that he would do just what I asked, I had to
leave him to do it, as I never accompanied him on his daily
ride round the battalion at work. Fortunately I had for long
been accustomed to giving informal talks to each company
in turn on the latest stage of demobilisation regulations, so
that I could summon this company for a talk on Saturday
morning without attracting suspicion. I did so, and made no
direct allusion to the Monday plan. But I made various remarks which might have been relevant had anybody a bad
conscience.

I then had only one question to decide. Should I break all
precedent and appear on my own parade on Monday morning,
or should I leave it as usual to the R.S.M.? I decided to risk
it, and in fact the parade passed off without anything happening. Without the colonel, the R.S.M. or myself ever giving
any direct hint to the potential ringleaders, we had succeeded,
as the R.S.M. subsequently discovered, in leaving them completely uncertain how much we knew, but unable to convince
themselves that we knew nothing!

It was not long after this that I collapsed again with the old
effects of gas, and did my best to expire in a hospital in Norwich.
The day I came back the War Office sent us instructions on
carrying out its final attempt to introduce some order into
the chaos of demobilisation. It was an immense form with over
two hundred and fifty pigeonholes; and it was divided by a
broad black line down the middle separating those who were

compulsorily retained, because they joined the army after
January 1, 1916, from those who might volunteer for retention.
Unfortunately (for them) they drew the line one column too
far to the left. I was Category E (in and out of hospital and the
lowest category) and was compulsorily retained to my great
indignation, as I had come over to England to volunteer, and
was already in France when conscription was introduced in
April 1916. I should have been in the last column of those
retained. Instead Category E occupied the first column of the
volunteers.

There was the opportunity for which I had been waiting.
I had completed my work on disbandment; I had everything
organised to meet the problems of demobilisation. I could
honourably quit my job, and the Colonel had agreed a little
before that at the first available occasion I could arrange my
demobilisation. Knowing by this time War Office mentality,
I had been sure that in some obscure corner was a 'Section B'
for officers who did not fit any of the innumerable categories;
and I was also sure that the War Office reaction to finding
anybody in such a complicated situation that he had got into
Section B would be 'For Heaven's sake get rid of him'. So I
went to the colonel, explained to him that my logical mind
refused to volunteer for compulsory retention, and that, anyhow, as I was Category E, I was not eligible to be a volunteer.
I therefore proposed to put myself in Section B. The day I came
out of hospital we were ordered to demobilise all officers in
Section B forthwith.

I was entitled to three weeks convalescent leave, so I told the
colonel I would take this, take a bunch of the necessary forms
with me, and demobilise myself at the end of my leave—if they
did not catch me by finding out the error. There was only one
form which the colonel had to sign. The others were signed by
the adjutant, the demobilisation officer, or the officer to be
demobilised. I was all three—the perfect Pooh Bah. If I may
be vain for a moment, the form signed by the colonel was an
appreciation of the character of the officer concerned, and an
estimate of his potential value to the army if he stayed. He
had to state whether the officer was capable of regular infantry
work, of staff work, and up to what rank his capacities would

allow him to rise. Naturally all the officers' forms passed through my hands, and the colonel had been very scrupulous in answering the questions. Mine was the only form in which he had said that one of his officers was capable of rising to any rank, that he was a good battalion officer, and that he could also rise to any rank in staff work.

At the end of my leave, I went to the nearest demobilisation centre, sat down in front of the demobilisation officer, pulled a set of forms out of my pocket and, before his astonished eyes, filled them in and signed them one by one, except, of course, that signed by the colonel. I had taken the precaution of bringing with me the extract from army orders gazetting my adjutancy and captaincy, and the two battalion orders, one appointing me demobilisation officer, and the other naming me for demobilisation. A week after I had returned to Guernsey the error was discovered, and a new form was issued. But by that time I was safely a civilian.

As a postscript to my military career, I wish I could remember all my experiences of generals between 1917 and 1919. Both in France and in England they were a remarkable collection of absurdities. At Lowestoft we built some special coastal fortifications—I forget now what was special about them— and the corps commander came down specially to inspect them. I, of course, was in attendance as adjutant. He had to cross half a mile of open gorse common. Half way across he suddenly stopped, listened acutely and gazed around with wonder. "There it is again," he exclaimed, "it *is* a cuckoo. Now that is very odd. Cuckoos are usually found where there are trees, and there are no trees here." Meditating on this strange phenomenon, and ignoring his own staff officers and the 19th Queen's, he turned round and returned to his car, having entirely forgotten the inspection.

When we were being demobilised one of our generals came down to say goodbye. Like most of his kind, he had only one speech. His was on the need to keep one's rifle cleaned daily. Saying goodbye to us, he exhorted us to remember to treat our wives as he had always told us to treat our rifles. Then, his mind running in the well-worn grooves, he added : "Wipe them over with an oily rag every morning."

When I returned to civilian life it was with a fairly clear belief that I wanted to be ordained. I had not completely made up my mind, feeling that Oxford would give me the opportunity to reflect and decide. As well as that change in career, the army, or rather long and frequent periods in military hospitals, had instilled two habits which have remained with me all my life. Hospital beds were always left open at the bottom. I still like to be able to poke my toes out at the bottom of the bed—causing some complicated bed-making when I got married! Secondly, if one is only out of bed for one's daily bath, one finds it much nicer to shave in the bath than in bed. I still always shave in my bath if I can!

More important is that I had become a keen and fairly competent sketcher in the army. It had started with military sketching as a scout, but it soon went on to filling sketch books with records of the towns and villages of Flanders, and of the trenches. As it was strictly illegal, the necessary care not to be detected added to the pleasure. On the other hand, I never named a place or the site of a bit of line. In one of my billets I found some pastels, and took to them as my chosen medium when I began to do landscapes on my demobilisation. It was not really surprising that I took to drawing and painting. My father excelled at figures—which I was never any good at—and my mother was a charming water colourist, both of landscape and of buildings. My father's elder sister, my Aunt Annie, was an even better water colourist, so that I had inherited a potential talent on both sides.

III

POST-WAR OXFORD 1919–1923

I WAS IN no state to go straight up to Oxford when I was demobilised. I spent a long and lazy Spring and Summer at Maxstoke and in the Islands, spending some time in both Jersey and Alderney, and building up a collection of pastels of the cliffs, bays and old forts and castles of all the islands. But first I had to create a room for myself at the bungalow. There was only my father and myself to occupy it, but we reduced its size by leaving the West family, who had looked after it during the war, in possession of the kitchen and the rooms at that end of it in return for Mrs. West doing the cooking for us. What we were left with had been the drawing room and five bedrooms. I was determined to knock two bedrooms together to make a sitting room for myself, and to furnish it out of my gratuity.

My parent was completely uninterested in anything but the cheapest and most efficient way to get a required result. Shelves were cheaper than chests of drawers or cupboards. Linoleum was easier to sweep than carpets—and so on. His lack of interest in possessions extended to any possessions I was rash enough to leave at home while I was at Oxford. I was a born collector, but was quite likely to find he had given away books or other things which I had acquired on a previous vac. This was particularly trying with old family possessions. We did not have many, so I tried to preserve what we had. But a lovely and ancient Irish 'damask table cloth, which was always on request for any lunch party on my staircase at Hertford College, illustrates my problem. When I went into Ripon Hall, I did not need it, and took it home. When I returned the following vac, my father had discovered it, and cut it up because he was short of tea cloths and floor cloths!

My father had been a popular pen and ink artist in his day, composing text and drawings of books like *The Man who would like to Marry* and *The Girl who would not mind getting Married*. He produced the first limericks with a completely new last line, breaking the Edwin Lear tradition. They were the result of a bad evening's tooth-ache, which he alleviated by drawing ridiculous people and then writing limericks to fit them. On his way to the dentist the next morning he passed by his publisher and sold them. I once produced a book in five days, but never equalled my father's record! They were good limericks. I liked particularly:

> There was an old man of Dundee
> Who sent me some gunpowder tea,
> But the first cup I tried
> Exploded inside
> And rather disorganised me.

Gunpowder tea was, I believe, a cheap but popular Victorian brand. My grandfather had produced the same kind of illustrated books—though his were for private circulation, as commerce was not, to his mind, genteel enough! With considerable difficulty I had gathered together all my grandfather's and father's books, but returned one vac to find he had burnt or given away the lot, as he wanted the space to keep tools in!

In October 1919 I went up to Hertford. Oxford then had about 4,000 undergraduates. Hertford was a very small college with little over a hundred. Hence we knew all our fellow undergraduates by name. Our Principal was the Nestor of the university, Dr. Henry Boyd, well on in his eighties; but every member of the college had breakfast or lunch with him every term, a delightful occasion, for he had been everywhere and his memory was prodigious. Oxford was a stately university when Lord Curzon was Chancellor, for on any important occasion he appeared in full court dress as well as the usual gorgeous black and gold robes. My first English passport was issued by him, over his signature and coat of arms. With his full list of titles and orders, it made a sonorous document to impress a foreigner —very different from the machine-made impersonality of today. This was my first *English* passport since I had previously had one issued, most ungrammatically, by: 'We, His Excellency,

the Lieutenant Governor of Guernsey and its Dependencies'.
The first rooms I had in college were next to the old hall, in
the old quad. From my bedroom window I could see the Rad-
cliffe dome, with St. Mary's lovely spire behind it. My first
tutor was E. A. Burroughs, followed by J. D. Denniston. In
contrast with the 'rat race' of today, both of them accepted
that I was not interested in exams but wanted to work at things
that interested me for their own sake. Actually I was not fit
enough to do the hard work which would have got a first, and
was very satisfied when I got a good second in classical Mods.
I then went over to theology, arguing that it was absurd for a
man to pretend to be a student of philosophy before he was
forty. I have never regretted that I preferred theology to
Greats.

In both Schools I had tutors whom it was a delight to tease.
Denniston was an impeccably correct classical scholar, wanting me to write good Livy and philosophical Cicero, while in
Greek verse he considered Sophocles the only model to follow.
I wrote him Latin proses in the style of Cicero's letters, larding
them probably with quotations in English and French as well
as Greek, on the reasonable grounds that, if Cicero had been
writing in the twentieth century, he would certainly have been
vain of his knowledge of those languages. Alternatively I
offered him epigrammatic Tacitus, which was a pleasant
contrast to my Greek offerings of highly emotional Euripides,
or sesquipedalian Aeschylus—not to mention Thucydidean
anacolutha. It was great fun, especially as he would probably
catch me out with some frightful grammatical howler. But, as
Burroughs once expostulated with me : "I realise that the rhythm
of your sentence required you to write *hominorum*, but you must
adjust your sense of rhythm to *some* knowledge of simple
grammar !"

When I came to do theology I had the immense advantage
of having Cyril Emmet as a tutor, and I discovered that it was
a waste of a good tutorial to produce something with which he
completely agreed. If he disagreed, then a really valuable
discussion followed. I also discovered—a fact which amazed
my colleagues in Ripon Hall —that he enjoyed having his leg
pulled. We had a great battle once over the Servant poems,

which he held could not have been written by the Second Isaiah, as they were on a deeper level than anything else in his writings. He told me to sort out my views in writing an essay on the subject for my next tutorial. The essay I produced proved there could not be a spire on Salisbury Cathedral as nothing else in the building prepared one for its height. On another occasion I held something to be by a single author, which he considered to be a composite work. When he adopted the same strategy, I produced an essay which proved quite conclusively that Rupert Brooke's *Grantchester* was a composite work of many dates and many authors. How could the man who wrote

> "Cambridgeshire of all England
> The shire for men who understand"

have written

> "Cambridge people rarely smile,
> Being urban, squat, and packed with guile?"

I also discovered a reference to the bishop in the 'clerical interpolation'. In fact I ended by doubting myself whether Brooke really wrote all of it!

I discovered to my delight that I could take Early Christian Art and Architecture as my Special Subject. As it was included in the Faculty List, they could not refuse, though they were somewhat annoyed. It had been included for twenty-eight years, and nobody had ever taken it before! Moreover there was nobody at Oxford who was considered suitable as a supervisor. I was asked with whom I should read it, and suggested Mr. Dalton, who was in charge of that section of the British Museum. I used to spend a day with him every term. They also had to find an examiner to set the paper, and for this they secured Percy Dearmer—all rather expensive for the university!

In the summer of 1923 I sat for my finals. On the afternoon of the second day the Supervisor approached me and studied me carefully.

"Excuse me, Sir," he said, "are you feeling quite well?"

"Perfectly well," I replied. "What's the matter?"

"Are you aware, Sir, that you are all over spots?"

I hastily pulled up my sleeve, and spotted I surely was. Measles! I retired to bed, and by the morning had a high temperature. I had done the required minimum papers for an *aegrotat*, so the faculty was notified. During the morning there was a knock at my door, and there entered a superb procession in full academic dress—Dr. Major, Principal of Ripon Hall, Mr. Emmet, my Tutor, Dr. Counsell, my Doctor, a representative of the Faculty of Medicine, and another of the Faculty of Theology. Standing as far away from me as was possible in a small room, they all raised their squares, and chanted in unison, "Good morning, sir," They then continued antiphonally:

"I think he has got measles."

"He appears to me to have measles."

"I believe we might certify that he has measles."

"Indeed, it would appear to me to be certainly measles."

Then they all raised their squares, intoned, "Good morning, sir," and the vision faded, leaving me wondering whether it was a delusion of fever. However, it was genuine, and in due course I was called for a *viva*. I had been an expensive item, requiring a special supervisor and a special paper, for which Percy Dearmer told me later he had received a fiver, so the examiners felt that they could examine me themselves without incurring further expense.

They thus afforded me the final joy of undergraduate life, that of flooring my examiners! They produced the exam paper, asked me how I would answer this question and that, until, gaining confidence, they adventured in too deep.

"Now, Mr. Parkes, Question 8, how would you answer that?"

Question 8 was deceptively simple: *How do you construct a dome?*

"Just in a sentence or two, Mr. Parkes, how would you construct a dome."

I gazed at them with infinite compassion: "I cannot tell you that in a sentence or two," I replied. "You must first tell me whether it is to be an in-centric or an ex-centric dome, and am I to construct it on a horizontal or vertical axis?"

"Thank you very much, Mr. Parkes, that will be all," they quavered gasping, and I departed rejoicing.

When I came to supplicate for permission to study for a

Doctorate of Philosophy, I produced a letter which had been
signed by all the examiners, saying that so far as I had got, I
had reached the level of a First. The Registrar was very upset
that they had expressed such an opinion on Faculty notepaper!
He accepted it as a qualification for permission; but he insisted on keeping it, on the grounds that they never ought to
have written it!

Outside work, the Don with whom I had most to do at
Hertford was the admirable chaplain, John McLeod Campbell.
He was an excellent college chaplain. In those days of universal
limericks—of which Canon Streeter was a prolific author—
it was said that:

> The Chaplain of Hertford, called John,
> Is a singular man for a Don;
> For he actually says
> He believes what he prays,
> And preaches his sermons upon.

'Holy John' quickly found out that I was thinking of ordination; he introduced me to the Student Christian Movement,
and persuaded me to go to its great missionary Quadrennial
at Glasgow in 1921. These were the great days of the S.C.M.,
and the platform at Glasgow was crowded with national
figures in Church and State. In the sectional meetings we could
find and talk to men and women who could speak from experience on the problems of all the continents, and of almost
every career which offered opportunities for Christian service.
It is a measure of the significant change after the second world
war that at the Westminster Quadrennial of 1947 the students
wanted only to hear each other talk, and to discuss on a level
we would have found inadequate in a study circle of freshmen;
while the general meetings were reduced to four in the whole
conference. Of these one was inaudible, one incomprehensible
and only two both relevant and by competent speakers.

Glasgow had been preceded, and prepared, by a campaign
in Oxford with the title *Religion and Life*. The biggest halls of
the university were filled night after night, when men like
William Temple, Baron von Hugel, W. Maltby would draw

hundreds to discussions and questions after their meetings. Though the S.C.M. was very active in Oxford in those days, I did not see a great deal of it, mainly because after Mods I was engulfed in the League of Nations Union. I joined it when I came up, because my desire for ordination was not based on any wish to escape from the contemporary world, but was tied to the conviction, which I shared with so many of my generation, that we had to discover the moral foundations of a way of life for the whole world which would make a repetition of the war impossible.

There was nothing inconsistent in my finding my interest in the L.N.U. rather than the S.C.M., for membership of the two bodies overlapped a great deal. In fact, wherever one was concerned with political or social progress, one would find members of the S.C.M. in on the ground floor. In those happy days neither 'liberal' nor 'humanist' was a term of abuse, and humanist and committed Christian worked together over a wide area of life. Nor were we ashamed to speak of the possibility of 'progress', nor, because we did speak of it, believe in it and work for it, were we utopians or shallow and superficial. It was a generation which had seen too much of the reality of war, and which saw too clearly the immense gaps in the Christian tradition in so far as human community was concerned, for it to be legitimate to call it 'starry eyed'. Of course it failed to achieve the realisation of its hopes; and that will be a very present reality during the later chapters; but it was a noble failure.

The term before I took Mods, I was asked whether I would take on the University secretaryship of the L.N.U. Before I agreed, I talked to John Campbell, and got him to arrange for me to put it before the Senior Common Room. I explained that I was not going to accept except with their consent, since I was a scholar, and it meant that for a year the L.N.U. would come first, and theology second. At that moment the Union had no special activities for a university section, and the university members were simply part of the city branch of the national Union. I wanted to make the union effective in the University, but that would mean considerable work in devising appropriate activities. The S.C.R. agreed to my doing it; and, for the next year, at my appearance before the terminal 'Don Rag', I was asked how the L.N.U. was progressing and not what progress I was making at work.

I came to the conclusion that the presence of undergraduates from many nations at Oxford gave us an immensely valuable basis for an international assembly based on, but not copying, the Assembly of Geneva. Because we were an exceptionally mature generation, I was able to set my sights very high, and to devise a technique of representation and discussion which soon made the Assembly the most popular regular meeting in the University. We met three times a term in the hall of the Union. We were equally open to men and women students. Each nation was represented by three persons from that nation.

There was provision for 'expert delegations' in cases where there were no citizens of the country concerned at Oxford, but where the position of that country was too important for its problems and point of view to be omitted. There were then no students from Germany or the Soviet Union, and both countries had 'expert' representation. At first bright young things thought it would be great fun to represent Azerbaijan or Ruritania. When they came to me and offered themselves, I sent them to the 'Committee of Delegations'. Were they sufficiently persistent to appear before the committee, they found themselves closely questioned. Unless they could answer positively to three basic questions they were at once rejected. The questions were: When did you last visit the country? Do you speak its language? What steps are you taking to remain continuously informed on its problems?

I had to devise the whole of the procedure for our meetings, for I was convinced that we must not be a 'debating society' where nations were committed in advance to opposing each other. I therefore proposed that for the first term *I* should be the constitution, that there would be no appeal from my rulings, but that at the beginning of the second term, when we would all have some experience of what we wanted, and what pitfalls we had to avoid, we would make a constitution. To my private surprise the proposal was accepted.

Each meeting of the Assembly was preceded by a Report prepared for it by a special committee of members on the subject which had been chosen for discussion at the previous meeting. This gave a fortnight for the work. Any nation might request permission to attend the committee, but then had to attend all its meetings. These were in my room though I was not present; I was, however, responsible for preparing material for the meeting. Sometimes the committee would meet three or four times before it was ready with its report. To cram three or four extra meetings into a fortnight for the kind of people we had on our delegations meant that they were really taking their work seriously. I remained secretary, but a new president was elected at each meeting for that following, so that as many nations as possible could receive the honour. The issues we debated were the burning issues of the day, and at times the Assembly had to be suspended before it broke into furious chaos. Distinguished visitors could be invited by any delegation. They sat with the delegation, and enjoyed the same right of speech as all the other delegates—but no more. At one tumultuous meeting Lord Olivier, later Secretary of State for India, had been invited. It was a meeting that ended in disorder—I think it was on the admission of Germany, but I am not sure—and I went up to Olivier afterwards to apologise. His comment was: "Yes, perhaps it was unworthy of the Oxford International Assembly, but what a perfect picture of the Supreme Allied Council."

There were two other issues on which I had no precedent to follow. We could not expect that voting would be unnecessary; at the same time we did not want intriguing and indignant minorities all the time. So we had three categories of decision. For a report to be 'accepted' it had to get the approval of two-thirds of the members of the Assembly—each delegation counting as a single vote. To be 'rejected' it had likewise to be refused by two thirds. In between, the report was 'not accepted'. The other issue, which I left to the Assembly to decide, was the admission or non-admission of states which were identifiable entities on the political map, but were not sovereign. Class A Mandates were an obvious example. The Assembly decided that, as it had no sovereign or executive power, but purely an educational function, these communities were eligible for full membership.

The Assembly was too complex and mature a body for the much younger generation which followed the ex-service men and women for whom it had been devised. It came to an end, I think, in 1925. But it was not my only activity as university secretary. I had a college secretary in all the colleges who recruited members. I, or someone else, spoke in most of the colleges. In addition to this, I spoke on the League in many of the villages and towns surrounding Oxford, dining with the squire or the rector before the meeting, and usually finding a courteous but invincible opponent of the possibility of any international development. Support of the League was dismissed as 'unrealistic'; the British Empire was the only permanent factor for peace; and admitting all these 'lesser breeds' to equality on the League Assembly was merely giving them ideas above their station!

These excursions into the countryside gave me an insight into the basic political problem of my generation—in all the countries which had won or lost the war. The older generation saw the war as an unfortunate—indeed tragic—lapse in a political world with which they were otherwise contented. My generation saw the war as proof that the distribution of political power and responsibility had failed and needed to be radically changed. The second war was largely due to the misfortune that all the positions of authority in between the wars were occupied by those who rejected a new world, and wanted to return to the old.

I collected a superb library of nationalist propaganda which, alas, my successors neglected and lost. I wish I could quote from its magnificent English. One Hungarian pamphleteer was a little vague as to the use of 'bulk' in describing population. Instead of saying that "the bulk of the population was so and so," he wished to be more specific and wrote that "this town contains ten thousand Hungarian bulks". Then there was the printer more accustomed to setting Arabic who, when his nationalist sentiments were aroused, began to set his English type backwards, and who, at the end of a pamphlet, set the whole peroration from right to left!

My position as university secretary of the L.N.U. naturally brought me into close touch with the undergraduates who were running the other main activities of the university, successive presidents of the Union and the political clubs, editors of the *Isis*, then at a very high level, and leaders of the S.C.M. and the religious societies. I became successively 'Idolet', 'Idol', and 'Man of the Year' in the *Isis*, and occasionally contributed to it. My most successful contribution arose accidentally from my calling on the editor, Alan Colingridge, and finding him lamenting that his poetess had failed him for the Eights Week number by getting chicken pox. "Come on, Parkes," he said; "produce me a poem." To my great surprise I did. It was intended by the 'poetess' to put the men whose invitations she accepted in their proper place.

> Because you're President of some
> Society you think I come
>   To see the play with you
>   But No,
>   I came to see the play!
>   And so,
> *Voila! C'est tout.*

She successively liked the cakes, the rooms, and the punts of her hosts but accepted their invitations solely for her own pleasure! I learned by a side wind that the poem had caused the most magnificent rage in the women's colleges, that angry resolutions of condemnation had been passed at turbulent meetings, and detective work had been undertaken to unmask the traitor. It was fortunate for me that Dorothy Sayers could not put Lord Peter on my track, or I should probably have suffered severely. In fact, my identity was never revealed.

The president of the university branch of the L.N.U. was inevitably Professor Gilbert Murray, and my greatest privilege was that I was allowed to visit Yatscombe on Boar's Hill whenever I wanted to. Mr. Murray—as he wished to be called —would always make time to help me with any problem, to secure any speaker I needed, or to expound what had actually happened at a League meeting. For he was at that time, with Lord Robert Cecil, appointed by Smuts as official representative of South Africa on the Assembly. I could also call on Colonel

Borden Turner who always accompanied Lord Robert to
League meetings as his secretary. The high water mark of these
contacts came when I was invited to meet Nansen at breakfast
at the Murray's. Nansen was in Oxford raising funds for
famine relief in the Soviet Union. He described to us graphically
the appalling situation in province after province of Russia,
and admitted with horror that in places this had led to canni-
balism. Murray's reception of this news was memorable. "I am
so glad," he said. "I have always hoped that, if I was in a famine
and not likely to survive, other people would save their own
lives by eating what was left of me."

Needless to say, these activities indicate that I was a good
deal fitter in my third year than I had been in my first. Nevertheless an eight week term was about all I could stand; and
by the seventh week my memory had almost completely gone.
In fact, I celebrated the laying down of my offices in an unusual
way. Sir Patrick Agnew, who presided over the L.N.U. in the
city and, I think, the region, held a little dinner in my honour.
Having observed the fact in my diary, I went to my bedroom
to change into a dinner jacket . . . Some time later I perceived
that I was half undressed, so I completed the process, put
on my pyjamas, and went to bed! Moreover, when I was not
running round the university, I was usually lying down. I
constructed a most complicated reading desk which could be
attached to an arm chair, and which would hold several books,
a cup of tea, and space to write an essay without moving, and
I did all my work thereon. It proudly displayed a motto from
that delightful old cynic, Qoheleth: *God hath made man upright;
but they have sought out many inventions.*

After I had retired from the L.N.U. to prepare for my theology
finals, I had to emerge once more into the political field. Gordon
Bagnall, who was president of the Union at the end of 1922,
headed an invitation to twelve German students to visit Oxford
for a month in the summer term. In February 1923 the rector
of the City Church took up his cudgels against the invitation,
preached a sermon in which he declared that it was "an offence
against all decency, the mere mention of which shocked and
disgusted him", and sent the text of his discourse to the Oxford
Chronicle, which was a paper which had always backed the

L.N.U., and had been very friendly to my Assembly. So I went to the Editor on the Monday and asked him if he would print a letter from me indicating that the rector was free to adopt what attitude he liked to his German contemporaries, but could not decide the attitude to each other of those who had borne the brunt of the fighting on both sides, since they had mostly been at school when war broke out.

The letter duly appeared, and then the *Morning Post* entered the fray with a whole column from an Oxford correspondent devoted to abuse of the project, and of me in particular. I had written it in agreement with Bagnall, for I was not a member of the committee and they could disavow me if they wanted to; in addition to which I left them anonymous and would draw the fire of the opposition months before the Germans were due to come. The correspondent misrepresented what I had said, so that I appeared as a schoolboy attacking the ex-service men. However, their most interesting comment was that I was the natural product of the pernicious teaching of

William Temple, Bishop of Manchester
Dr. Cairns, Professor of Dogmatics at Aberdeen University
William Inge, Dean of St. Paul's.
Dr. Selbie, Principal of Mansfield College, Oxford.

Later I met all four, and informed them that I was the natural result of their pernicious teaching! There was a Union debate on the invitation at which I followed Evelyn Waugh who produced a somewhat artificial support for the City rector. The voting was in favour of the invitation by 177 to 74.

These tactics were successful in drawing the fire at a time when the Germans were not there, and the visit passed off perfectly peacefully. There was only one moment when the committee regretted they had left me to do the job; that was when I received an anonymous letter threatening to shoot me at sight! I had until then no suspicion that the receipt of a anonymous letter was so envy-making a distinction.

My years at Oxford were not all serious, for I was privy to some of the most successful fake meetings of those years. I had no part in the meeting on 'Freud and the New Psychology' of

3

which Edinger was, I think, the hero, and Balliol the origin. But Hertford was the source of the very successful lecture of Dr. André Veulotte (actually a Cambridge undergraduate) who described his experiences in Africa where he had discovered a tribe so primitive that he could actually see their minds working, and so could establish the link between physiology and psychology. I believe references to it caused much puzzlement in the following year's medical schools, for it was mostly medical students who were invited. The source of the idea lay with the late Kenneth Franklin, who became Professor of Physiology in London University. He lived on my staircase, and we usually shared lunch.

There was also a lecture on the revolution in Mexico, attended by American students, which was given by 'an American journalist' with the implausible name of Sam Hill—at that time a common American expletive. It succeeded in enraging the audience (for which purpose it was designed). Sam Hill was actually a Christ Church undergraduate. He displayed a stone which was treated with unusual respect for one picked up in the Meadows, since he alleged it was taken from the top of Popocatepetl. His best remark was a comment on the revolutionary leader's knowledge of English literature. "He has just retired and told me that it was from that famous English dramatist, Shakespeare, he would take a description of his action: 'It is a far far better thing that I do now than I have ever done before.' Now I don't pretend to be an expert on the subject, but I knew that came from Thackeray's *Mill on the Floss*." This glorious howler was received with complete courtesy and acceptance by the well-bred Oxford audience!

My vacations were spent at Maxstoke or in the cottage the Lee-Elliotts had at Blakeney, and in the Channel Islands. I had very little money and, anyhow, hitch-hiking was not then invented—there were not enough cars on the roads of Europe to make it possible. Some of my contemporaries did, of course, travel in various ways. Were there a prize for originality it would certainly have been won by a Rhodes scholar from America who travelled as far as Constantinople on a Life Insurance policy, which he assured frontier officials was a diplomatic passport. Needless to say he chose remote spots for crossing a frontier. The first few were, he admitted, difficult, but when the policy was well decorated with stamps it was willingly accepted. The adventure was worth while, for in those years transit visas to Constantinople would cost an American citizen more than first class with sleeping car on the Orient Express!

When I got home to Guernsey, often with an Oxford friend, I worked hard and also painted. Harold Mulliner, later Chancellor of Truro, profited most, I think, from such a visit. I gave him measles, and in return, took him over to Alderney to convalesce. We spent our days happily building sand castles, and I taught him all he knew of medieval fortification in so doing. We started with a joint effort on a carefully chosen rock, beginning with Norman keep and walls. The sand of Alderney was excellent, fine and firm, so that one built a three story keep of vaulted chambers. Then one continued to fortify the site, right down to the heavy bastions against the cannon of the Tudors. If a building collapsed one rebuilt it in the period at which one was at that moment working. The 'show castle' completed, we chose two sites, and fortified them against each other, following the same historical sequence. He took a first in history the year after my *aegrotat*, and was commended for his paper on medieval fortification.

I painted fortifications as well as built them, and the results of my painting I took back to Oxford the following term, and succeeded in selling quite a number. All the money I made went into making a very pleasant collection of Jacobean and eighteenth century furniture. In 1922 there was an exhibition of undergraduates' work at the Oxford Arts Club. Of one picture I exhibited the *Oxford Chronicle*'s critic wrote that "there is assuredly nothing more agreeable in the whole Exhibition than his *Mists* where he gets almost Whistlerian effects of pale, soft colour touched with the sense of mystery". I had tried for a long time to get the effect of the sea disappearing into the mist, without the adventitious aid of ever paler rocks to mark the perspective, and here the foreground is simply sand without a single rock. I had sold the picture to a fellow undergraduate, John Bird, within half an hour of painting it, and had begged it back from him for the exhibition. After Oxford I often used to visit him and his mother at Radlett. When she died he got a job in New York. The following Christmas I received a large parcel. In it was my picture, and a letter saying that he had noticed that I always sat in a chair opposite the picture, so that he suspected I was sorry I had sold it. Now that he was quitting England he was sending it me as a Christmas present on condition that I never sold it to anyone else.

Before I left Oxford I had a curious experience with my pastels. The measles left me at Ripon Hall for the vac, looked after by the Norwegian housekeeper, Miss Kleppe. She was most anxious to have one of my pastels so, when I became convalescent, I produced my sketch books and asked her to choose one to be turned into a picture. But she insisted that she wanted one of Norway. I said that I had never been there, and had never seen a mountain, a lake, or a forest in my life. She produced a coloured postcard which she wanted me to turn into a pastel. Thinking that, if I used a sunset, I would cover my ignorance of the colours, I consented. But she followed this by producing several more. In all I did her nineteen pictures. I had to do them when she was in the room, and she had to imagine herself looking at the scene I was trying to transfer to my picture. She was quite hopeless at explaining any colours in words, but if she imagined herself looking at the scene I could pick out the colours from my tray. I could say to her with complete certainty: "you have stopped thinking about it", and if she left the room I had to stop. The last two I did were of her own island, and she had no picture for me to take as basis. I had to do it entirely out of her mind. But some time later, when all my pictures decorated her walls, she gave a Norwegian evening, and I stood behind two Norwegian students who were identifying them one by one. When they came to the two of her island, they proceeded to identify it correctly.

During my period at Ripon Hall I was accepted by the Bishop of Lichfield. The Parkes family came from the Warwickshire-Staffordshire border, and I thought it would be pleasant to begin my clerical career there. But in March 1923 I received, quite unexpectedly, an invitation to join the staff of the Student Christian Movement, and accepted it.

After Oxford I was inevitably much less in Guernsey. I got

over when I could to see my father, but it could be only for very short visits. He stayed in the bungalow till the middle of the twenties, when he sold it, and had very pleasant rooms with the widow of an old artisan friend of vinery days, Mr. Crocker. There he remained until he died during the German occupation.

IV

THE STUDENT CHRISTIAN MOVEMENT AND THE STUDENT MOVEMENT HOUSE

In 1923 the Student Christian Movement of Great Britain and Ireland was at the height of its influence and its authority. It was ahead of other student organisations for two reasons. It was the only one which had existed before 1914 in all universities in the British Isles, for the National Union of Students and the University League of Nations Society were both post-war creations. Even more important was that its two leaders, the Rev. Tissington Tatlow and Miss Zoë Fairfield, were both of pre-war vintage. "T" had come on to the staff in 1897, and had been General Secretary since 1903; Zoë had begun to work as Assistant General Secretary in 1909. Their different qualities made them a remarkable partnership. Both had a deep and unassuming religious sincerity. T. had a genius for training his juniors without fussing them, and often understood the movements of thought among students better than his younger colleagues. Zoë had an ever-fresh imagination and intuition joined to an extremely wise understanding of how things got done—and by whom. Both were completely without any denominational narrowness; and the contribution they made to the developing ecumenism of British Christianity was immeasurable. Both had been planning all through the war how to meet the problems of the new university world to which—on both sides—men and women would come back.

Unlike the situation in most continental universities, the S.C.M. was jealous of nobody and, generally speaking, nobody was jealous of the S.C.M. It provided a solid backing for other student societies, and it provided equally often the kind of student who was prepared and fit to undertake the strenuous task of moulding and leading the new Student Unions or Representative Councils which were springing up in all the universities except Oxford and Cambridge. Typical of the situation was an incident which befell me at an autumn Council meeting of the N.U.S. I got up to say something. The President pulled me up, saying that I had not given my name, and there were a number of new Union Presidents and Committee members present. I looked round the room, spotted the newcomers, and had met them all at the summer conference of the S.C.M. at Swanwick.

The full-time staff of the S.C.M., when I joined it in June 1923, was about forty. There was a headquarters, based on London, which included the Study Department under 'George' Cockin, later Bishop of Bristol. I was in charge of International Study, H. A. Mess of Social Study, R. O. Hall, later Bishop of Hongkong, of Missionary Study, while George himself specialised in Bible Study. Then there were the special Secretaries for Training, Theological and Technical Colleges, a London University staff of four, a man and a woman looking after foreign students, of whom one, Louise Royaards, a witty and delightful Dutch girl who married the Business Secretary, 'Johnny' Walker, was specially linked to international study. She was invaluable for her understanding of the continent and her knowledge of languages. When I got involved in profound theological correspondence with German students, she translated all my letters until it occurred to both sides that it would be easier if we corresponded in Latin.

In the 'outback' there were secretaries who were in charge of the S.C.M. at one or more universities, travelling secretaries, and the Welsh, Scottish and Irish staffs. In all it was a goodly company.

Almost immediately after I arrived in London, I took part in an Anglo-American conference, the first to take place in the new house of the First Conference Estate, High Leigh. None of the extra buildings had yet been erected; it had only just ceased to be the home of the Barclays, the parents of the Treasurer of the Movement. Its gardens were still in all their cultivated and elaborate loveliness. After High Leigh I went to Switzerland to a conference of the World's Student Christian Federation at Heinrichsbad in the north-east corner of the country. It was a very moving conference, for it witnessed the first meeting since the war of the French and German Christian

Student Movements. In the words I have just written there is a distinction, which implies also a difference. I was a member of the staff of a Movement for students whose object was to create or deepen their understanding of Christianity. The continental movements were movements for Christian students. The British Movement was interdenominational, and only the Roman Catholics—by their own choice—abstained from it. The continental movements were primarily confessional.

The culmination of Heinrichsbad was a Communion Service, held in German, French and English. We all felt it to be the only possible consummation of a deeply stirring experience. We had to compose the service. The actual words of consecration were read by a Danish pastor; I took the English part (I was not yet ordained), and a French student read the French part. The whole was presided over by the Swiss pastor of Heinrichsbad, which was a small Protestant spa. This was the beginning of what was to be a somewhat odd clerical career, conducting strange services in strange places under strange language conditions.

My concern with international study brought me naturally into contact with various other bodies. I became a member of the British Institute of International Affairs, soon to become 'Royal', and owner of Chatham House in St James's Square. I was very much younger than the average member, but my value was that I could tell them of promising members in the British Universities, and also report on conditions in the European Universities, which were intensely active political bodies. In fact a good half of the political assassinations between the wars were committed by University students.

I came later to know quite well one of the group that murdered Rathenau. The desperate despair of Germany after the first World War is something which it is almost impossible for us to realise. There was starvation everywhere. To the young intellectual, worse than the physical starvation was the appalling sense of moral isolation, of being regarded by the whole world as moral lepers. The demands of the Allies grew every day more exhorbitant. The currency was falling every hour. Every hope, every dream was shattered. Many committed suicide rather than face the future; many abandoned themselves recklessly to the pleasures of the moment such as could be got. In Berlin there was a small group of very serious students, high minded, patriotic, and intellectually of the first water. Day by day they discussed what could be done to save Germany. For them the most awful thing was the apathy and despair. Nobody seemed to care if there was a solution, or to believe one possible. They felt that the vital thing to do was to wake people up to the seriousness of the situation. But how? The people were exhausted. There was no new horror which could stir those who had already been through so much. How could they attract the attention of the people? Their final decision, taken, one must realise, with a kind of mystical exaltation very foreign to our calmer temperaments, and in a spirit of fanatical self-sacrifice, was to decide who was the greatest man in Germany, and to assassinate him as a demonstration! Their choice was unhappily correct, and in the hour of her greatest need, their insane crime robbed Germany of the one man whose brilliant gifts might have rendered her enormous service, Dr. Walter Rathenau.

It is on such a sombre background that European student life was lived, and that work like mine had to be done. British students, in their secure a-political world, had little idea of the stresses and tragedies of their European brethren. I was staying once in a student hostel on top of an Austrian hill—Sontagsberg. Walking one day with an Austrian student, we came to a point where we looked down on the picturesque town of Waidhofen. There was a bridge over the Ibbs which was obviously an excellent position to sketch the castle from. When we reached the bridge—a quite new one—the parapets were seven feet high. I asked her why they made parapets like that in Austria, and she replied, as though it was the perfectly natural and reasonable explanation: "I suppose it is more difficult for people to jump off."

I had a special relationship with the National Union of Students. In fact, Ivison Macadam was one of the young men I recommended to Chatham House membership. I had known the N.U.S. since it was brought into existence to provide a national body which could combat the anti-German policy of the *Confédération Internationale des Etudiants*; and I became a

3*

visiting member of its executive, as representing the S.C.M.
As the years passed I came to occupy a difficult position.
Students came and went and I remained, by far the most
senior member outside the permanent officers and the natural
consultant on difficult internal matters. For in many cases I
knew presidents and secretaries of local Unions from my visits
to the universities and their visits to Swanwick. The international battle was the main interest of the N.U.S., but it was
very difficult and puzzling for British students to meet the
skilled intrigue of their continental opposite numbers. I remember attending an Autumn Council meeting where there was
general disappointment at the failure of all their efforts, combined with an equally general unwillingness to reproach anyone for the failure. The whole morning was taken in the attempt
to put these complicated feelings into a Resolution. So I
suggested a simple formula: "This House endorses everything
which anybody has done anywhere, and regrets it."

My third special contact was with the League of Nations
Union and its distinguished—but odd—secretary, Maxwell
Garnett. I used to report to him how things were in his branches
in the universities, and never ceased to plead for an autonomous academic organisation with its own secretary. In the end
this was done. C. W. Judd was appointed, and held the post
for many years.

My joining the S.C.M. had put an end to my Lichfield
project, but the Bishop of London was accustomed to ordain-
ing secretaries of the S.C.M. and accepted me. He told me,
however, that I should have to pass his exam. I asked him
whether it was the usual cram exam, in which I had to answer
questions on all kinds of matters I would, for the rest of my life,
look up in a book if it became necessary to inform myself about
them. The Bishop replied that I had done with all that kind
of thing, and that now he wanted to know what I thought about
things, and what I was interested in.

The result was, so far as routine was concerned, disastrous.
When I sat for the exam I found a set of mid-Victorian questions of which the first I read—a 'gobbet'—indicated the kind of
rubbish which was provocative to my extremely bad temper,
for I had had to cancel a quite important piece of work to sit

the exam. It was: "Give the speaker and context of: (a) 'Is thy servant a dog that he should do this thing?' " Avoiding saying that the obvious context was the bishop of London's ordination exam, I passed on hurriedly to the next question. This, following the Bishop's expressed wish that I should say what I thought about things, I dismissed succinctly by saying: "this is a silly question." But on the next I shipwrecked. Of all ridiculous questions to ask, it was: "Explain the causes of the ruptures of the kings of Judah and Israel." This also required only a one sentence answer: "I am not a doctor." I still regard as complete justification for my explosion the next question, which was: "Outline the development of the ideas of (a) God, (b) morality, (c) immortality *in the whole of the Old Testament*!" What a question to put on a par with the ruptured puppets of Syria and Egypt!

The result, of course, was that I was ploughed in every paper. The Bishop—it was Winnington Ingram—wrote to me and explained that he had been bishop of London for I forget how many centuries, and that this had never happened before. Would I go and see him? I went, and told him he had asked me to answer the questions in such a way that he could see what I thought about things, and what I was interested in. He said he understood, was perfectly sweet, and gave me his blessing. He then sent me to his senior examining chaplain, who was not and didn't. The result of a two hours' interview was that I refused on principle to take the exam again. The bishop of Manchester heard of this strange young secretary of the S.C.M.—a movement to which he was very sympathetic— and said he would like to see him the next time S.C.M. business took him to Manchester. So the next time I went to Manchester, I stayed with William Temple.

The actual cause of my coming was quickly dealt with. Having heard the whole story, William remarked that he did not know which was the bigger fool, me or the examining chaplain of the Bishop of London. He then wrote a long letter to the bishop, as a result of which I was duly ordained. This was only the first of many visits to Temple, who remained a much-loved guide and friend to the end of his life. The last letter I had from him was typical of the trouble he took even

with apparently minor matters. I had, as he demanded that
I always did, sent him something I had written in the theological
field. He answered me saying that if I meant so and so, he
agreed; but if I meant so and so, then I had not sufficiently
taken this or that into account.

My curacy at £5 a year was with Archdeacon Sharpe at
St. Stephen's, Hampstead, and it perfectly illustrated my basic
problem. Sharpe was a saint in many ways. He had a men's
club (which to be 'with it' in those days you called a Moot),
and asked me to speak to it on my work in the S.C.M. In the
course of my remarks I said that, if the Church of England was
in some sense the conscience of the nation, then it should call
the nation to repent and make atonement for many things that
had happened and were happening in the British Empire.
My dear Vicar picked out this remark for his closing address.
It was not the duty, he said, of the Church of England to call
the English people to make atonement and restitution, but to
preach Christ to other people so that they should forgive us
without asking for restitution. And this was a most earnest and
devout Christian, who once said to me, when I queried his
giving to someone at the door: "I know as well as you that nine
out of ten who come and beg from me are frauds, but I cannot
guarantee to pick out the tenth; and I cannot bear the thought
that a man came to a Christian priest in his need and was
turned away empty. I would much rather give to the nine
others."

Heinrichsbad involved me at once in the controversy with
which I lived continuously until I came home from Geneva
in 1935, the controversy with German Protestant theology
about the nature of 'the Fall', and the basic relationship between God and man.

Fortunately for me the leaders of the German Movement for
Christian Students (the D.C.S.V.) were not the only German
students with whom I came into contact. The World's Student
Christian Federation had, in 1921, founded a Committee for
European Student Relief (later the International Student
Service, now the World University Service), and I was a mem-
ber of the English Committee, responsible for raising funds in
England. The S.C.M. always took the lead in this fund-raising,

usually with the loyal co-operation of the N.U.S. The E.S.R. brought me into touch with another strand of German student life. Moreover immediately after I joined the staff we were all appealed to by E.S.R. to take on German students individually with a scholarship which amounted, if I remember, to £2 per month. For isolation was as deeply rooted an evil in Germany as starvation. I said I would take two.

Nothing after the second war equalled the currency collapse after the first. In 1923–4 E.S.R. had already the most phenomenal budget ever put before the student world to raise. It was the year of the Russian famine; we were feeding over 30,000 students a day in Russia, as well as supporting all the Russian refugee centres in European universities; and the budget had come to £80,000. Then came the German collapse and £50,000 was added for Germany. Of this vast sum the students of the world failed by only one thousand. They raised £129,000. My two students were Franz Schmal, who became a priest and with whom I have kept contact ever since, and Hans Becker, with whom I lost touch in the Nazi period. But I still have the whole sum earned by Hans as a miner during the summer of 1923. It amounts to seventeen thousand seven hundred and twenty-two million, two thousand seven hundred and ten marks. The whole of this sum would not buy him a roll of bread when he returned to Wurzburg University in the autumn. The mark was stabilised in November at one million million paper marks to one new mark! On this basis his earnings amounted to much less than a farthing.

It was typical of the attitude of the D.C.S.V. that, when the proposal was made to increase the budget by £50,000 for German relief, the only voice raised in opposition was that of the D.C.S.V. spokesman. He insisted that feeding the starving had nothing whatever to do with preaching the Gospel, and was no responsibility of a Christian student organisation. In every way we could, the British S.C.M., in full co-operation with the N.U.S., sought to reach all sections of the German student body. For we knew that there was just the same fight for a new world among them that there was among us. But the battle was much more difficult in Germany, where the liberal Christian tradition, concerning itself with political and social questions, was very much smaller and weaker. We reached it through E.S.R. better than through the W.S.C.F.

In February 1924 I paid a much less exhausting visit to the continent than Heinrichsbad had been. I went as representative of the British S.C.M. to the Jubilee of the Norwegian S.C.M. The high-water mark of the celebrations was a banquet attended by members of the Government, in which we had three courses and twenty-one discourses. Mine was the only short one, for I made it in Norwegian and had learned it by heart for the occasion. But I was immensely impressed by the Norwegian student president, who in every case welcomed the foreign guests in their own language. I could never rise to that linguistic eminence, but, inspired by him, I did achieve being able to say "Good Morning", "Goodbye", "Please" and "Thank you" in every country I visited. The visit introduced me to all the beauties I had not known when I did the pastels for Miss Kleppe, mountains, forests, lakes and fiords.

My main work at home was the building up of study programmes based on serious reading. I gradually collected the necessary books on current international questions, and these I was ready to lend out, if I could not get them into college libraries. I tried to wean students from being satisfied with potted and popular works, valuable though many of these were. I caused some amusement to my colleagues when a very pious branch came to me for advice on Lenten reading, and I recommended Parker T. Moon's *Imperialism and World Politics*. However, that does not mean that I did not do a good deal of devotional work, especially in taking pre-terminal retreats for committees and small gatherings of the faithful. These, in fact, were the backbone of the term's multifarious activities. As far as possible we headquarters staff tried to arrange our travel economically, each of us combining general religious work with our own speciality. In this way R. O. Hall did most of the Scottish travelling, and I did most of the Welsh. I was completely at home among the Welsh, feeling the affinity between my island and their mountains, each harbouring a small people with their own history and identity.

The three main topics of international study at that time were war and pacifism; the League of Nations; and the problem of

AN HONORARY JEW

Voyage of Discoveries. By James Parkes. (Gollancz. 2gns.)

THE Rev. James Parkes is what one might call a Jewologist. His clerical training of necessity gave him an interest in the Jewish people, but it was some years later, while working for the International Student Service in Geneva, and observing the spread of Nazi ideologies across the Universities of Europe, that he became acutely interested in the Jewish question.

He began to look into the origins of anti-semitism and found that Jews were the victims of what was essentially a Christian disorder. It was, he discovered, "the Christian church, and the Christian church alone, which turned the normal xenophobia and normal good and bad relations between the two human societies into the unique evil and . . . most crippling sin of Christianity." From there he went on to launch what was virtually a one-man ecumenical movement.

We are all ecumenists now, but this was in the 1930s, and his work was greeted with less than a chorus of approval. Some of his Christian colleagues tended to dismiss it as mere philo-semitism, while Jews, if gratified by his findings, were a little doubtful about his intentions.

This was a time when Jews could be forgiven for being cynical even about philo-semites, and there is a tendency, especially among Orthodox Jews, to beware of clergymen bearing gifts, for behind every act of Christian goodwill they "smell the incense of the missionary." It says something for the trust which Mr. Parkes inspired that he has come to be accepted almost as an honorary Jew.

I still recall the terms in which I was introduced to him: "He's a *goy*, but one of us." He is today perhaps the only gentile in the English-speaking world who can be critical of Jews—as he sometimes is in this book—without being thought an anti-semite. One cannot be more accepted than that.

"Voyage of Discoveries" is aptly named. It is the story of a life spent in search of the truth behind the "truth." Revelation to him is never wholly revealed: he wants a second opinion. Can it be that Mr. Parkes is not merely an honorary Jew, but that he has become Jewish by contagion?

Chaim Bermant

through and every viewer must have felt pleased that Henry was defeated and Lucy released from the fantasy.   M. M. C.

long finale and to omit altogether the second trio of the second minuet.

Between the two orchestral

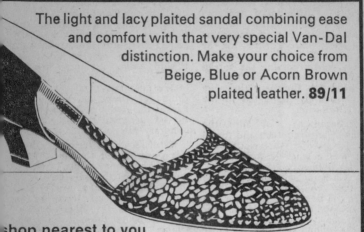

Africa and India. The first two subjects are obvious. On the third, we worked closely with the missionary department, for medical and educational work had become as much a feature of the missionary department as straightforward evangelism. In view of the present situation in 1968 it is interesting that we were telling our contemporaries in 1923 that the mere fact that white women could bear children in some particular African climate did not give Englishmen the right to take over African land; and that, while they might enjoy possession for the rest of their own lives, their children would not. We were helped in this aspect of the work by the friendship of the two leading opponents of the Colonial Office policy in Kenya, Dr. Norman Leys and Mr. Macgregor Ross. In 1924 J. H. Oldham published his epoch-making *Christianity and the Race Problem*, which ran through five editions in a year. In its demand for intellectual integrity as well as sympathy, and for knowledge and research before the Church made pronouncements, it was a welcome addition to the material available to both the missionary and the international study programmes.

Though I was basically sympathetic to the pacifist point of view, I abstained from joining any of the pacifist organisations. I always felt that our slogan needed to be 'much more peace' rather than 'no more war'; and that the latter slogan concealed the real issue. War was a very expensive and wasteful business, and no nation would go to war if it could obtain its just needs by a peaceful method, while no 'rogue nation' would dare to go to war if the world were effectively organised to restrain it. Hence I encouraged positive study of all the machinery of the League of Nations rather than abstract study of the rightness or wrongness of war.

These different activities took up all my time between September and July. Then came Swanwick, two general conferences sandwiching a special conference for the staff and the student officers of the different branches. After the first general conference, and that for the officers, I departed for the continent with a rucksack and a programme of travel, holidays and conferences until the Secretaries' meeting towards the end of September.

I had a unique position in these wanderings. I have already

mentioned the mutual hostility of almost all student organisations in Europe, and this made it very difficult for the ordinary
English student to penetrate into more than one student circle
on the continent. But, in addition to being a secretary of the
Christian group, I was founder of the League of Nations
group at Oxford, I was a member of the executive of the
National Union of Students, and I was also a member of the
executive of the British Committee of European Student
Relief. Whatever student group I wanted to meet, I came with
a visiting card which proclaimed me a colleague. This pleasant
chameleonesque diversity was put to full use in the summer of
1924. Between July and September I attended the annual
conference of E.S.R. at Schloss Elmau in Bavaria, that of the
C.I.E. at Warsaw, and the study conference of the W.S.C.F.
at Bad Saarow in Prussia. In addition I gave my two German
scholarship recipients a holiday in Austria. In between the
conferences I also had some personal holidays. I spent a week
in the glorious city of Prague, where a Czech lady revised my
views of university precedence. For she asked me what university I came from.

"From Oxford," I replied with pardonable pride.

"Oh, then you are an American?"

"No, an Englishman."

"Oh, and is there an Oxford in England too?"

What the story really illustrates is that Americans had the
money to travel in the long vacations, and that all the Oxford
undergraduates she had met were American Rhodes scholars.

The contrast between Elmau and Warsaw was fascinating
and educative. We were asked to arrive at Elmau a day or two
early, so that before the conference opened we could digest
the more than one hundred pages of reports of the administration of relief, the building-up of self-help, and the projects for
the coming year. It was an intensely serious and realistic
conference. At Warsaw Franco-Belgian-Polish politics dominated the entire proceeding.

Adequately to describe the Warsaw conference would take
at least two chapters. The central issue was the admission or
non-admission of Germany. Those who sought her admission
were led by the President of the Swedish Student Union, and

Ivison Macadam, outstanding member of the British delegation. Those who opposed it were the French, Belgian, Polish and Czech student bodies—or the national Foreign Offices behind them, which had so devised the constitution of the C.I.E. that Luxemburg, which had no university, was a member, and Germany, with the largest student body in Europe, could not be. My own part in the proceedings was amusing. By a series of intrigues the Poles had prevented the Ukrainian Union, which was affiliated to the C.I.E., from sending any representatives to Warsaw. In despair the Ukrainians had telegraphed to the English N.U.S. giving them *plein pouvoir* to represent them. Macadam came to me and asked me to do the job. Not being an official member of N.U.S., but only a visitor to their executive, I would not commit them by anything I did. So I became *Chef de Délégation* of the Ukrainian students, and a member of the secret meetings of the *Chefs de Délégations*—incidentally the whole idea of 'secret meetings' was a little puzzling to the Anglo-Saxons; I was also a recipient of the 'secret dossier'.

In this capacity I found myself possessed of a superb and doubly secret document, of Czech origin if I remember, which drew attention to the improper disparity between the budget of an unofficial and partly religious organisation, E.S.R., and that of the government recognised and official student organisation, the C.I.E. It drew up a pretty little plot by which the religious organisation should be left the burden and expense of raising the funds, while the official organisation should, as was right and proper, arrange and control the spending of them. In that year the budget of E.S.R. was in the neighbourhood of a hundred thousand pounds, that of the C.I.E. may have amounted to that number of sous. Alas for the clever little plot: the Ukrainian *Chef de Délégation* took a copy of the document and communicated it to himself as a member of the executive of E.S.R.!

The following January there took place another Missionary Quadrennial of the S.C.M. This time it was in Manchester; and, if I remember, it was attended by over two thousand students, several hundred of whom came from the Christian Student and Student Christian Movements of other countries. As international study secretary, I was mainly occupied with

our foreign guests (the whole conference enjoyed the hospitality of the citizens of Manchester) who were entertained by
a different Manchester public body each day. It was as outstanding a gathering as Glasgow had been, and it was a triumph
of the organising powers of T. and Zoë. At it I met Pastor
Médard, a member of the French Movement, and a southerner.
We happened to get talking about the effects of the war. I told
him how foreign travel had already modified my habits in that
at first I had kept myself wrapped up all the year, but a doctor
had suggested that I copy the German students, and harden
myself with an open collar and, where possible, sandals. This
had done marvels, but I still found the English winter—to
which, after all, I had never been accustomed—extremely
trying. Pastor Médard suggested that it was not too far to
Provence, and that there I could get dried out in winter sun.

So began a long-drawn-out love affair with the triangle
bounded on the north by Montelimar, on the east by Cassis
and on the west by Carcassonne. It was charmingly said of the
Midi by Daudet that "they do not tell lies, but the sun causes
them to exaggerate". At first I explored the region on foot, for
one could find a clean bed in the humblest village; but towards
the end of the twenties the 'autobus' came to the Rhone Valley
and the inns in the small hamlets ceased to provide shelter.
"On ne le fait plus, Monsieur. Il y a l'autobus. Vous pouvez
aller à Avignon." When that had been said many times to me
I had to take to a bicycle. With a heavy rucksack another five
or ten miles to a larger village is no holiday enjoyment, but on a
bicycle it is possible.

I do not know how many times I have been down to the
magic triangle, always sleeping the first night at Avignon, always
renewing the magic of the South. I left the North, grey and
damp, when the train passed into the night as it swayed through
Burgundy, to find the South as one looked out in the morning
at blue sky and a branch of mimosa blowing across the window.
I came up once into the sun from the shady side of a long hill
to see the whole line of the Basses Alpes in a panorama before
me; and I understood, as never before, what the psalmist
meant when he spoke of the mountains and little hills skipping.
For, as the clouds passed across them, there were the high

mountains slowly galumphing along like dignified dowagers while, at their feet, the little hills skipped merrily from sun to shadow and back again.

Where, but in Provence, would one be arrested because, not having a hat, one was clearly a *vagabond*? Happily the *garde champêtre* did not discover that I had no socks either, or I should still be languishing in some rural dungeon left by the Middle Ages.

Where, but in Provence, would the Old Man of Courthézon reduce a compartment to tears while he recounted the terrible cultural privations of his only son, a French soldier, who for some obscure reason was fighting in Serbia, and ended his account with the words: "Not that I have a son, but *if* I had a son, and *if* he was in Serbia?"

Where, but in Provence, in a region which I believed I knew as well as the back of my hand, would it be possible to find, unannounced by any written or illustrated advertisement, *on an eleventh visit* to the region:

A Cathedral of the time of Charlemagne—at S. Paul Trois Chateaux

A Cistercian Abbey, complete in all its thirteenth century buildings, but now a farm—at Silvacane

The largest renaissance chateau in the south of France—at Grignan?

My trips always ended at La Rolane outside Marseilles, the delightful farm house where Madame Cru and her two daughters, Alice and Helène, lived. Helène was a keen member of the French Movement, and we had met at Heinrichsbad. The mother came from Gloucestershire, the father had been a Protestant missionary. The first peak of the Chaine de St. Cyr, the mountains around Marseilles, rose in their back garden. They kept the house until after the second war, and had many adventures, to which I shall come later, during the occupation.

In my second year of work I began to be conscious of a void in the middle of my activity as a promoter of the study of international questions. I was doing my best to teach the student generation to discern where the real problems lay, and along what line they could be tackled. I was developing in them a sense of the moral and the immoral in politics. But I could not

give them a solid basis in a *theology* of politics. It was not only
that many of my own Christian fellow countrymen disagreed
violently as to what was a 'Christian' line on any concrete
political issue, but that I was all the time in close contact with
continental theologians who denied that politics had anything
at all to do with religion. I have already quoted the D.C.S.V.'s
attitude towards feeding the starving students of their own
country.

The climax came in a visit which I paid to Mirfield. I had
come for a discussion on some precise international problem—
I quite forget what it happened to be—and, after the usual run
of services E. K. Talbot announced that we now had forty
minutes for the discussion—before we had to go to Compline.
Well, it was something that Compline was two hours late that
night, and that the students had to be dragged away to it.
Talking to Talbot after Compline, I spoke of the void I felt.
He could not see it.

"Surely," he said, "where you have a banker who is a regular communicant, there you have the Church in banking."

"Would you say, then," I replied, "that where a nursemaid
reads her Bible regularly, there you have the Church's understanding of the Scriptures? And if so, why do we want all the
academic Chairs of Bible and Theology? The problems of
banking are surely just as difficult as those of New Testament
criticism?"

Here was the dilemma to which I could find no solution,
not even in discussion with William Temple, though it was he
who always encouraged me to go on puzzling. To my colleagues
in the S.C.M. I think I became something of a bore. Somehow
I felt it must be tied up with our doctrine of the Trinity, and I
argued that we had a full time occupation for the second
Person, but the vaguest ideas about the activities of the first
and the third. But it made no impression on anyone except
Zoë. To the rest it was "Jimmie's bee in his bonnet about God".
I had too much respect—not to mention affection—for them
to be unmoved by this attitude. But I put the problem into
cold storage rather than abandoned it.

I was also getting more impatient with my pacifist friends.
More and more I was convinced that the attempt to create a

pacifist nation, a whole nation which would voluntarily allow itself to be destroyed, was following a wrong line altogether. This was before Prohibition had shown the disastrous result of making a nation vote on a moral issue which it had not wholly understood. I wanted the pacifist to concentrate on a devotion to making 'much more peace', but my arguments had little effect.

I was busy enough with the study groups, conferences and retreats which occupied my time. In addition I ranked as a sub-warden of Student Movement House in Russell Square, which had been founded in 1917 as a Club for students, especially foreign students. It was created as a war memorial to the students of all nations who fell in the war. S.M.H. was always short of money and full of problems. One of the most useful contributions which I made was to build up a 'Guild of Happy Carpenters' who undertook the repair of furniture and fittings, which were constantly being damaged. I defined 'happy carpenters' as those who would not use a chisel as a screwdriver, but who would not refuse to do a job on the grounds that it needed a completely different set of tools from those we had. The fact that repairs were made by members had this useful effect—that a member could say: "Don't do that, or I shall have to put it right" without creating offence. If an official of the club said it, it was more likely to be resented, and was usually ineffective. For Student Movement House was not the easiest club to run.

In the summer of 1925 I prepared for a repetition of my 1924 trip. E.S.R. had its conference at Gex above Geneva; the W.S.C.F. Conference was also in Switzerland, at Oberaegeri, near Zug. After that I had to go to Venice, and then to Belgrade. While in Yugoslavia I attended a conference of the Russian Orthodox Church at Hopovo. Both the E.S.R. Conference and that of the W.S.C.F. were important for the future.

In 1925 the relief work, which E.S.R. had been founded to perform in the whole of central and eastern Europe, was coming to an end. The different governments and universities were becoming capable of meeting their own needs, and were becoming self-conscious about receiving outside 'charity'. The Gex Conference was given the task of weighing up the problem, and of recommending whether E.S.R. should be gradually closed down or not. The secretaries of the Commission which had to handle this vital issue were Bettina Warburg, daughter of the great American banker, Paul Warburg, and myself.

The suggestion that E.S.R. should close down met with an unanimous wail of agony from the whole field in which the work had been done. Speaker after speaker, from minorities like the Jewish students as well as from government sponsored organisations, insisted that E.S.R. had been the only organisation where they all met each other, and which inspired universal trust in a situation where trust was a very rare quality. We just did not realise what we had been doing if we thought, firstly that there were two mutually exclusive groups of givers and receivers, and secondly that it was just material goods which had been given and received. As to the first, all countries were giving and receiving, and as to the second, it was the all-inclusive co-operation which was the real value which they appreciated.

Behind this appeal lay the basis on which the work had been built up since 1921 when it was founded. E.S.R. would work in a country only through a committee representing the whole student body of that country. If any group tried to monopolise its activities and collect all its funds, E.S.R. refused to remain. The most amusing example of this happened during the Russian famine. The Soviet Government tried to make it a condition of accepting help that no help was given to refugee Russians. The refugee Russian students tried to make a comparable corner in our interest. To both we replied that we thought that, if we were giving the funds, it was we who made the conditions, and that we were interested in genuine students anywhere and in their politics nowhere. So in all the countries of central and eastern Europe the E.S.R. committee was unique in containing members of staff and students, nationalists and socialists, majorities and minorities. Nowhere else did all these groups meet, and they met because they had a practical programme to carry out, which none of them could afford to forgo. What the Gex commission asked for was that a new department should be opened to develop "cultural co-operation". The executive of E.S.R. took note of the change in the situation by changing its name from European Student Relief to International Student Service; but it postponed any consideration of the proposed new department to a later date.

The W.S.C.F. Conference at Oberaegeri, of which I was chairman, was of interest to myself because it brought me into direct contact with the Jewish problem. Hitherto it had just been one of the many contemporary problems of which I was aware. This conference made me conscious of its violence and special quality. The W.S.C.F. had invited a member of a Central European Christian Movement to open a discussion on the Jewish question. It had also invited a Rumanian Jewish student to be present. The Christian's speech was so venomous, contained so many accusations and innuendoes that I was sure were false, that I took the unusual step of saying from the Chair that I could not accept the speech as the introduction to a discussion among Christians of the problem. I would invite no one else to speak until the speech was withdrawn. I then sat down, and a deathly silence ensued. After five minutes two officers of the W.S.C.F., who were running the conference, came and sat on each side of me, and assured me that, whatever the practice in England, in Europe a chairman could not do such things. If I insisted I would wreck the conference. I told them they could remove me from the Chair if they liked but that, while I was in the Chair I had nothing to add. Finally the speaker got up and said that he must have been misunderstood if he had appeared to be antisemitic, which was enough for me to accept. But the silence had lasted over twenty minutes.

At every conference of the W.S.C.F. there was a—usually unspoken—conflict between students influenced by Anglo-saxon theology (this included British, Commonwealth, American and Asian students) who wanted to discuss Christianity's relation to social and political questions, and students influenced by German theology, who opposed the idea that Christianity was concerned with such questions, and who demanded unlimited Bible Study, usually of the worst passages of St. Paul's letters. The Germans—I say it regretfully but objectively—usually won by the blackmail of sulks and intolerably bad manners if they were opposed. I think it was at this conference that all social and political interests were reduced to a single meeting; and even that meeting was to be opened by a German student. The usual procedure was that an opening speech of about ten minutes defined rather than solved the problem for the session. This particular speech went on for a quarter of an hour, and was still in full spate after twenty minutes. Thereat I called the leader of the German delegation to my side, pointed to my watch, and asked him whether the speech could not be shortened. At that time I spoke no German, but he assured me that every word was pertinent, and that nothing could possibly be omitted. He spoke for forty minutes. With the translation that filled the whole hour allowed for the session. There was no time for any discussion.

When we had the translation, it was the seventh speech we had had at the conference on the subject of Grace; and the first and only mention of social or international issues was the last sentence: "Grace can forgive our international sins also".

The Orthodox conference at Hopovo was, in its way, quite as novel an experience. I was the only non-Russian present, and found it a very strange world. I was a little astonished when I was asked whether we in the British S.C.M. still used John Chrysostom for our Bible study. But that was nothing to the meeting on social and political issues addressed by an important looking bishop. His familiarity with an enormous Bible, in which he could at once turn to any page he wanted, was impressive, but I was not really convinced when he proved a passage in the book of Joshua by a verse in Ezekiel, or supplemented a sentence in the Psalms by an apparently completely disparate passage from Leviticus. The pages of the Bible whirled round and round like a helicopter! On the other hand, Russian worship was an overwhelming experience.

I cannot imagine myself enjoying, in a language of which I did not understand a word, any service that had been arranged by the Anglican Church, which lasted from one and a half to three hours before breakfast, and at which I had to stand. But the liturgies which we had at Hopovo were a profound spiritual experience. I had been taken to the conference by the Court Chamberlain of the unfortunate Alexander who was later assassinated in Marseilles. We did the last nine miles of the journey in an immense and springless ox-cart. But I never saw Mr. Nenaditch at the Conference. When I returned to Belgrade I asked him what had happened. He replied: "J'ai vu les chambres; j'ai vu les W.C.'s; et je me suis dit, 'Alors, mes chers camarades, restez si vous voulez; moi, je me sauve. Et je suis rentré a Belgrad par le même carosse.' "

In the spring of 1926 I was asked to continue my work for another three years, and gladly agreed to do so. But in the same winter a crisis occurred at Student Movement House, and I was asked to become Warden. The House, with its financial, moral and intellectual problems, had exhausted my excellent predecessor, Josephine Currie, and she had had to retire. The wardenship was unquestionably the most difficult job in the S.C.M. On the one hand the House served as a rallying point for organised groups of Christian students from overseas— Indian, Chinese, West Indian and others—and on the other it welcomed the presence of non-Christian students, of whom there were many hundred in London's huge and cosmopolitan university. At that time there was no other place where such students could find the social life and activities of a club.

This second purpose gradually came to predominate, largely because there was no alternative club. It became a centre for all foreign students with what would today be called a 'Christian presence' in its leadership. The social life of the House was run by an elected Club Committee on which the S.C.M. came to have no special authority; and it will easily be seen that the genuine effort to maintain equally the original dual purpose of its foundation contained within itself many possibilities of tension.

The main cause of the trouble was that the Club was now nearly ten years old, and that a small group of ex-students had remained members—as the constitution permitted them to do— and had become a not very good influence for the younger members. It was not possible simply to change the constitution, so that the membership was limited to full-time students, because it was among the younger ex-students that we also found our most valuable helpers and committee members, providing an element of stability in our rapid turnover of undergraduate members, many of whom spent only a year in England.

Besides the problems of membership, there was the serious financial problem that the House always had a considerable deficit, which the S.C.M. had to meet. There was a restaurant, but we had always employed as bursar an S.C.M. member who had just graduated from a School of Domestic Science. It was much too difficult a job for such a novice, and I insisted on advertising for a Bursar, appointing Miss Agnes Griffiths, a middle-aged and very experienced manager, though my Chairman protested violently. When I also insisted on paying her the salary that she asked for, he protested still more. I told her that I would be satisfied if her accounts broke even during the summer, but that I would expect a profit when the Autumn Term opened. But she made a profit from her first month, and was soon turning in a monthly profit well into three figures.

It was very hard work for both of us, for I also had to cope with the moral issue in the Club. While I was at Swanwick my Chairman got a letter of resignation from Agnes, saying the work was too hard for one person. He brought me the letter with obvious satisfaction. I immediately telegraphed: "Don't resign. Go summer sales and get assistant bursar." My chairman was furious, and I had my only personal quarrel during my S.C.M. days. I told him that it was much easier to get a chairman than a warden, but that one or the other had to go. Zoë took his place, and we began to get things straight all round.

Success at the house was like liberty. It was only gained by perpetual vigilance. The House was open to any genuine student; and our main problems were with students, young and inexperienced, and probably living abroad for the first time in their lives. We could *obtain* the right atmosphere only by attracting the right students, and that meant by having the right activities, physical, intellectual, aesthetic and religious to attract them. We could *preserve* it only by having a sixth sense for possible casualties. In this difficult task I was enormously helped by an honorary sub-warden, Jean Brants, whose understanding and sympathy rescued many youngsters, boys and girls, when life in London was becoming too much for them.

One of our perennial problems was the breaking of barriers

at the beginning of their stay. We used to have 'New Members' Parties' at regular intervals, and I was lucky enough to hit upon a perfect ice-breaker. We always had a number of good actors in the Club, and it depended on them. It was a dramatic entertainment which I called "As you like it". I devised a series of plays in which the action turned on periodical rhetorical questions, which required simply *Yes* or *No* as an answer. The audience was asked to vote as to which it should be. Writing the play was like composing a genealogical tree, as the action changed according to the vote. The actors composed their own dialogue, taking care not to introduce rhetorical questions of their own, and remembering to bring in, and act on, the ones I had devised.

The opening of one of our most successful ones will illustrate this admirable way of breaking ice.

Enter the wife, riffles through her husband's letters on the breakfast table, and sees the one which is going to destroy her home. "My God! Shall I destroy it?" The audience always voted that she should. When finally, after furious argument, she was refused permission several letters later, the husband enters and reads it and, of course, exclaims, "How can I live when you have so disgraced me?" The audience almost always thought that he could manage it quite easily. So the play went on. By the end of it there was no ice anywhere!

I was beginning to enjoy my period at the House when, in the winter of 1927, Dr. Walter Kotschnig, general secretary of International Student Service, came unexpectedly to see me, told me that the Assembly of I.S.S. had decided to adventure on the programme of cultural co-operation outlined at Gex, and invited me to come to Geneva to put it into action. I was naturally thrilled, and we went up that evening to see T. who was chairman of the I.S.S., as well as general secretary of S.C.M. T. asked Walter where the money was coming from, and Walter admitted that I would have to raise it. But T. had had experience of my complete ineffectiveness as a financier. I had not only not produced any cash when all the secretaries were sent out on an emergency campaign to meet a deficit, but had once been put in charge of the finances of a conference, and my accounts had shown that the conference had resulted in a deficit larger than the total expenses *plus* the total amount of fees paid. So T. at once negatived the proposal, told me to be content with the job I was doing, and told Walter that he could not start a new department of I.S.S. until he could show that there was the money available to pay for it.

At that time Bettina Warburg was in London, doing some postgraduate work, and we met very occasionally, for both were very busy persons and it took some preparation to find a free date which suited both of us. The morning after Walter and I had visited T. I was in my room at the House when a message came up that a Miss Warburg wanted to see me. I came downstairs at once.

"Hullo, Bettina," I greeted her. "What has brought you here unexpectedly?"

"I don't know, Flibberty," (by which nickname she always called me), "I just had a feeling I would see how you were."

Without telling her of the financial difficulties at all, I said:

"You remember the Gex programme. What would you think of my trying to put it into practice?"

And she replied at once: "If you're going to do that, Flibberty, you know the family will be responsible for your finances."

V

GENEVA 1928–1935 AND
INTERNATIONAL STUDENT SERVICE

IN MARCH 1928 I joined the staff of I.S.S., and spent my first month in the lovely city of Prague, staying with the sister of Jean Brants, whose husband was a Czech patent engineer, Jannik Voyaček. There I imbibed something of the atmosphere of central European student and political life. The staff of I.S.S., were all relatively newly appointed. Walter Kotschnig, the general secretary, was a brilliant Austrian. His Welsh wife, Elined Prys, had been a secretary of the S.C.M., working in Rumania. Then there was a Russian (but Parisian by choice), Michel Poberezski. A number of other people joined us during the period I was in Geneva, especially Rena Datta as administrative secretary, and Gustav Kullmann as director of social services.

I.S.S. was a body without a student membership. It consisted of a small and self-perpetuating Assembly, registered under Swiss law. The fact that we did not seek members in the universities meant that we did not compete with other student societies; we were protected from becoming a remote bureaucracy by the fact that the annual programme was fixed at the summer conference, and that at the same time plans were made for raising the budget required by the programme from the student bodies of co-operating countries.

The conference was one of the big annual occasions in the student world, being a unique meeting of staff and students from many continents. During my period we met at Chartres in 1928, then in the following years at Krems on the Danube, at Oxford, at Mount Holyoake in U.S.A. and at Brno in Slovakia. Of the 1933 meeting at Kloster Ettal in Bavaria and Festung Luziensteig in Liechtenstein I shall have more to say later. The French Ministry of Education had invited us for the 1928 conference. I went with one of our French committee to see various Lycées. The Lycée Marcel at Chartres was a very attractive possibility. But I knew that a bevy of British and

American girls were coming, and that proper sanitation was essential. My French student was clearly too embarrassed to ask the headmaster directly about his arrangements. So, after watching him skirt round the subject for some time, I plunged in and asked him directly what his W.C.'s were like. Where but in France could the smelliest arrangements be so superbly described in the words: "Ah, Monsieur, ici nous sommes un peu du grande siècle!" The situation was saved by our finding a modern hostel adjoining the Lycée where all was as it should be, and Chartres provided a delightful backcloth for the conference. It was at Chartres that I put forward my general plans for the department of 'Cultural Co-operation'.

By the summer I had settled down happily in Geneva. My first Sunday I went to the early service at the Anglican church, and introduced myself to the chaplain as a secretary of the S.C.M. coming to do a difficult job. As soon as I mentioned the S.C.M. I received a blast of thundering abuse of everything the S.C.M. stood for. As I felt this was scarcely the spiritual background I needed, I went after a few Sundays to the early service at the American church. As I came out the chaplain stopped me and said: "You are a newcomer. Are you a visitor, or have you come to live in Geneva?" I told him I had come to live, and gave him the address of my newly-found flat. On the next Wednesday evening there was a knock at my door. There was the chaplain, Dr. Everett Smith, to see how I was, and to ask if there was anything he or his congregation could do to make life easier for me. I remained a member of the American church while I was in Geneva and came to be acting chaplain on most occasions when Dr. Smith was away.

Lest, however, my American readers fall into the sin of *superbia*, I must add that no Anglican chaplain ever had me arrested for trying to steal the communion plate, a misfortune which befell me when I asked if I might celebrate communion in the American church in Dresden. The manner of it was thuswise. Dresden was a frequent host to our conferences, for it was the home of the national organisation which grew out of our work in Germany. It pioneered every kind of student social activity with German thoroughness under its leader, Dr. Reinhold Schairer. A new chaplain had altered the hour of the early service, with a result that the Anglicans at one of our conferences arrived just as the service was ended. I went to the vestry and asked the chaplain if he could give us a short service. He said he could not, so I asked him if he would allow me to celebrate. The one excuse for his refusal, superficially good but psychologically rotten, was that I had a beard but not a clerical collar. A fake parson would certainly have had a collar, and probably not a beard! For he refused, on the grounds that my licence was English and not American.

We were saying our prayers quietly when the caretaker turned us out—into the arms of the police waiting outside! So three of us, Harry Baines now Bishop of Wellington, impeccable with a rolled umbrella and *The Times* under his arm, Outram Walsh, later Vicar of Hitchen, and myself, were marched through the streets to the police station. Dresden had the system of a police magistrate permanently on duty, so that I soon found myself, as the ring-leader, 'before the beak'. I gave him my passport. He had fortunately heard of student conferences being held in the old royal villa above the city. He asked whether anyone could identify me in Dresden, and I suddenly realised it was the most fortunate city in the world for such a thing to happen to me.

Three months previously Dr. S. K. Datta, husband of our administrative secretary, and I had received lovely Dresden shepherdesses from the Saxon government for our services to German students during the collapse of the mark, and we were then given a civic luncheon—one of the two occasions when I have eaten off gold plate! So I referred the magistrate to the Burgomaster of Dresden, and the Saxon Minister of Education, our hosts, and to all the other dignitaries I could remember.

"There has clearly been a mistake," he said. "You are quite free to go."

"Thank you," I replied, "but why were we brought here at all?"

"Do not blame the police. The American chaplain telephoned to us urgently to send police to the church at once as a gang of robbers was trying to steal the communion plate."

My flat in Geneva was in the *Cité*, Calvin's old hill town above the lake, whereas nearly all the foreign colony lived in the modern city which surrounded it. It was the top floor of a sixteenth century *bourgeois* house—a *maison de maitre*—where the servants of all the lower flats would have been housed. For the flat system on the continent is not a modern invention but has long historical roots. The family flats below me had all been remodelled in the eighteenth century, but the servants quarters, of course, had been untouched. I had wonderful ironwork on my doors, curly hinges, lovely key plates and latches, immense bolts and locks, all of which I cleaned and oiled. There was an enormous larch beam right across the flat nearly forty feet in length and ten inches in girth. In my work room it rested on two complex struts, one of which stood up from the floor on a wooden pillar.

Lit with wax candles, and with all my old furniture, 3 Grand Mezel came to rank with Versailles as one of the places an American student tried to visit on a trip to Europe. And it was more difficult to do so, for an introduction from the American Consul was the only *open sesame*. Growing out of my membership of the American church, I came to be 'at home' to American students every week of the summer that I was in Geneva. The American consul, Gilson Blake, arranged the invitations, American wives from the consulate and the Y.M.C.A. took charge of catering, and I was responsible only for the discussions. When I could, I met the students somewhere in the modern city, and guided them into the *Cité*, which was full of entrancing and unexpected stairs, passages and courtyards. The culmination came with my candle-lit flat. When I had a full evening, it took sixty candles, all in ancient sticks and sconces. It was a unique occasion for most of the guests who could handle antiques and sit on furniture they ordinarily saw only in museums and show places.

Because I had very pleasant old furniture, as well as plates, glasses and such like, and because students are, by reputation, careless and irresponsible, I would like to pay them here a very warm tribute. As with my previous flat in England, the key was always with my colleagues when I was away and they were free to lend the flat to anyone they thought fit. And this permission was consistently used over a period of twelve years. Yet during that time I never had any damage done to my furniture; on two occasions when a jug was broken, I only realised it when I found a new jug in its place; and I never lost a book. I never found the flat dirty on my return, and often only found that it had been used when I went to the office and they told me.

Typical of the situation was an incident in Vienna. At a meeting an unknown student asked me whether I was Mr. Parkes from Geneva. I said I was, and he thanked me warmly for the loan of my flat during his week's stay there attending a course. I asked him how he had got it, and he said that X, another Austrian student, had lent it to him. I had never heard of X, and asked him if he knew how X had got it. He said that he thought Y had lent it him. Two years previously I had met Y in a train somewhere in Europe, and he had told me of his desire to go to Zimmern's summer school in Geneva. He said he could meet the fees, but did not know what to do about lodging. I told him he could stay with me, or could get the key of my flat at the office, and he had done so.

The Cité was a delightful place to shop in—before the depression of the thirties. Within two hundred yards of my flat I could get any article in gold, silver, copper or iron made for me. I could get cloth woven for furnishing or for dress. I could get a dinner service made and painted. I could get furniture made or repaired. I could get jam and cakes or a whole dinner cooked for me; and in addition, for groceries, fruit and so on I had delightful little shops where I was served by the patron, and we knew each other by name. But I used also to enjoy making my purchases early in the morning at the admirable markets of the city, where one could get anything from meat to mushrooms—except the English taste in Gruyère cheese. For that one had to cross the French frontier to Annemasse. The Swiss taste in Gruyère is quite different from ours.

The beauty of my flat was a perpetual refreshment to me in a very exacting job, concerned almost always with the ugliness which men had made of their common life. The fact that I.S.S. committees were exhausting assemblies which lasted a whole week—for it was too expensive to gather men and women from all over the world every time we wanted a discussion—enabled me to enrich the flat in an unexpected way.

4

My temper was usually exhausted by the end of the first day of the committees, with the result that I was a burden to my colleagues and myself for the rest of the week. I was wandering through Geneva one evening contemplating with disgust the fact that the whole of the following week I should spend in committee, when I found myself gazing at a shop window full of wools and tapestries. The thought occurred to me that the people who bore with the committees best were the women who knitted. They did not talk when they had nothing to say. They had an uncanny faculty for seeing the way out of a dilemma in which the rest of the committee had got itself bogged down, and their dispositions remained sweet and sunny the whole week. I could not knit, for I cannot count above four without insisting on complete silence and isolation, and these feminine marvels would count up to hundreds without losing the thread of debate. But why should I not make tapestry? I wanted a new tea-cosy. Why should I not make it? So, knowing nothing of the technique of the job, I went into the shop, bought canvas, wools and needles and became a model committee member. I also—gradually—learnt the different stitches properly for the making of very pleasant tapestry for chairs, stools, cushions and so on. I only stopped recently when my Dupuytren's contraction curled my fingers up too much.

During my seven years in Geneva there was only one occasion on which I slept for twenty-eight consecutive nights in my flat. Much of my work had to be done by personal visits, and I spent a considerable part of each year in the universities of central and eastern Europe. Every country was different, in every country the nature of our relations with that particular country had to be taken into consideration. In some, different groups would co-operate happily, in others we had always to look out for trouble. The country which I found most trying was Rumania, where the National Union was entirely political, and where I kept all my plans in my own hands, trusting nothing to them to arrange for me. I 'gave audience' on one occasion to the leaders of the National Union, when they had been behaving more than usually disgracefully, and after an hour's questions and answers where I had replied quite freely to everything they had asked, I terminated the 'audience' without their having learned where I had entered the country, which universities I had visited, where I was going to from Bucharest, and whom I had seen in Bucharest. All three of us were experienced diplomats—when necessary. Fortunately it was not often necessary!

Apart from personal visits, and attending conferences arranged by others, much of my work was the evolution of a special brand of 'study conference' where we severely limited the numbers, spent a whole week together on a very carefully planned programme, and came to be able to secure the attendance of almost anyone we needed for expert help. The gradual evolution of competent plans for such conferences was my main contribution to the academic field. It led to the appearance of a book in 1933 entitled *International Conferences*; but every conceivable misfortune attended its publication, and it never got any circulation. A pity, because it was a very good book, based on extensive experience, and also, as one critic said, excellent bed-side reading.

My conferences were designed to deal with sore spots in the body academic, conflicts of nationality, of race, and of political party. We usually met in country hotels in beautiful corners of Europe, moving north or south according to the season—and the rate of exchange. I can mention only a few. Of the conference between Jewish and antisemitic student bodies I shall write later; but we tried to cover all the main groups of students studying in Europe, and our general principle was to examine a question in which we could get a definite student slant, and so rouse a definite student interest. Thus we had one which gathered students from many universities of Europe who came from all the countries bordering on the Pacific. Another brought together European students with those from India. A whole series dealt with the conflicts arising out of the first world war and the succession states. A European-American conference had as its subject "Why do we so dislike each other?" It had no set programme and met in a delightful ex-monastery in the Austrian mountains.

Our general purpose I find expressed in notes prepared for some lecture which I gave somewhere in the days before I was careful to date and identify every document I typed. It runs:

"The main task of those who, like myself, are engaged with students in Europe on the political side is to introduce the idea of discussion with those who disagree with you. It does not necessarily matter what is discussed, so long as it is a really controversial issue." In the same notes I find this comment on Hungarian student standards: "*I* can make a remark to a Hungarian which may make him white with rage; but, because it is useless to challenge me to a duel, he has got to justify himself on the plane of morals and intellect, when he would never dream of doing so to another Hungarian, whom he would either challenge at once, or insult with impunity if he was a Jew or not of his class." I was once in Budapest when the Magyar National Union was invited to some centenary celebrations of the Oxford or Cambridge Union. The President asked me to explain what the Union was. When I described it as a debating society which discussed all the burning topics of the day, he said to me, with eyes round with wonder: "Do you mean to say that you have been discussing political questions for a hundred years and have never had an assassination?"

English debating was still an inexplicable mystery to the student of the continent. The idea that you sat in your seat and let others ridicule your arguments and your person, and neither challenged them to a duel nor rose and left the room, was incomprehensible to them. Thus, in addition to the subject discussed, our discussion conferences had a value in themselves, simply in our bringing together many points of view in an atmosphere where duels were *out*, and walking out of the room was discouraged.

In addition to travel and conferences I had one amusing task. We had a restaurant in Paris, largely for the benefit of eastern European students whose currencies were always letting them down, and I kept a 'headquarter's eye' on it with regular visits. This was usually a somewhat Erewhonian adventure. I would arrive, and be saluted by its delightful and devoted creator, Marguerite Zagarowsky, with: "Look how much profit I made last month. I have eight thousand francs in the till." Then I would get down to the books.

"Marguerite," I would call out, "why have you given up serving fish?"

"But I serve fish every day."

"But you have not put any amount for fish in your accounts."

"Of course not; I have not paid the bill."

This would go on, covering the fuel used as well as the food served and the size of a portion. In the end I would arrive at a figure of the actual situation, and would carry back to Geneva a bill for several hundred pounds. But, as our main purpose was to enable foreign students to get a square meal for a few pence, and not to make a profit, and as Marguerite was a most devoted worker for those same students, we would end up by paying the deficit. But she never grasped that the money in the till at the end of the month was not net profit!

During my first years at Geneva I still had contact with the W.S.C.F. At one of their discussion conferences in 1928, held in a delightful *pension* high up above Gex, I was responsible for the morning meditations. The whole of the rest of the morning was given to an address in German, to be followed by translation and discussion. The lecturer was Fritz Lieb, Karl Barth's assistant. It was my first encounter with the full blast of the abominable heresy of Barthianism. Lieb had four periods, and his four subjects were *The Fall*, *The Incarnation*, *The Atonement*, and *The Holy Spirit*. The secretary of the conference was Henri-Louis Henriod, general secretary of the W.S.C.F. The conference committee used to meet at breakfast, and on the third morning Henriod expressed his anxiety.

"Look, Fritz," he said. "This is the third morning, and you have not yet finished your address on the Fall. We still have to have translation and discussion. There are only two more days of the conference, and you have three addresses to give. How much time are you going to need for the Holy Spirit?"

"Oh, the Holy Spirit," replied Lieb, "a quarter of an hour is enough for that."

This, after five and a half hours on the Fall, was an admirable introduction to Barthian theology! That this evil doctrine spread over Germany is understandable, even though supremely tragic. For young Germans had to have great courage to resist so comforting a doctrine of the universality and inescapability of human sinfulness, and of human inability to do anything about the evils of the social and political worlds. It rid them of any sense of responsibility for the war and its evils. A sense of social and political responsibility was a very young and tender growth among members of the Lutheran tradition. Instead of fostering it, Barth's influence destroyed it, and thereby made the surrender to Hitler in the vital academic field so much easier to achieve.

This is the point at which the core of my story begins inevitably to include something of a theological detective story. I was still looking for a real theological interpretation of the divine relation to our social and political life. I could not accept any doctrine of a purposeful creation which did not include the ultimately complete responsibility of the Creator. Anything less seemed to me just immoral. Now along came Barth proclaiming a godling who, apparently, revelled in making himself totally obscure and incomprehensible to his creation— causing unending suffering and misery thereby—and who accepted no responsibility for the result. He had been so inefficient or malicious a creator that man, his creation, could not understand his purpose or nature, however hard he tried. In fact Barth's godling was so egotistical that he regarded it as blasphemous if man tried. It made no difference whether Barth ascribed this situation to man's 'fall' or to man's basic nature. For the godling who gave man freewill, and did not take into account the possibility of a 'fall' was so grotesquely incompetent that he had no right ever to have created man at all. Barth's perpetual insistence on the *otherness* of God merely enfolded him in a fog too thick to penetrate rather than in a light too brilliant for human eyes.

Barth's 'incarnation' was no better; for the human life of Jesus did not grow organically out of the continuous divine-human relationship in creation, but had struck the earth like a bombshell, making a large crater in human history—an exquisite metaphor which is Barth's, not mine.

Apart from his commentary on *Romans* Barth was introduced to English readers by a work entitled *The Word of God and the Word of Man*, a title of inherent and inescapable absurdity for a work by any human being. For 'the word of God' was inevitably represented by the opinions of Dr. Barth, and in 'the word of man' were inevitably included all the opinions from which Dr. Barth dissented. It is extraordinary that so perverse a theology had so overwhelming an effect. Part of the effect was, perhaps, due to Barth's attractive personality. I quote from a letter of June 1930, written by David Cairns, son of the Principal Cairns mentioned earlier. After expressing his complete disgust at Barth's theology, he described him as "one of the most charming people I have ever met", and goes on to say: "He is quite a young man, and gives the impression of extraordinary defencelessness and also of humour, enthusiasm, and a certain dramatic power which came out in gesture and simile even in his bad English." This reminds me of an occasion when I sought to defend Dr. Major, Principal of Ripon Hall, from a violent denunciation by a conservative Oxford theologian. I said that there was no question of Dr. Major's Christian piety and attractive personality, to be met with the withering reply: "That's the damnable thing about him. If he wasn't such an attractive personality he wouldn't influence so many people with his abominable views."

The growing effect of Barth began to be pitifully and tragically evident in the students who came to international gatherings from the Christian Student Movements influenced by him. All social and political striving was dead. All interest in any kind of political or social problem was condemned. The last study conference of I.S.S. where German students were present was one where they met French and Belgian students, and where we had tried to get all academic faculties and all political opinions represented. Consequently there were two theological students. There were also two Nazi students. They were the same two, and both were Barthians.

Later, of course, when Hitler was in power and turned to attack the Lutheran Church, the disciples of Barth were the backbone of the *Confessing Church*; but in the years when Hitler might have been prevented from ever achieving power Barth was silent, and the immense majority of Protestant leaders were silent under his influence. Yet these were years when the danger was already evident, and when the Jewish community of Germany was making instant appeals for Christian backing in their warnings to President Hindenburg and the nation of the danger which was menacing them. The record of Martin Niemöller is a little better. Silent, and even approving before 1933, he was already known for the shelter which he gave to persecuted Jews by the summer of that year.

Made to think furiously by the increasing influence of Barth, I produced in the Spring of 1929 a tentative trinitarian theology. Accepting that God in his 'home life' was wholly other and unknowable, I argued that he had from the beginning of creation revealed himself and accepted responsibility for it, and was himself the inspiration of its development. He was its ruler and inspirer as well as its redeemer. My essay had the advantage of criticism and encouragement from people like Temple, Lionel Curtis and others, and led to my being asked by Francis Millar, Chairman of the W.S.C.F., to give three lectures at the summer conference at Glion near Montreux. My title was *Politics and the Doctrine of the Trinity*, and I did not so much fall between two stools as disappear into a crevasse between two towering cliffs! For the Anglo-Saxons were irritated that I spoiled sensible remarks about politics with medieval obscurantism like the doctrine of the Trinity, while the Barthians, of course, found it blasphemous to mention politics in the same breath as the *arcana* of theology.

The real significance, however, of this attempt to sum up my thinking from Oxford onwards was that, though I conceived of the Trinity as a meaningful doctrine of the total involvement of God in the whole of his creation, yet I had not discovered any clear guidance to a theology of politics. And there the matter rested for some years.

By this time W. A. Visser t'Hooft was looming very large in the life of the W.S.C.F., of which he was to become General Secretary in 1931, and t'Hooft was a complete disciple of Barth. In fact he introduced Barth to English theological students in a tour of theological colleges in 1930. That the Protestant continent went Barthian is explicable; that Anglo-Saxon theologians succumbed to its evil influence is still an unexplained mystery. But by the beginning of the thirties I was out of sympathy, not merely with the W.S.C.F., but with the S.C.M. itself in which the same influence was becoming paramount.

I am not sure whether an authoritative history of the change in atmosphere and temper from the twenties to the thirties has yet been written. The economic depression was naturally an important cause of increasing pessimism, but I believe that the failure of political leadership to make any use of the League of Nations, together with its conviction that the old type of political relationship was unalterable, and the old white supremacy eternal, were still more responsible. People of my generation were still regarded as unpractical 'idealists'; the men who were leading the world straight into another war were 'realists'. Nothing that we could do made any essential difference, whatever victories we might score in the lesser seats of power. The Briand-Streseman hope had been a brief interlude. The United States remained aloof from the League. All these things provide the background for the failure of theological nerve and the disgraceful collapse into the pessimism of German Protestantism.

In 1932 I was so exhausted by the beginning of the summer that I was unable to go to the annual conference at Brno, and I think I would have resigned from I.S.S. the following year if it had not been for the accession of Hitler, and the immediate obligation which fell on I.S.S. to deal again with relief, this time in the persons of the Jewish, non-Aryan and Left Wing students expelled from Nazi Germany. Because I had already begun my studies of the Jewish question, as I shall describe in the next chapter, it was inevitably on my shoulders that much of the responsibility fell for dealing with this particular crisis, though it would be wrong to think of it as a task into which the whole staff did not throw itself with energy.

The two vital questions were, firstly, what countries would accept the studies they had already done in Germany and, secondly, what countries would allow them to stay and work, once they had obtained their degrees. The whole world was our field, and each of us could contribute something to the picture. As soon as we had mapped out our needs, I came over to England to find new funds for meeting them. I learned that the Marks family had set aside a considerable sum which they wished to be asked for; so I got an introduction to Simon Marks, who saw me at once. Saying that he had to go to a meeting, he took me to his brother-in-law, Israel Sieff, and

4*

said: "Talk to him. It is just the same as talking to me." Fortunately I had already published *The Jew and His Neighbour*, so I was known to them. I told Mr. Sieff what I needed at that time, and said that I would probably come back, once we had to deal with personal cases. At the moment I wanted to get my organisation and information. I went back to Geneva the next day with a cheque for the amount I asked for. As Israel Sieff comes into the story a good deal, and as 'Israel' by itself is liable to ambiguity he appears henceforth by his initials 'I.M.S.'

I had stayed with T. during this visit to England, and I spent the first evening telling him of the anti-Jewish measures which were actually in force in Germany, and the threats of what was to come. I had taken the precaution of bringing with me the actual official texts of the German laws. T. was amazed by what I showed him. He told me that he had been with the Archbishop of Canterbury (Dr. Lang) earlier in the day, and that Lang had assured him that the allegations that Jews were persecuted in Germany were largely false; that he had been to see Ribbentrop—the German Ambassador—himself, and that Ribbentrop had assured him that all the stories of persecution and violence were fabrications. The Archbishop was planning to make a speech in the House of Lords on the following day repeating the assurance of Ribbentrop. T. rang up the Archbishop's secretary, Alan Don, later Dean of Westminster, and arranged for me to go down to Lambeth in the morning with the texts I had brought with me. The speech was not made!

I.S.S. dealt with students only—telling those who had not completed at least a year that they would have to give up university studies till they could look after their finances themselves; reorienting the many students who had entered the law faculty; sending advanced medical students to the countries where they would be welcome; and so on. Young graduates we passed on to Miss Ginsberg, Librarian of the League; professors had a generous and compassionate co-operative by which, once they had a place, they taxed themselves to help the unplaced.

In spite of all the new work involved, we tried to keep on all we could of the old. The annual conference of 1933 involved the most difficult decision. In 1932 we had accepted a German invitation to hold the conference in Bavaria, at Kloster Ettal. Fritz Beck, one of our oldest collaborators, was most anxious we should not cancel it, hoping we might still be of some influence in the universities. But, of course, no Jewish student could attend, and I felt it impossible to go in such circumstances. In the end two of us felt we could not go, two of us felt that we should seize this last opportunity. There followed a most moving experience. Each of us perfectly accepted the decision of the other. We planned the whole conference in complete mutual trust, each caring that the part in which he could not himself participate was given every chance of success. So Walter and Rena Datta went to Ettal, Pob and I awaited them in Liechtenstein at Festung Luziensteig, and the second half of the conference was held there. By that time the situation in Germany had become so much worse that a continuation of collaboration was impossible. Fritz Beck, when he left us, told us we should not see him again, for his murder was already planned by the Nazis among his own students. He was brutally killed very shortly afterwards.

In the autumn of the same year I went over to the States to raise more money. While I was in New York I met one of our collaborators in Germany—now an exile—who had been very friendly with Elsa Brandström, an elderly Swedish lady of such eminence and distinction for her services to war victims in the past that even the Nazis could not touch her. Dr. Brandström was completely anti-Nazi and had let it be known that she would help any of their victims that she could. She was to be regarded as a last court of appeal, and certain refugee organisations had been told that they could get in touch with her as a last resource. She was interested in students, so that we were one of the organisations who could call on her.

With considerable precautions, because of the number of Germans in New York, we met and I was given a code in which to communicate with her. One copy I was to take back to Geneva, the other was taken to her in Berlin. All through 1934 the code was in my flat in Geneva, while I was (as I subsequently discovered) constantly visited by Nazi spies. Taking

into account that it was a bachelor flat, I think I had devised
a perfect hiding place for it. I was always one meal behindhand
in my washing up. There was always a pile of dirty plates on
the kitchen table. In the middle of that pile was a clean plate
on which the code reposed.

During my visit I went to Canada to preach in Holy Blossom
Synagogue, Toronto whose rabbi, Maurice Eisendrath, had
visited me in Geneva. While in Canada, I received a telephone
call from James G. Macdonald. He had just been appointed
High Commissioner for Refugees—born, as he said himself,
of the League of Nations, and abandoned forthwith on the
doorstep of public charity. He asked me to return at once to
New York, so as to sail back with him. Being a European, I
asked for the next plane to New York, and arrived shortly
after in James G.'s office. He was dumbfounded, and said that
he thought I was in Canada, and would not arrive till the next
day. Americans had not begun to regard flying as a normal
way of getting around in 1933. In fact the routine daily plane
in which I travelled from Montreal to New York had four
basket chairs tied with string to the linoleum floor!

I explained to the new high commissioner that I had to have
the money I had come for before I could sail back to Europe.
He sent me to Mr. Felix Warburg, whom I had already met
while staying with his brother Paul on their beautiful estate in
White Plains. Felix gave me the money I needed, and I left
on the *Ile de France* with James G. It was really an extravagance
to travel first class with him—though very pleasant—for he
would not discuss work at all until he had met his adviser,
Mr. May, in Geneva. It was unfortunate that he had brought
with him an American secretary, who spoke neither French nor
German, and set on his other side an American adviser. Both
were in their own way, competent, but neither brought the
high commissioner into real understanding of Europe. Though
I could not discuss his work during the voyage, I could estimate
his knowledge of French. So, as we approached Le Havre
where he rightly expected to be received with diplomatic
status, I asked him how he intended to present himself to the
French authorities.

"It is not difficult," he replied, "to translate high commissioner into French. I shall explain that I am a Haut Commissionaire de la Société des Nations."

Fortunately he did believe me—though his American adviser was not present to endorse it—that he proposed to introduce himself as head porter and that *Haut Commissaire* was the French for high commissioner.

I soon found that the High Commission was not work for which I was well fitted. McDonald was a man of complete integrity and devotion, but he was given neither the authority nor the respect by the governments of the League which the job required. He had fixed the salaries of himself and his immediate staff at a figure which seemed to me far too high, and which he justified by saying that he would be so much judged by his salary that he would lose prestige by taking less. I was supposed to be his non-Jewish expert, Norman Bentwich his Jewish expert. Both of us were serving for little more than pocket money, because we were conscious all the time that the whole cost of the High Commission was being met from refugee funds. I told him that I could not accept his argument and resigned. It was a measure of his fundamental greatness that he bore me no resentment, and we met in the most friendly fashion on subsequent occasions.

I continued with I.S.S. through into 1934, and then resigned, handing over the continuation of the job to a very competent young Swiss, Dr. Schnaebeli. But I stayed in Geneva, having made up my mind to go deeper into research on the Jewish question, but not sure whether it would be better to remain in Switzerland or return to England. I did not want to pack up at once, as I was looking after a refugee student at Geneva university. I had offered him a room in my flat, telling him that I would need his help in the domestic work. This he promised to give, and would, I am sure, have given, had he had the very slightest competence in that direction. As I was living on odd earnings, and had to meet his university fees as well as his board, it turned out a difficult year. I know we lived on less than £150. I ended up a very competent laundryman and sempster as well as cook. For he could not even wash up or make his bed without some completely unexpected disaster. His one thought was to get his mother out of Germany into

Israel, in which plan, I am glad to say, he ultimately succeeded.

The rest of the story of Geneva properly belongs to the next chapter and to my involvement in the Jewish question. Here I need only say that the fall in the value of the £ brought me home in the spring of 1935.

VI

INVOLVEMENT IN THE JEWISH QUESTION

IF 1929 SAW the end of any creative relations with the
W.S.C.F. it also saw the beginning of my real involvement
in the Jewish question. It may not have been more acute than
other political or ethnic conflict in any particular university,
but it was undoubtedly the most widespread cause of disorder.
Riots between nationalist and Jewish students were tragically
common in Germany, Austria, Hungary, Rumania and Poland.
The aggressors were, inevitably, the nationalists, for the Jewish
groups wanted nothing except to be left in peace. In some cases
the riots caused deaths, in many severe injuries, and, especially
at the beginning of the academic year, it was not uncommon
for the whole university to be closed down until the authorities
could regain control of the situation.

Consequently among the conferences which I proposed at
Chartres in July 1928, there was one between the nationalist
and the Jewish student organisations. I knew enough already
about the academic situation in the countries affected to realise
that there were problems on both sides, and that the two sides
never met under any circumstances which would make possible
a cool appraisal of the real issues and what to do about them.
I was generally regarded as mad for proposing such a conference, and both sides tended to inform me that I was insulting
them by suggesting that they should sit down with the other
side. It was hopefully foreseen that the conference would end
in bloodshed; but I was given permission to try the experiment.
So was born the Bierville conference of January 1929.

I reversed all my usual methods of choosing site and time.
Usually we went to the most pleasant places available in the
most pleasant season. For this subject my problem was to keep
the two sides together, to make it unattractive for either side
to walk out, and to eliminate all counter-attractions. I chose
January because it was the wettest month, and I set out to find

a place which was five miles from any café, cinema, or other distraction, and which had only one large room properly heated. If it had two rooms, I knew that in between the formal meetings all the Jews would go into one room, all the antisemites into the other.

I found exactly what I wanted, deep in dank woods, surrounded by water, five miles from Etampes, with accommodation for the twenty-five I proposed to invite, but with only one *salle de conférence* properly heated. It was the seventeenth century chateau de Bierville, belonging to Marc Sagnier of the *Jeune République*, who gladly gave it to us, and allowed me to arrange *kosher* cooking from Paris. To gather the members I paid a visit to all the countries of central and eastern Europe whose presence was essential, and secured from all of them the acceptance that I wanted. Nothing better illustrates the respect with which I.S.S. was regarded than the fact that every member of this conference was either president or a high official of a Jewish or national student body. But I also made certain solemn pledges. There would be no voting at the conference and no resolutions, so that members could not be put into embarrassing opposition or still more embarrassing support of unwanted developments. Further no official report would be published, and members could decide for themselves whether to make known their attendance or to keep it confidential. I.S.S. would mention no names.

The president of the Deutsche Studentenschaft—the official German national union—was one of the conference members. He courageously published his attendance at the conference, and in consequence received thirteen challenges to a duel for insulting German honour. To have fought the duels would have been a trifle for an expert duellist. But I was immensely pleased that he had the moral courage to refuse the challenges on the ground that he did not admit that German honour was involved in his attendance.

All three of us were at the conference, and were together capable of dealing with all the problems of translation. I chaired it, and made continuous use of the period of translation as a cooler of the atmosphere. It was an unfailing resource. A member from one side would make a very provocative speech.

At once half a dozen members from the other would leap to their feet and burst into excited protest, till the Chair interposed: "Un petit moment s'il vous plaît; faut avoir la traduction." Down went the temperature. Most of the crises at the conference were the unexpected ones. The most serious arose from our excellent intention to have a quiet cultural evening after the battles of the day.

I looked for a Jewish speaker who could introduce us to the non-controversial aspects of Jewish culture, helping us to understand Jewry more positively, and to see something of its inner life. Enquiries at Geneva all suggested that M. Josué Jehouda, the novelist, was just the man. I offered him all four evenings to develop as he liked. He accepted. For his first evening he chose Jewish Mysticism, a subject which, in my ignorance, I regarded as exactly what I wanted. I forget for how many hours he spoke, but it was several times the offered length, and he succeeded in uniting the whole conference in frustrated fury, both at what he said and at the time he took to say it. By the next morning it was evident that the continued presence of M. Jehouda would wreck the conference. The Rumanians demanded an equal length of time to expand Christian mysticism—about which they knew nothing; most of the Jewish members demanded similar opportunities for denying that the speaker had represented *their* views on Jewish mysticism.

I have mentioned before that we were all qualified diplomats! I had the task of persuading M. Jehouda, whose feelings we did not want to hurt, to take the morning train back to Geneva. This I did on the specious grounds that the conference was much smaller than I had expected when I asked him to give four days of his invaluable time to addressing it, and that, with our small numbers, he had already given us much to think over and discuss during the remaining evenings, whereas I was sure he had most important tasks awaiting him in Geneva. I left him, dashing to his room to pack and catch the train. On the way he ran into Walter, and told him of his decision. With true Austrian courtesy and charm, Walter expressed such regrets that he decided to change his mind and stay! Luckily Walter met me, and told me of the disaster. That M. Jehouda caught his train, that we remained good friends till his death, and that he was delighted with the report I gave him of the conference when I returned to Geneva, is the basis of my claim to some diplomatic talent!

The most important results of the conference were that, firstly the leaders of the two sides met each other personally, and actually heard from the other side what their claims and complaints were; and secondly that the 'Christians' present heard very competent lectures on Jewish history and the contemporary Jewish situation, lectures they would certainly not have attended at home. Moreover both sides wanted me to visit them in their own universities, and wanted I.S.S. to continue the work of mutual understanding which the conference had made possible. When the three of us reported to the Assembly our opinion of the opportunities opened by the conference, we had also to report that all the addresses already referred to were given by Jewish scholars. We had combed Europe unsuccessfully for a Christian scholar who could talk objectively either about Jewish history or about the contemporary Jewish situation. The result was that the Assembly suggested that I should spend what spare time I could extract from a pretty busy life to make a study of the Jewish question!

I had from the beginning to make an important choice. Should I seek to know Hebrew, or to know Jews? I had not time to do both, for they made opposite demands. To do the first I should spend all the time I could spare in study; to do the second I should go out and meet people. My travelling life made the choice of the second the obvious one; but I also realised that in the atmosphere of the antisemitism of the thirties I had much better not get involved in arguments about the Talmud unless I became an acknowledged master of rabbinic Hebrew. It was a work which antisemites freely quoted, but it was much wiser for me to confine myself to pointing out the conclusions of acknowledged Christian scholars like Hermann Strack or Herbert Danby. So I bought Graetz's *History* instead of a Hebrew grammar, and read the whole of it in the next six months. But I also made use of the unrivalled knowledge of central and eastern Europe of our old friend, Alexander Teich of Vienna, to meet as many as possible of the Jewish leaders of the day.

I became familiar with most of the Jewish student centres in Poland, Hungary, Rumania and elsewhere, as well as keeping in touch with the habitually penniless World Union of Jewish Students. Its President was Hersch Lauterpacht, then a young lecturer at the London School of Economics, and I always saw him when I was in London and gave him news of Jewish student life in Eastern Europe. I gradually built up a group of Jewish scholars who showed infinite patience in answering my innumerable questions. Professor L. Hersch of Geneva had been one of our lecturers at Bierville. In London there was Dr. Charles Singer, Professor of the History of Medicine, and Rabbi Dr. Mattuck who, a liberal himself, was one of the most coherent and sympathetic expounders of traditional Judaism imaginable. In Oxford and Cambridge there was Herbert Loewe, who spent half the week in each university. He introduced me to Claude Montefiore. In Paris and Berlin I discovered the most learned booksellers, Nathanson and Louis Lamm, who helped me with the beginnings of a Jewish library. In Geneva there was M. Slatkin from whom I got many treasures.

While I was developing this new work, my previous interests had all to be maintained. The result was that my visits to my flat at Geneva were short, my opportunities of getting over to Guernsey to see my father were restricted, and all the time I was trying to become something of an expert on European Jewish history with especial reference to the Jewish student. My colleagues were, in fact, just as busy, for the work of I.S.S. was growing steadily more difficult during those years of the depression. It was no unusual thing for me to come back to Geneva for a few days, and to find the office so busy that I had to engage a typist from one of the pools that existed in that city full of organisations. On one occasion I came back from Poland, where I had been studying especially the Jewish student houses and their social and economic life. I dictated a long letter to Lauterpacht on this visit. When my temporary typist brought the letter, the key word was spelt throughout juice!

I had not been long in the field when I was brought smartly up against the fact that any Jew automatically suspected an interested Christian of having missionary motives, and that he deeply resented the Christian attitude of superiority. Conrad Hoffmann, previously an American Y.M.C.A. secretary, had been the first secretary of European Student Relief. He had been deeply loved throughout the universities of eastern Europe, especially by all the minority groups to whom he brought moral as well as material encouragement. When Walter Kotschnig succeeded him in I.S.S., he became a secretary of the W.S.C.F. with the special task of developing work for foreign students. About this time Dr. John R. Mott, a great Christian leader and the founder of the W.S.C.F., but a good deal of a 'Christian imperialist' took him from this work and made him first secretary of the new committee on the Christian Approach to the Jew, created by the International Missionary Council.

Dr. Mott's choice of Conrad was based on the confidence which he had won among Jews in central and eastern Europe, and was a naked piece of religious aggression, since Conrad had earned their love by the complete equality with which he treated them. Shortly after the appointment I was in Vienna where I met, as usual, Alexander Teich. When I told him, he just sat there and sobbed. "But Conrad would not do that to us," he whispered, with tears running down his cheeks. "He would not do that to us," he kept repeating, while I began to understand what Jews felt about the Christian missionary approach.

Conrad Hoffmann was not an intellectual. I do not think that he ever realised how deeply he had hurt those Jewish students who had trusted him, nor did he realise how universal and profound was the suspicion in Jewish hearts of any Christian approach. I was at that time silent on the relationship of the two religions. My Oxford background had been conventional. I had, up to then, had no reason to ask myself whether our relationship to Jews and Judaism was something different from the relationship of Christianity to any other religion. The missionary department of the S.C.M. had been concerned with Asia and Africa, and I do not remember missions to the Jews ever being discussed.

My own work did not touch the religious issue. I was con-

cerned with antisemitism in the European universities. But
Conrad regarded me still as a colleague, and our relations
became very embarrassing. I found it was unsafe to express
any opinion to him. He would misquote it to the next man he
met. When my first book was in the press, he tried to get me to
suppress it, on the grounds that it would damage my reputation to publish a book which both laid the chief blame for
medieval antisemitism on the Christian Church and, in discussing the remedies, made no reference to the necessary conversion of the Jews. I had a similarly embarrassing relationship
with William Paton, secretary of the International Missionary
Council, but also an old S.C.M. secretary who had left the staff
a year before I joined it. His argument was, I felt, completely
bureaucratic. It was that to approve an attitude to Jews and
Judaism different from our attitude to any other people and
religion undermined the whole claim of Christianity to be of
universal significance. My suggestion that our connexions and
relations with Jews and Judaism had been unique, so that our
attitude to Jews might also be considered as not deciding our
approach to other non-Christians, was met by the somewhat
discourteous reply that I had better go and read my Bible. I
learned very early that to evolve a new attitude to Jewish-
Christian relations was to be a lonely job.

In the spring of 1930 I decided that, as I had not found a
competent short study of antisemitism in English, I would
write one. It was to be the only book which I have ever dictated straight on to a typewriter. But, with my constant
travels, that was the only way I could get the book written,
and I was lucky enough to find in Geneva Mrs. Spender who
was quite equal to the job. Though she had never been in
England her English was faultless. When completed, the
typescript went straight to the Student Movement Press, and
I did not see it again until the book appeared in October 1930.

It was published in America by Richard Smith. When,
shortly afterwards, he decided to specialise on travel, he sold it
to Harpers. When I was in the States in 1933 I had two contrasting experiences of it. Knowing that it was the only book
on the American market dealing with the causes of antisemitism, I hoped that the prominence given to the subject by the

accession of Hitler to power might mean that it had had reasonable sales. So I went hopefully to see Harpers. There the manner of my reception raised my hopes. I almost understood that the sole business of a directors' meeting was to see how further to extend the sales of the book. Finally the executive who received me said: "Let me show you, Mr. Parkes, how we present the book in our catalogue." Seizing a large tome he began to leaf rapidly through the pages. Ignoring history, sociology and international relations, all of which seemed to me possible categories in which the book might appear, he slowed down as he reached religion. Religious education became a cause of further deceleration. Finally he reached 'Sunday Schools' and to my astonished gaze showed me the entry. Instead of *The Jew and His Neighbour*, it read:

James Parkes: *Jesus and His Neighbours*.

They had sold eleven copies. A few days later I was in the library of the Jewish Theological Seminary, talking to Dr. Marx the librarian, when the president, Cyrus Adler, came in. Marx turned to him and introduced me. With a beaming smile Adler turned to me and said: "Well, and how is the neighbour?"

In 1931, under much more normal conditions, we held a second conference on the Jewish question at a pleasant hotel in Nyon on the lake of Geneva. Our two Jewish speakers were Nahum Goldmann and Hermann Badt. The latter was then the highest placed Jewish civil servant in any German Ministry. He was in the Prussian Home Office. So that they could not complain that their philosophy was ignored, we invited the Nazi students to provide us a speaker. They chose one of their leading theorists, Dr. Wilhelm Stapel, who explained that the Jews had 'a differentiated plasma' and the Germans 'an undifferentiated plasma' which prevented any *symbiosis*.

I suppose I went to bed on the first night troubled that the conference was going to be haunted throughout by the absurdities of plasmic philosophy, but in any case I woke up with a pleasant jingle in my head based on 'My bonnie is over the ocean'. Being unable to sing in tune myself I passed the new words to my more musical colleagues who immediately saw the light. They came down to breakfast humming the tune, which is a catchy one. The Germans, and others, soon wanted to know the words, which began:

> My plasma is over the ocean
> My plasma is awful to see
> My plasma is all of a muddle,
> Oh, who'll differentiate me?

By the end of the second day the *plasmalied* had become the official conference tune, and solemnly opened every session. When Drs. Goldmann and Badt left Nyon, they were escorted to the station by a choir, headed by the president of the Deutsche Studentenschaft, singing the *plasmalied*. We had indeed progressed since Bierville, and it was not our fault that the advent to power of the Nazis, and their influence in other countries, made further progress in understanding impossible.

Both our Jewish speakers left Germany when the Nazis came to power, Dr. Goldmann to his consummate leadership in the World Jewish Congress and the World Zionist Organisation, Dr. Badt to retirement. But before he retired Dr. Badt made his own contribution to the annals of German Jewry. It was well known that the Nazis intended to murder the Prussian Prime Minister, the Socialist Dr. Braun, under whom Dr. Badt served. When none of his own staff would lift a finger to help him, Dr. Badt donned his chauffeur's uniform, took the largest, most official car from the ministry, and drove Dr. Braun and his wife through the night across the frontier. When Nazi patrols tried to stop him, he relied on the official markings of the car, put his foot down on the accelerator, and drove straight through them. He rightly calculated that precise instructions would not have gone out to every corner of Germany on their first night in office. In the morning Dr. Badt was at his desk in the Ministry as though he had spent a quiet night in bed at his home.

After Nyon, I visited Poland, as the official guest of the Polish National Union of Students, even though the purpose of my visit was to study and discuss with them the problems of Jewish participation in academic life. The impetus to this invitation came from Jan Wroczynski, vice president and foreign secretary of the Union, and an old member of the Assembly of I.S.S. It was a most interesting visit, in which the Polish student leaders were completely loyal, if rather bewildered, co-operators.

It became evident to me, from this and other visits, that if I were going to get anywhere in so controversial and difficult an issue, I had to become *Herr Doktor*. It was not that any doctor was automatically a learned man, but that, if a man was not even a doctor, he could not be a learned man. I had begun the story of *The Jew and His Neighbour* with the massacres of the First Crusade. But the question was always in my mind: why did these massacres take place in cities where there was already a long Jewish residence, and no tradition of violence? So I determined to take as my thesis a study of the period behind the crusades, and of the beginnings of antisemitism.

I.S.S. allowed me to spend one term a year at Oxford for three years, the minimum required if I was to try for an Oxford Doctorate of Philosophy. I was very fortunate in that Helen Ellershaw, whom I had met when she was a sub-warden of Student Movement House, offered to come out to Geneva at her own expense and help me with secretarial work and the considerable job of typing the thesis. Oxford accepted *The Jew and His Neighbour* as the equivalent of a first research degree, and my illegal letter from my theological examiners as evidence that I could have got at least a second. Professor (Later Sir Maurice) Powicke undertook to supervise and guide my work. Finally Exeter College, which was a beneficiary of the closed scholarships from Elizabeth College, allowed that, as a born Guernseyman, I was entitled to at least a modest post-graduate scholarship, since such were definitely part of the foundation. So in the summer of 1931 I spent a whole term at Oxford.

My subject was an enquiry into the origins of antisemitism. I could not more closely define it, as I was in considerable doubt as to what I should find. I had been a classical scholar and was familiar with the dislike of Jews and other orientals among Romans of good old Latin stock. I knew Cicero's pretence that it was dangerous to offend the Jews of Rome—

though I did not know whether it was a typical Ciceronian flight of rhetoric or a genuine fear. But I knew very little either of patristic attitudes or of later Roman legislation. Of post-New Testament Judaism I knew nothing at all. I had understood from my teachers at Oxford that all that was good in the Old Testament had passed to the Christian Church, and I had been content to leave it at that.

Treating the subject chronologically I soon saw that the dislike which one found in the Hellenistic world was directly related to actual facts, or to reasonably assumed facts. Jews *were* clannish, and a soured historian might well attribute to them—as he did to early Christians—a hatred of the human race. They inspired intense dislike in Egypt, but, after all, they did celebrate annually a story which was very unflattering to the Egyptians. And so on. Hatred, dislike or contempt in the classical world were examples of normal human reactions, normal human xenophobias.

My next discovery was that the rabbis who rescued the Jewish people and their religion from the nationalism of the wars with Rome were not contemptible themselves, nor was the Judaism which they rebuilt from the ruins of temple and national autonomy a contemptible religion. If there was 'a fence about the Torah', it was a reasonable reaction to an actual spiritual need. A sympathetic knowledge of post-Christian Judaism is an essential foundation for an understanding of Jewish-Christian relations during and after the separation of the two religions. For it is only by being fair to both sides that one can understand both the hostility and the friendship which is revealed by our sources.

I discovered this in a suitably dramatic fashion. I was working always under the pressure of time; and, when I found that Catholic, Protestant and Jewish scholars all agreed that the martyrdom of Pionius, Pontius and Philip, supported by various patristic texts, proved Jewish responsibility for the persecution of the Christians, I was very disposed to take it as something I could assert without verification. I was working in the Bodleian, in the Duke Humphrey, at the time, and went down to the Selden End to find the *Lives of the Saints*, to see if it was something I could verify easily. When I was confronted with the sixty-six fat folio volumes of the *Acta Sanctorum,* I felt it would have to stay unverified.

I started back to my place, but my conscience got the better of me! I knew that I could not quote Pionius and company without checking. That meant a week learning how to use the *Acta,* which are a highly specialised type of literature. I then approached the sixty-six volumes. I found the three saints, and was rewarded by the discovery that:

the life of Pionius was a most moving document by an eye witness;

the life of Philip was a late and unreliable account;

the life of Pontius was dismissed by the Bollandist editors themselves as *acta fabulosa et minime credibilia*;

but all three documents had one feature in common. They did not mention any responsibility of Jews for the death of the martyr! If Jews were mentioned at all it was simply as part of the crowd. So I sat down and read all the lives for the first six centuries of Christianity in the sixty-six volumes. I thought that I might as well do the thing thoroughly, so I followed this with the lives of the saints of the Eastern Orthodox Church in Greek, and then the lives of the Arab Jacobite, the Ethiopian, the Armenian, and the Georgian Churches, fortunately all in French translation. Some of it was very amusing reading. There is Saint Juliana of Spain, obviously patron saint of women's hockey, and few people know that aspirin seems to be named after Saint Asprinius, Bishop of Naples and patron saint against headaches—but his remedy was a little drastic, for he is one of the saints who goes about with his decapitated head tucked under his arm!

I wonder who started the story—I suspect the Abbé Fleury, but I have never proved it—but it is not the only completely false accusation against Jewry which I found deeply embedded in Christian historical writing, and which contributes to the general atmosphere in which I was inevitably labelled 'philo-semitic' by the mere fact of drawing a very different picture of post-Christian Judaism and Jewish history. I suppose no historical scholar is completely objective, but I certainly tried to give both sides their warts—as well as their attractive features.

This was all the more necessary because I was completely unprepared for the discovery that it was the Christian Church, and the Christian Church alone, which turned a normal xenophobia and normal good and bad communal relations between two human societies into the unique evil of anti-semitism, the most evil, and, as I gradually came to realise, the most crippling sin of historic Christianity. It was not any particular contemporary fact on either side which led to this tragic result, nor was it any deduction by the Christians of any one period from the behaviour of their Jewish contemporaries.

Antisemitism arises from the picture of the Jews which Christian theologians extracted from their reading of the Old Testament, a work for whose every word they claimed divine authority. The Old Testament is very frank about Jewish sins and very definite in its certainty that they earned divine punishment. But it also dwelt on the love between God and Israel, and the promises of the Messianic Age. So long as both elements in the story are accepted as being about a single people, a lofty balance is retained. But Christian theologians divided it into the story of two peoples—the virtuous Hebrews, who were pre-incarnation Christians, had all the praise and promise; and the wicked Jews had all the crimes and denunciations. This was the interpretation repeated over and over again, in every possible variation, and in every century from the third onwards. In the leading Church historian of the fourth century, Eusebius of Caesarea, Jews and Hebrews are biologically two distinct races.

During the whole of this study I was immensely helped by Herbert Loewe, who, in his generosity, kindliness and deep religious conviction was a veritable saint of Torah, and a living denial of all the stock charges that Judaism is legalistic, unspiritual, formal and so on and so on.

I carried my study right down to the end of the Roman influence on the first barbarian societies, Visigoths, Vandals and the rest, and ended in the Dark Ages. It was longer than was necessary for a doctorate, but it completed a period, and left the Middle Ages for subsequent study. I duly got my doctorate, and my examiners paid an official visit to the University Press, to make a special recommendation that they should publish the book. This resulted in the first of a series of paradoxical contacts with that famous press. In due course I was summoned by one of the Sindics.

"We have a rule," he said, "that we do not publish a work which has been submitted for the D.Phil. in more than sixty thousand words. You would have to reduce it to that."

I pointed out that the book contained 135,000 words, apart from five appendices, so that he was asking me to cut it by more than half. But he had not finished his conditions.

"Why do you need all these footnotes?" he asked.

"Surely it is usual in a serious but controversial work to give your sources and your authorities?" I replied. He did not think so. But his next objection was even more stunning.

"You do not bring in England," he complained.

"But the book goes down only to the Dark Ages and there were no Jews in England before the Middle Ages."

"Bring it down to the end of the Middle Ages."

"If I double the length of the period treated, and halve the length of the book, there will, perhaps, be a paragraph dealing with the unimportant Jewish community in England. In any case they were expelled in 1290."

"Bring it down to 1290, an excellent date."

"But, sir, that is like writing a history of the interwar period and bringing it down to the birth of your second child. It is a totally unimportant date in medieval Jewish history."

And thereon we parted. Returning to London, I called on Jack Davidson of the Soncino Press, whom I had never met before.

"I have written a book on the origins of antisemitism," I told him.

"Good. We will publish it."

"Be careful. It has 135,000 words and five appendices."

"I don't mind if it has a quarter of a million words."

Jack not only published *The Conflict Between the Church and the Synagogue* as it stood, but had to reprint it, and sold nearly two thousand copies. I.M.S. helped us to keep the price down, because it was still in the middle of the depression, and public libraries were severely restricted in their budgets. It was made a paperback in 1961. Probably the greatest compliment paid

to it is that the material of single chapters has twice been successfully pirated by American graduates seeking a Ph.D. In
one case the textual identity was such that it could, technically,
have made *me* infringe *his* copyright did I secure an American
edition! So that had to be straightened out before 1961. But I
have often wondered whether, if I was interested in acquiring
as many degrees as possible, I was not entitled to call myself
Ph.D. Columbia and Ph.D. Johns Hopkins. It was undoubtedly
on my work that the degrees were given, but I have never put
it to the test.

At some time during this period Walter came back from
America with what he hoped would be welcome news for me.
He knew I would not stay much longer on the staff of I.S.S.,
but wanted to go deeper into the Jewish question, and he had
met members of the Crane Foundation in New York who were
interested to hear that a Christian scholar was concerning
himself with this subject. The Foundation dealt with contemporary problems, having a number of regional centres, each
with a staff of experts. The results of their work were circulated
rather as memoranda to the sources of power than as books
for the general public. There was such a regional centre concerned with the Middle East; and Walter brought me a firm
request that I would meet its Chief, George Antonius, in
London with a view to joining its staff as their Jewish 'expert'.
I already knew and respected Antonius as author of *The Arab
Awakening*, and was encouraged by the fact that he was a friend
of Blanche Dugdale, Balfour's niece and biographer. This
suggested that he was a serious and objective scholar of a very
controversial subject!

I met Antonius at the Reform Club, but his proposition was
more in the nature of a bribe than a serious opening for
scholarly work. He offered me a salary of £1,200 a year—
three times what I was quite satisfied with in I.S.S.—together
with a house in Jerusalem which he would get me from his
friend the Mufti. At the end of my service there would be a
substantial pension. In return, everything that I wrote would
be subject to his over-riding censorship. I would pledge myself
never to put anything on paper on the subject of the Jews except
for the Crane Foundation, and this condition would continue

after my retirement. I did not become an officer of the Foundation.

During my last year in Geneva I made a more detailed study of the Gospels and the Pauline letters than was possible in the doctorate. This was published, after I came home, with the title *Jesus, Paul and the Jews*. It was, I believe, the first book by a Christian writer on Jesus and Paul which had a Foreword by an orthodox Jew. For Herbert Loewe very generously consented to write an introduction for me. Reviewing the relation between the two religions as my two books had revealed them, I realised how false it was to say that 'the Jews rejected Jesus'. The immense majority of the Jews had rejected a Gospel account of the life of Jesus in which he was made to exaggerate their faults and to distort their religion, a distortion which in Paul became at times a completely false picture. To this must be added the tragic attitude of patristic writers who did not conceive of the Church as sharing the Old Testament with the Jews, but claimed an exclusive right in it, and exclusive authority for their own interpretation, an attitude which some 'biblical theologians' of our own day seem ready to repeat, but which Jews have always quite naturally rejected.

At that time I had come to believe that the missionary approach of different Churches, intended to turn Jews into Anglicans, Lutherans or other Gentile forms of Christianity, was a mistaken approach. Did Jews ever come to accept Jesus as Messiah, I believed it would be in their own way, not in terms of our Hellenistic theology, or our interpretation of Old or New Testament. But my view at that time was mainly negative. I knew what I rejected, but I had no clear picture as yet of any positive belief.

The period 1934–1935 saw an extraordinary trial going on in Berne. The Jewish community was trying to get a court declaration that *The Protocols of the Elders of Zion* were a forgery, and were to be classed as obscene literature whose distribution should be prohibited. I received a number of visits from 'Swiss' students who said that they had become interested in *The Protocols* because of the trial, and had been told that I was the person who could explain what they were, and what it was all about. Naturally, when one comes to a scholar and asks him to explain his speciality, he is delighted and pours forth the riches of his treasury on the head of the enquirer. Besides, I had one of the rare originals from which the Protocols were plagiarised —the *Dialogue aux Enfers entre Montesquieu et Machiavel*, and showed it willingly to them, together with all my own notes and studies. Though I officially resigned from I.S.S. in the summer of 1934, I continued to be interested in the refugee students, and they used to come to the flat one night a week. Older exiles from Germany, professors and others, also visited me quite frequently. The enquirers, in my innocence, I invited to come too.

There was a time when it would have been unnecessary to explain what *The Protocols* are, for they were blazoned over the national press, and agonised discussions were held as to whether they were genuine or not. They purported to be the elaborate plans of a group of Jews to take over the control of the world, destroy democracy and Christianity and subvert or enslave the whole non-Jewish population. In the early days of communist revolutions, with Jewish personalities like Trotsky, Rosa Luxembourg and others so prominent among their leaders, it appeared to many *just* possible that there was such a world plot. Then the correspondent of *The Times* at Constantinople discovered that they were a plagiarism from the *Dialogue aux Enfers*, a satire on Napoleon III, and the world relaxed. But Fascist and Nazi propagandists continued to republish them, to translate them into many languages, and to proclaim their authenticity. Hence various trials instituted by Jewish communities to get them officially established as a forgery.

In the beginning of 1935 I was invited by the S.C.M. to give a series of lectures on Judaism and Christianity in the theological colleges. I had by that time decided to try and find means of making my speciality a whole time occupation. This I wanted to discuss with old S.C.M. friends and with William Temple, who by now was Archbishop of York. I don't think my lectures in the theological colleges were a great success. One lecturer at St. Aidan's, Birkenhead protested that what I had said about Judaism could not possibly be true as, if it were, Christians would have to study it and there was no time for extra studies in the curriculum ! In another college I was greeted with a tirade of abuse of Claude Montefiore, whose noble study of *The Synoptic Gospels* was described as a deliberate and malicious smear. Towards the end of the tour, I came to York, where I stayed for a few days with Temple, and got his complete approval of my desire to give my whole time to a deeper understanding of relations between Jews and Christians, Judaism and Christianity. "I shall not always agree with your views," he told me, "but I want you always to keep in touch with me."

From York I went to Birmingham to give my last lecture to the staffs of the Selly Oak group of colleges, who always invited a speaker to their corporate lunch on Thursdays. At the end of my talk an Anglican professor said to me, very reasonably, "This is very interesting, but I would like to know whether these are just your personal views, or whether they are accepted by any recognised authority?" I replied that I did not want to appear boastful, but that I had just been staying with the Archbishop of York, and that he seemed disposed to agree with my basic hypothesis that the separation of Christianity from Judaism was a schism which, like all schisms, left truth divided. This apparently serious remark was greeted with a universal outburst of laughter. I turned to my host, John Coates, and asked him what I had said funny.

"You would not realise it, Jimmy," he replied, "but standing behind those yellow tulips last Thursday William Temple used exactly those words. Then we heard it from the throne, now we hear it from the power behind the throne."

But William Temple did not take other people's remarks and repeat them. If he was prepared to use the same words it meant that he had considered them with his own much vaster understanding and experience, and was prepared publicly to endorse them. I could not have had a more encouraging experience.

From Birmingham I came to London, and went to see I.M.S. I told him what I wanted to do, and that I was sure it would be a long time before I could get Christian support adequate to enable me to do it. I asked him whether he would guarantee me an income on which I could give my whole time to research.

"How long do you think the work will take?" he asked.

I had no idea what kind of answer would appeal to him, and I said what I believed to be true: "About three hundred years."

I.M.S. laughed and said: "Good, I am prepared to help you. Had you said 'twenty-five years' or 'my life time' I would have told you to go away because you did not understand what you were talking about."

The state of sterling *vis-à-vis* the Swiss franc made it inevitable that it should be in England that I tried to establish the work. I had to decide which of the three great libraries should provide a background. I did not want to live in London, not only because I am a countryman, but because I thought that a certain geographical separation from as many storm centres of my problem as possible would be wise. I did not want to return to Oxford, because I had experience of reading in the Bodleian, and because I found the Thames valley relaxing. Cambridge had a modern library, open shelves, and, if one had a Cambridge degree, the right to take books out. I had already discovered the pleasant line of bracing hills twelve miles south of the city, and it was there that I looked for a house, and found one in Barley.

While I had been Warden of Student Movement House, I had had an excellent handyman, called Thomas Thomas—he invented the Christian name 'Len' because he did not like the two Thomas's. It had been an understood thing that if I came back from Geneva and set up house in England he would come and be my factotum. So I went to see if he was still willing to come. When he said 'yes', I told him that I would take him back to Geneva to help me close the flat and pack up, but that first I wanted to spend a few days in Guernsey with my father. When I got to Guernsey I found a whole batch of letters waiting for me which told me that my flat was in police occupation, and that there was even a policeman in the street outside the house. My more candid friends warned me not to come back, as they assumed the police were there to arrest me. Walter had gone to the police to find out what it was all about, and was told that they were there to protect both me and my possessions. He begged me to send him at once a *plein pouvoir* to take any steps which might be necessary until I came back.

It was fun being asked in Guernsey for an official document

5

for use in Geneva, for the official and legal language of Guernsey is French. I went to Eugene Carey, our family solicitor, and he prepared a lovely screed. "I think this would look better if we had some seals on it," he said, admiring his handiwork. He produced the impressive seal of the Carey's. Not to be outdone, I produced my great-grandfather's. "As it is for use abroad," he said, "we must get it authenticated by the island authorities." So he managed to get an official seal of the bailiwick of Guernsey attached. The net result of our handiwork was unexpected. It was so splendiferous a document that the police of Geneva could not bear to give it up, and I have never been able to recover it! As soon as Walter got the *plein pouvoir*, he was able to find out what it was all about. The Berne police had obtained information that the Swiss Nazi organisation, the *Eisene Front*, had received instructions from the World Antisemitic Service, *der Antisemitische Weltdienst*, in Erfurt to arrange for my liquidation and the collection of a number of books and documents from my flat. All my 'Swiss' students had been Nazi spies.

Thomas and I duly arrived in Geneva one Thursday evening. Shortly after we arrived the telephone rang. As soon as I lifted the receiver and gave my name, the caller rang off. We were proceeding in the best *whodunit* manner: it had been ascertained that I had returned. Friday passed peacefully. On Saturday morning Thomas and I went to the market. He was in his best suit, and walked beside me while I did the bargaining and buying, since Thomas did not speak French. Obviously we were identified during this excursion, but the appointed thugs decided that Thomas was the scholar and I was the *valet de chambre*. I should add that all our goings out of, and comings into, the flat were surveyed by a large policeman reclining in my best armchair at the head of the stairs outside our flat door.

We were busy all the rest of Saturday. When my post came, I threw the envelopes with foreign stamps over to Thomas, who put them as they were into his pocket book, since his younger son, Johnny, collected stamps. In the evening he said he would post my letters, and take a walk. Now comes an important point. The dear little part-*concierge* and part-owner of the house, Mademoiselle Campiche, had to put outside the front door late every night the heavy dustbins of the whole house. They lived behind a glass door that shut off the back stairs down to the cellars. When I was in Geneva I had always done it for her. I told Thomas that, as I was now a *bourgeois* with a *valet*, I would leave him to look after the dustbins.

The next thing that I knew was that, an hour or so later, Thomas staggered into my room and collapsed dramatically at my feet. I rushed to the telephone, but my doctor was out. I had to call the police and ask for their doctor. He was clearly instructed before he came to deny that anything had happened. He examined Thomas on the floor and looked up brightly: "It's influenza."

"But my dear doctor, is it normal that a man should feel perfectly well, then suddenly fall unconscious, remain unconscious for between half an hour and an hour, recover consciousness saying that someone had hit him on the head with a ton of bricks, and *all the time that his temperature should remain perfectly normal?*"

Looking at me with owl-like wisdom he replied: "Ah, la grippe, vous savez, ça prend des formes diverses." I have kicked myself ever since for not being bright enough to ask whether this was the political form of influenza (grippe).

During the whole of the vital period my policeman remained fast asleep in my best armchair outside my door. He refused to descend the stairs after Thomas had staggered in, on the grounds that he had no electric torch.

There were enough incidents in the 'affair' to fill a detective story. The British consulate was completely unhelpful, in fact rather offensive. The Geneva police, who detest affairs with a political undercurrent—and I sympathise with them in this— maintained that either Thomas had invented the whole thing, or that he had taken a young man down to the cellar for improper purposes, and that the young man had turned on him. In furtherance of this point of view the next morning a police officer arrived and informed me that, as there was clearly no need for any guard, the policeman was returning to more important duties. At least I could once more enjoy my best armchair!

I was, in fact, completely dependent on the American community, and they looked after me and Thomas with the utmost generosity. On the ground that I was temporarily American chaplain, the consul took a semi-official interest, and was an invaluable counsellor. The American ladies provided Thomas with invalid food and, as soon as he was well enough, took him daily for a drive. The Swiss legal adviser of the consulate briefed me, through the consul, on how to establish that Thomas had actually been attacked, and drew up for him an official *plainte d'une aggression livrée sur moi par un inconnu*! This had the interesting consequence of acquainting me with the procedure of a *juge d'instruction*. Two of the important pieces of evidence were Thomas's pocket book and his silver cigarette case. But first we had to explain how it came about that Thomas had been behind the glass door leading to the cellar stairs.

The explanation, fortunately, was found reasonable. I had told Thomas he would have to empty the bins. Coming in from his walk, and getting up to the first half-landing where the door was, Thomas thought he would just look in and see how the land lay. He found it was not lighted, and drew on his cigarette to get enough light to see the bins. Just below him the stairs turned, and the attacker was presumably hidden round this turn, waiting to mount to the flat later. I might add that our policeman's snores were quite audible from the bottom of the stairs, so that he would know when it was safe to come. When Thomas appeared he thought he was discovered or, at least, suspected, and laid Thomas out with a sandbag or rubber cosh, before Thomas could expose him.

However, he thought it was the scholar not the valet. The pocket book contained the perfect evidence that this was so, and that important material had been secured. It contained two pieces of this evidence. There were all the envelopes with foreign stamps addressed to me. I love to think of Nazi back-room-boys taking off the stamps for messages underneath, trying the paper for invisible ink, in order to explain why Dr. Parkes kept the envelopes in his pocket book! Its other contents arose from another of the hobbies Thomas shared with young Johnny. It was a collection of autographs of football teams. So there was just the name of a town, then a list of signatures—could they be the secret local anti-Nazi organisation? There was no single item in the pocket book to identify Thomas. It had been torn completely to shreds and the debris was lying on the stairs.

The silver cigarette case was also lying beside where he fell. Each side had been twisted out of shape—presumably to make sure it had no secret lining. At the interrogation Thomas insisted firmly that the case must be returned to him. After the hearing, the detective in charge of the case came up to me and confessed himself to be very puzzled. He wished to maintain the official view of the police that Thomas had invented it—possibly to explain a disreputable incident—but he was honest enough to admit that Thomas had given his evidence as an honest man would. He was impressed by the fact that Thomas knew what he ought to know and was ignorant of what he ought not to know—assuming his story to be true. The detective had asked several test questions, and Thomas had not betrayed himself by any false answer.

"But I ask myself this question," the detective explained to me. "Thomas collects the autographs of athletes. Do you think it possible that he believed it would be easier for him to get these autographs *s'il se faisait un peu de reclame?*"—if he got himself a bit of publicity?

"My good detective," I replied, "you saw that Thomas insisted on the return of his cigarette case. This was because it was given to him by the Prince of Wales for his victory in an army athletic championship. Thomas has also played football for the British army. Now do you think he will get the autographs of athletes more easily because of these facts, or because someone hit him on the head in a cellar in Geneva?"

The detective was an ex-athlete himself, and this won him completely to the innocence of Thomas. But we never got any satisfaction out of the Geneva police. To the end they maintained that 'the incident' had never happened.

While I had Thomas in bed at the flat I refused to see journalists, but a day or two after it had happened I was rung up by Paynter (I think that was his name) of the *Daily Telegraph*. He had been beaten up by the Nazis in Germany a little time before. He used this as an argument for seeing me.

I told him I wanted to see him. When he came, I explained that my father always read the *Telegraph* and asked him to play the whole thing down as much as was consistent with his journalistic conscience. My kindly intentions towards my lonely parent had unforseen consequences. When I next got to Guernsey and told him all that had happened I found him very sceptical, and convinced that I was exaggerating a great deal. When I protested at his suspicion of my accuracy he quoted at me the much reduced account—in the *Daily Telegraph*. The nicest detail in the whole affair was a postcard from Gilbert Murray:

> I hope you are not upset. This is probably
> the greatest honour you will ever be paid.
> G.M.

I stayed in Geneva for three weeks after Thomas had been sent home with the doctor's permission. One of the Russian students whom I.S.S. had helped insisted on coming to the flat every night and sleeping at the foot of my bed! I was really quite grateful, since every window in the flat could be got into from the roof, and the roof of my particular house could be reached by entering the staircase and climbing up to the loft of any house in the whole block bounded by four streets. By day it was a curious sensation to carry on a normal life, taking bicycle rides into the country in the afternoons and so on, and wondering whether a car or something would suddenly descend upon me.

For some time it was equally difficult to carry on a normal life in England. Thomas was still a very sick and disturbed man when he returned. But we were fortunate in that a very able medical student, who had known us both at Student Movement House, Dr. Augusta Bonnard, had graduated and had specialised in psychiatry during the years that I had been in Geneva. She undertook to look after Thomas and he gradually seemed to get better. But after some weeks she asked me to go and see her, and told me that Thomas was still in a dangerous state of mind. He was suffering severely from ambivalence. On the one hand he was very attached to me but, on the other, he felt victimised by the appalling headaches which became his

lot while I went scot-free. He laboured under the impulse
actively to make me share the fate which, although intended
for me, had instead been inflicted on him. It was a situation in
which he might at any moment succumb to a brain-storm, and
suddenly attack me, if only to repent it bitterly afterwards!
"Did I mind living alone with him?" she asked me. The essential condition for his recovery was, she felt, that he should come
himself and tell me of this periodical impulse to do me harm, and
ask me to let him go. On the other hand, if I dismissed him,
she felt that he would be blocked from recovering his equili-
brium.

It was not an easy decision, but it was obviously my duty to
take the risk. It was about a month later that Thomas came to
me and told me that he must leave me. I let him go, let him
find another job without it being in any way dependent on me,
and we remained good friends. But I did not see him again
until we retired to Dorset, and found him living only half an
hour away. He died early in 1968.

So, much as I had loved my Geneva flat, I was glad to leave
it in the spring of 1935. Apart from its charm it had one special
association for me. When I originally found and rented the
flat I had no special interest in the question of relations between Jews and Gentiles. Also at that time the study of medieval
Geneva was incomplete. When, several years after I had come
to Grand Mezel, a medieval map was compiled, I found that
I was living in the bridge house between the Jewish ghetto and
the Christian city.

VII

BARLEY 1935-1939

THE VILLAGE OF Barley lies high up in a fold of the hills between Royston and Saffron Walden. It is Danish in origin and its name means 'Barley field', for the land is mostly too light for wheat but grows barley excellently. It was actually the first village in this corner of England I visited, since its chief citizen was Redcliffe Salaman, a member of an old Anglo-Jewish family and a distinguished scientist, who had specialised in the potato. We had met because he wished to discuss *The Conflict of Church and Synagogue* with its author. During my first months in residence I was looked after by the fatherly police sergeant in Royston. The Geneva incident had naturally been reported, and for three or four months the police kept an eye on me to see whether the British Fascists or others might be interested in my existence. I was not only living alone, but I was often at meetings and committees in London in the evenings, driving home late at night. He taught me how to notice if I was followed, while patrols between London and Barley knew of my existence and knew my car by sight. I became very friendly with a philosophic constable in Ware whom I used to encounter in the early hours of the morning.

On two occasions in my early days at Barley I went to Harwich to meet friends from Germany who were coming to stay with me, and then return to the Nazi world. I found the police, passport officers and customs men there fascinated by the problem of ensuring that there was no risk of any Nazi seeing my friends meet me and so becoming themselves suspect. They devised a route by which they would see my visitor off until I could meet him safely, and held up all the rest of the passengers until he and I were out of sight.

The house which I had bought in Church End was half timber, though the studs did not show outside, as is the fashion in those windy hills. It had a vast chimney in the centre, with

three stacks. It had no documentary history but, as I became
familiar with every inch of it, visible or invisible, I realised
that it was basically a late medieval manor house of the simplest
kind, consisting of a hall on one side of the chimney, and on the
other a solar sleeping room, and a kitchen with huge hearth
below it. Later ages had added dairy and cellar, divided the
hall into a long parlour with two bedrooms above, and finally
turned the parlour into drawing room and dining room. Its
rarest possession consisted of some thousands of original roof
tiles. In the 19th century it had declined into being two cottages,
but when I bought it it was a terribly slummicky small holding
with two and a half acres of misused land. The small holder
was a war invalid unable really to cope with what he had.

Knowing that I knew nothing about English prices, I asked
my uncle, Sackville Bell (from whom I needed a mortgage),
to bring with him someone with a knowledge of building and
property values who could vet it before my uncle committed
himself to the mortgage, or me to the purchase. My uncle—
who was the solicitor of the family—said he had just the man,
an old friend and client of his. The man inspected all the
property, was entirely useless in dealing with the question of
price, was wrong on every point such as the ownership of
tumbling down boundary walls, and gave me a bill for eight
guineas and a certificate that adultery had not been committed
in the bedrooms. I had forgotten that my uncle had become an
enthusiastic spiritualist.

Thomas and I spent much of the summer of 1935 on the
house and garden, both of which needed enormous attention.
I put in two bath rooms and drainage for just over a hundred
pounds. I had a big barn and a granary, which gave me a
garage, and all the store room I wanted. The garden was full
of the debris of ill-built sheds, pig styes and fowl houses. By the
winter the house had begun to reveal some of the charm which
had been hidden in its previous existence, and its rooms were
beginning to be lined with the bookcases which ultimately
became the main 'wall-paper' throughout.

The garden was complete desolation with the only redeeming
feature of some big greengages and Bramley Seedlings, when
we could free them from the chaotic over-planting of the

5*

previous owner. Luckily we kept all the trees we cut down and dug up, for they provided me with fuel for a wood fire during the whole of the first winter of the war. I was not inexperienced in garden making. It had been a main hobby ever since my work had made me live in cities, and I had made a number of gardens for my friends. At Barley all the levels needed changing, but I kept an acre for orchard, gave half an acre to the village for gardens of three cottages the Parish Trust owned on the edge of my land, and which had no gardens of their own, and had an acre left to landscape into lawn, herb garden, rock garden, herbaceous borders and vegetable garden.

Thomas ran the house, but was obviously not really well. I looked round for a 'Mrs. Mop' to help, and was recommended to a villager who had had an illegitimate child and was looked on as almost a pariah in consequence. When after the second war illegitimate children tended to proliferate as a result of handsome prisoners of war on agricultural work, the results were paraded with pride to the Rector. But poor Rose always went about as though she had committed an unforgivable sin. I got her to come and see me, and asked her what she charged by the hour. She said 'sixpence'. I told her I could not possibly pay her that, and that if she came to me she would have to get accustomed to charging ninepence. It never struck me how unpopular I was making myself among the housewives of Barley!

When Thomas left me I had to look round for another factotum. After several failures, John McNeilage came to me for an experimental period. He had, as he said, been cooking one item for a whole restaurant and now wanted to cook a whole dinner for one person. Besides he wanted to get married to a girl whose parents lived in Barley. I suggested an experimental period to see if we liked each other. If we did, he could get married as soon as we could get a cottage. So in due course, John married Frances Newling, and both are close friends of ours today. John stayed with me after I married, and was an essential part of the work until we retired. He will reappear at many points in the story.

Barley proved, as I had expected, an ideal place for the work. It was an hour and a half from London, and half an hour from

Cambridge University Library. St. John's College generously made me a member of the Senior Common Room—a privilege I would have liked to make use of a lot more often than actually I did—and so paved the way for me to get a Cambridge degree. Being modest, I asked them only to make me an M.A., holding that it was absurd to be a double Doctor of Philosophy. Thereby I unintentionally created the precedent of not receiving the same degree (*ad eundem gradum*) as I had at Oxford, and all kinds of special formulas had to be composed for me. But it gave me not only access to the library shelves, but the ability to take books home to Barley.

During this period I had the advantage of a research secretary, Hermann Eschelbacher, who later wisely englished his name into Ashbrook, and served in the infantry throughout the war. He had worked with a bookseller before he came to England, and was of enormous value in building up the library. Inevitably we were always primarily concerned with books bearing on the particular aspect I was working on. At that time I was following *The Conflict* with a volume on the medieval period. In consequence we built up a very complete collection of local histories of the European communities, and acquired the basic periodica and reference books. Antisemitica and pamphlets were also being added to. The pamphlet collection ultimately numbered over two thousand items, with the oldest being dated 1497.

Correspondence as well as typing out articles and lectures soon made it evident that I needed a personal as well as a research secretary. I was lucky to find one in a local youngster, Kenneth Dodkin. Not particularly brilliant when he first came, and capable of making magnificent mistakes with my long words and his commercial shorthand he developed into a wonderful colleague, completely reliable in keeping both my diary and my accounts, and doing it all with a generosity and loyalty which always replied to any suggestion of an increase of salary that this had better wait until there was more money in the till.

In fact there never was 'more money in the till', though I.M.S. was reasonable about the inevitability of expenditure growing. But I never asked him for more than the minimum on which I could manage, for the calls upon him were far more than most non-Jewish millionaires would attempt to meet, and I was always conscious of the unfairness of a Jewish friend having to provide the necessary funds for fighting against the non-Jewish, in fact Christian, sin of antisemitism. But though I had quite a list of Christian supporters before the war, they would never have made a whole time job possible.

Every development was discussed both with William Temple and with I.M.S.—who were incidentally well known to each other—and I could not have had a more generous and understanding backer than the latter. What was absolutely fundamental, when controversial work was being made possible by a member of one side of the controversy, was that I.M.S. never attempted to influence my opinions, dictate the way in which the work should develop, or allow others to tell me what to do or not to do. I always stayed with him when I went to London, and conversations late into the night before the woodfire in his delightful library turned on most of the deep things of life as seen in Judaism and Christianity.

Most of my time was spent on the research needed for the medieval volume which was to follow *The Conflict*, and this occupied also almost all the time of Eschelbacher. But I was constantly lecturing up and down the country, for I was always conscious that historical research was justified because it was necessary for the understanding of a contemporary evil and its eradication, and it was here that my main task lay. Much as I loved history, it was never an end in itself, and consequently I left dozens of delightful bye-ways for later scholars to wander in. I hardly ever wrote the articles in learned periodicals, English, French or German, which do so much to make a scholar's work known.

It soon became clear that to do justice to the medieval period I would need two volumes. I concentrated first on the status of European Jewries as chartered property of the ruling prince, and on their economic role. Reading innumerable medieval history books, I became astounded at the frequency with which I met the phrase that "as the Church forbad usury, all the medieval money lending was conducted by Jews". This was just as true as to say that "as the Church forbad adultery, all the medieval adulterers were Moslems". Properly disentangled, the economic role of medieval Jewry was specialised and fascinating. Its basic difference from Christian moneylending was that it was thoroughly discussed by medieval rabbis, and was an occupation which, if no other was available, could be followed by an honourable man. Contrasted with the absurd and disastrous perambulations of Christian scholasticism, it gave me some initial insight into the fact that I was not going to find Judaism "just the same as Christianity but without Christ".

The second medieval volume, on the Church and the Populace, was well advanced when war came in 1939 and put an end to my first period at Barley.

From the moment I came back to England in 1935 I was naturally concerned to get as much Christian support as possible. I always had the backing of William Temple as well as George Bell of Chichester, and Tissington Tatlow and Zoë Fairfield of the S.C.M. But it was very difficult for the ordinary Christian to think of relations with Jews in any other terms than those of conversion to Christianity. Though I was not yet at all clear what I should substitute, I was by that time quite certain that a relationship which had produced such a uniquely disastrous result as antisemitism could not be the relationship divinely intended to exist between the two religions. Moreover I had discovered in the course of my medieval work that all the false accusations which had led to the deaths of tens of thousands of Jews had come from Jewish converts to Christianity.

It was one such who had invented the charge of ritual murder, another had evolved the poisoning of wells, a third had produced 'proof' from the Talmud that Jews had concocted a world plot to destroy Christianity. There was no parallel to this among the converts to Christianity from any other religion. Men whom I knew personally, like the Chinese scholar T. Z. Koo, were great interpreters of their national culture, not denigrators and betrayers of it. I did not find a single Jewish convert who defended his late brethren until the 19th century. It was my perpetual search for pamphlets which brought to my notice one produced during the Damascus ritual murder accusations of 1840 in which a group of distinguished Protestant converts from Judaism denied the truth of the accusation that Jews ever committed ritual murder.

I cannot, unfortunately, reconstruct the list of my Christian supporters of those days, or quote from the many interesting letters which I received in response to a circular I sent out at the beginning. When in 1940 we were warned that Barley was right in the middle of the area where an invasion by air might take place, I burned all files which showed other Christians, especially prominent ones, associating themselves in pro-Jewish activities. I have had great sympathy with members of embassies in difficulties ever since, for I found that papers take an infernally long time to burn!

I travelled abroad little in those years, but visited a good many parts of the British Isles, giving learned or popular lectures to Jewish and Christian audiences. I had become a member of the Jewish Historical Society, and enjoyed its evenings in London with their opportunity to meet most of the scholars of Anglo-Jewry. Besides, I had the privilege during those years of always being able to stay in London with I.M.S. There too I met many of the leaders of Anglo-Jewry as well as other interesting people.

Outside my research my main concern was the rise of British Fascism. I need waste no time on a general account of it, since it can easily be studied in other books, but I was concerned with its deliberate provocation of the Jewish community, and the vulgar antisemitism of its literature. I was in touch at that time with the Board of Deputies of which Neville Laski was President and A. G. Brotman Secretary—two men of whom any community might legitimately be proud. The amount of work they got through, the wisdom of their leadership, and their constant awareness of the total situation were outstanding.

In agreement with Laski and Brotman I prepared a book on the *Protocols of the Elders of Zion*. There was no intention to publish it unless Mosley increased his influence considerably, and unless he made direct use of the Protocols. But we agreed that, should these things happen, it would then be much too late to start doing the necessary research for a balanced and authoritative work, whereas, if the book were ready, it could in those days be published in a matter of weeks. The detailed work which I did then came in for the writing of short chapters in my two books on Antisemitism, but full use was not made of the material I had collected until Norman Cohn began his magisterial survey of the whole problem which was published in 1967 under the title *Warrant for Genocide*. It saved him at least a few weeks of research since I had by that time developed the use of card indices which could be used by other people as well as myself. Southampton University now has thousands of cards on a variety of allied subjects which could be used by other scholars.

I forget when and where I first published anything on the *Protocols*, but it was just at the end of the second world war. It produced a letter from an unknown Henri Rollin, who asked me to go and see him. I went and he explained that before the war his special subject had been Russian secret influence on European politics in the years before 1914, and in the course of that work he had solved one of the mysteries about the *Protocols*, namely who was their actual author. He had hinted so much in a huge tome he had published, unhappily, just before the fall of France and the entry of the Germans into Paris. Almost all the copies of *L'Apocalypse de Notre Temps* had been destroyed by the Nazis, but he had hidden a few. He had not done more than hint that the author was a certain Elie de Cyon, because he was in touch with de Cyon's widow, and did not want to shock her, but rather to persuade her to bequeath to him all her husband's papers. There, he was sure, he would find the evidence. Alas, Rollin died before he could return to Paris, and no more was heard of the papers. But he had told me where the copies of his book were hidden, and I told Dr. Wiener of the Wiener Library. He secured them, and there is now a copy of this rare but important work in the Parkes Library.

Besides preparing a work on the *Protocols*, I spent a good deal of time in the East End and became friends with people like Jimmy Mallon, Edith Ramsey, Basil Henriques and Father St. John Groser. They were the centre of action—and reflection—during those troublous days. I also spent some time with the Jewish People's Committee, which was at that time fighting the Board of Deputies over the right Jewish attitude to Mosley. The Board, and especially Sir Robert Walcy Cohen,

President of the United Synagogue, insisted that Anglo-Jewry must attack Mosley's antisemitism, but not Mosley's fascism. For Mosley *might* come to be Prime Minister, and then Jews would be in the impossible position of opposing the policy democratically adopted by the nation. East End Jews, suffering nightly from the attacks of Mosley's toughs and the insults of Mosley's speakers, insisted that it was everything that Mosley stood for that should be opposed. Both Redcliffe Salaman and I thought the People's Committee were right, and we got all the 'combatants' down to Barley for a day to argue with them—quite fruitlessly! The permanent result of the deliberations of those days was the excellent Committee of the Citizens of East London.

My Christian contacts were almost wholly with the Auxiliary Movement. This was a movement originally founded by the S.C.M. for ex-members who had ceased to be students, but it had come to have a life and character of its own. At the time Zoë was its secretary and moving spirit. T. was primarily occupied with a City church, and with the Institute of Christian Education which he had founded. The S.C.M. itself was becoming more and more Barthian in its theology, and less and less influential in its social and international studies.

I was often chaplain at the annual conference of the Auxiliary, but two occasions when they had expected someone else gave me an amusing insight into the variety of our cathedral life. On both occasions, as soon as I arrived at the conference, I was asked to be chaplain as the expected chaplain had not turned up. On neither occasion had I any clerical gear for the job. The first time we were near Chester, so I went to the cathedral, explained my dilemma and asked for help. "Certainly," was the reply. "What do you want, full vestments or just surplice and stole?" They also provided me with communion plate, linen, wine and wafers. The second occasion was at Durham. So I naturally went to the cathedral, explained my dilemma to a verger and waited hopefully. In twenty minutes he came back with this classic reply: "Well, sir, we *have* got a spare surplice, but we shall be having a service on Sunday, and we shall need it." My apologies to Durham. I am sure they are not like that today!

Zoë shared with me a deep puzzlement as to what was the right and creative attitude of Christianity to politics. Like me she was convinced that the most earnestly intended generalisations could not deal with the intricate concreteness of any political situation; while at the same time no amount of religious intuition could necessarily see what was possible to the particular people involved. We both felt that what was ultimately needed was a Christian Chatham House, with a regular daily round of prayer and worship, combined with full time residential study and facilities for the coming and going for longer or shorter times of men and women out in the field. We even on one occasion went to look at an enormous house somewhere in the outer suburbs, which was going very cheap because it was impossible to live in. It was in the most deliciously absurd Strawberry Hill Gothic, but I forget its name and where it was. Reluctantly she decided that the depression was no time to launch such a revolutionary project. So I stayed at Barley and developed my work in isolation there.

While I was still in Geneva I met two men who as I have already mentioned, greatly influenced me during this period. I had come over to England to collect a moderate fund for helping Polish Jewish students whom I used to discover stranded abroad by some personal misfortune or just the fall of the zloty. Both had helped me generously at that time. One was Dr. Charles Singer, and the other was Rabbi Mattuck, and I saw a good deal of both of them now that I lived in England. Dr. Mattuck, though himself a liberal, was by far the best lecturer to a Christian audience on the traditional values of Judaism I ever encountered. Charles Singer had just retired from his Professorial work in London University to Kilmarth a delightful seventeenth century dower house overlooking St. Austell's Bay in Cornwall which he had enlarged to make room both for his wonderful library and for the visits of his many friends. He and Dorothea were most generous hosts, and I spent many holidays with them. When I married during the war we spent our honeymoon there, for my wife had known Dorothea during her work at Bloomsbury House for refugees.

Charles Singer was one of the wisest as well as the most learned men I ever met. He and William Temple were the only two people who held three doctorates of the University of Oxford. But Charles made also a unique contribution to my spiritual growth by the quality of both his Jewishness and his humanism. He was not in any sense 'orthodox', though his father had been a much beloved rabbi, and the editor of *Singer's Prayer Book*, the liturgy used by the United Synagogue. It was in the contemplation of Charles's quality that I ended up with the phrase that "Jewry is a civilisation" to which I added, when asked by the Anglo-American Committee in 1946 what the particular characteristic of a civilisation was, that it was "easy to identify and impossible to define".

One typical aspect of his 'Jewishness' was his intolerance of injustice, which included injustice of thinking. This came out strongly in his very successful pamphlet on *The Christian Approach to the Jews* which was a Jewish reply to the missionary approach to Judaism, and which I had been primarily instrumental in getting him to write. I think that the deepest quality of all was his sense of membership of the Jewish community *once it was attacked*. Like other scholars of Jewish origin he lived his life almost wholly in a non-Jewish environment; but Nazism made him immediately accept his solidarity with Jews who were being persecuted. I realised this above all on one particular occasion. We were walking round the garden at Kilmarth discussing the enormous financial problem of meeting the needs of refugees, and the immense burden it was placing on the Jewish community. In the end we fell silent, and were just enjoying the evening beauty of the Cornish land and seascape when Charles murmured, more to himself than to me: "Yes, I can rarely meet my communal obligations with less than a third of my income." And Charles was not a rich man. I have never met a Christian who considered his 'communal obligation' on that scale.

From Charles also I learned a great deal of the real humanist approach to life. I think that what was most valuable to me was his discussion of the revolution caused by the emergence of 'the scientific method' in later scholasticism and the Renaissance. It was not that any particular scientific conclusion was important. What mattered was the new approach to any problem made by examining the actual data to elucidate concrete and contemporary issues, instead of seeking some previous authority, whether it was, for example, the Bible in astronomy or Galen in medicine. The second lesson was that, while Judaism and Christianity insisted on the personality of God, it was often more important for the scientist's understanding of creation to see the impersonality of truth and law. The intrusion of ideas appropriate to personality only confused the issue.

A third scholar, with whom I was brought into contact by Herbert Loewe, was Claude Montefiore, a friendship continued by his son Leonard. Montefiore had the amusing habit of reacting to anything which he happened to be reading by writing an immediate note of comment, approval, or criticism. Just as an eighteenth century drinker was a 'two bottle man', or a 'three bottle man', so one's friendship with Montefiore was estimated by whether one had received one, two, or three letters in a single day. I felt quite elated when the day arrived on which I received three letters from that delightful scholar.

While I was meeting scholars in many parts of England, scholars were also coming to meet me—or my books—at Barley. John Gwyer's witty exposure of the *Protocols* in *Portraits of Mean Men* made use of all my material on that subject. Louis Rabinowitz, whose doctorate was a study of the Jews of northern France during the early medieval period with which I was also involved, became a close friend. G. D. Kilpatrick, who was writing his thesis in Birmingham on a subject concerned with the rabbinic contemporaries of the New Testament, found many specialist works at Barley that he could not find elsewhere in England. The same thing happened during the war while Professor W. D. Davies of Union Theological Seminary and Duke University was writing his doctorate on St. Paul and Rabbinic Judaism.

There were also projects which ultimately came to nothing for one reason or another. During the period of potential danger from Mosley I.M.S. had the idea of publishing a periodcal broadsheet, patterned on the well-known broadsheets of P.E.P., and dealing with a wide variety of cultural, historical and contemporary aspects of Jewry. These would be circulated to a selected group of influential Gentiles. For the editing of

this broadsheet he chose Tom Martin, then diplomatic correspondent of the *Daily Telegraph*, and his brother George, who at
the time was working on a northern paper. Barley was to be
the 'Information Centre' for the project, and Tom and George
were frequent visitors, while specimen broadsheets were prepared. It was an interesting project, and I was very sorry
when I.M.S. decided to abandon it; for ignorance of things
Jewish is one of the most potent allies of antisemitism.

It might appear from the preceding pages that Barley was
something of an ivory tower, except for contact with Mosley
and the East End. But not all my Jewish friends were of the
level of Singer and Montefiore. Two of the projects which
failed were admirable illustrations of the fact that Jews are
human, and that you cannot put any human group through
the experiences which Jews had encountered in two thousand
years of dispersion and oppression without their developing
some awkward qualities.

At that period General Wigram was developing discussion
groups on various subjects at Chatham House, and he asked me
to come and discuss with him the possibility of a group on
Jewish issues, a subject which, he admitted, Chatham House
had thus far funked. What he wanted was a small group of
members which could meet regularly and, by a developing
intimacy, really get to the heart of the problem. He asked me
to help him in choosing the Jewish members to whom he should
issue invitations; and he admitted that the basic difficulty was
that, while the groups were 'private', it was technically impossible to refuse any member access to them if he insisted on
coming. He was anxious for advice as to which Jewish members
to invite as well as which—if possible—to deter. Looking through
the list of members, it was pitifully easy for me to pick out those
members who would contribute, and those who would, from
the noblest motives of passionate conviction, wreck any group
of people who did not think exactly like themselves. Needless
to say, enough of this latter type soon discovered that a group
on the Jewish question was envisaged, wrote rude letters to
Wigram asking why they had been neither consulted nor
invited, insisted on their rights as members of Chatham House
to be present, came to the first meeting, and produced the

foreseeable result that, at the second meeting, General Wigram, the proposed speaker, and myself were the only three present.

The other experience reflected another inevitable consequence of Jewish suspicion of any Christian, indeed 'non-Jewish', approach. I was very conscious, during the Mosley period, that a large proportion of Jewish defence literature, whether in the form of books and pamphlets or of letters to the press, was written by Jews, approved by a wholly Jewish committee, and offered arguments convincing to Jews. The misfortune was that it was the non-Jew to whom all this defence material was addressed, and again and again it missed its mark, sometimes disastrously. It was a period when I was seeing a good deal of the Martin brothers, and was profiting from both their political and their journalistic experience. I worked out with them the names of a small group of very prominent 'Gentiles' representing politics, the Church, the press, the universities, and philanthropy, who would agree to meet a group of Jewish leaders for a private lunch once a month to discuss anything which either side might wish to raise. I had men of the calibre of George Bell, Bishop of Chichester, and Sir Richard Livingstone, Vice Chancellor of Belfast University, who agreed enthusiastically to the idea, and were prepared to set aside the time to come to such a lunch. It was the Jewish leaders who turned it down.

An incident which occurred some months after Hitler had occupied Czechoslovakia goes a long way towards explaining this attitude. 'Rab' (Louis Rabinowitz) descended on Barley one night, blazing with anger. Relatives from Prague had asked him to go and see an orthodox Jewish boy who had been sent over to England to save him from the Nazis. His mother had signed a document proffered by the man who said he could bring the boy to safety. He told her this document was necessary to allow him to take responsibility for the boy with the British authorities. In fact the man belonged to one of the extreme Protestant missionary societies, and the mother had unknowingly given her agreement to the boy being brought up by the missionary society as a Christian. Rab had the address given to the mother, went to it, was refused admission, was unable to find out where the boy was, and was told that none of his Jewish relatives in England would have access to him. So, blazing with rage, he came down to me to do something about it.

The next three months were an extract from a 'whodunit'. We managed to trace the boy to an establishment which was in the diocese of Rochester; but, when we appealed to the bishop, he could only reply that this particular missionary society did not acknowledge his authority. I forget now the complicated steps which ultimately resulted in not only rescuing the boy—who was in his teens, and had just been Barmitzvah, so that there was no question whatever of his wanting to be brought up a Christian—but in finding twenty-eight other Czech Jewish boys who had been similarly kidnapped by unscrupulous missions. Incidentally, when English Jewish boys were evacuated, I was sometimes called in to help rescue them from well-meaning foster parents. The Czech incident closed with a telegram from Rab, which must be the oddest telegram sent by a rabbi to an Anglican clergyman: "Glad to say boy saved", meaning that he had been rescued from Christianity and come home to Judaism!

In 1937 I finished the writing of *The Jew in the Medieval Community* and it was published by the Soncino Press in the following year. I had inevitably in my search through medieval sources collected a great deal of the material necessary for the next volume, *The Medieval Church and the Jews*. In fact I needed only two sections, Judaism in medieval theology and the Jew in medieval drama, to complete my card indices. But just at this moment Gilbert Murray, who was literary editor of the *Home University Library*, asked me for a fifty thousand word book on the Jewish problem in the modern world. The opportunity was too good to miss, and I agreed. Its real history belongs to the post-war period, when the Home University Library had been sold to the Oxford University Press.

Its writing obliged me, for the first time, to study Zionism seriously, and make up my mind as to my attitude towards it. I had hitherto taken the reasonable position that antisemitism and European Jewish history was quite enough for one scholar to concentrate on, and it was up to another 'Gentile' to make a similar study of oriental Jewish history and the whole Zionist issue. But it would have been preposterous in 1938 to have offered a book on *The Jewish Problem in the Modern World* which did not have a carefully thought out chapter on Zionism and the actual problems of the Palestine Mandate. The words with which I concluded in 1939 the chapter on *Hopes and Conflicts in Palestine* remain as pathetically true as when they were written:

> Whatever its advantages, the Balfour Declaration has been a tragedy from one point of view. It has obscured from the rank and file of the Zionist Movement, if not from the leaders, the stark truth that the ultimate success of the National Home is its acceptance by the Arabs. Far too much reliance has been placed on its words, and on British bayonets and British imperial interests to enforce them. Much criticism can be levelled at the Mandatory Government, and at the Colonial Office which ultimately directs it, and the last Royal Commission was very open in such criticisms, but, whatever the faults of the British, that remains true. In its final analysis the success of the National Home must be based on harmonious Jewish-Arab relations, whatever the price at which they are achieved. (*The Jewish Problem in the Modern World*, 1939 edition, pp. 233f.)

In November 1938 I went on the *Normandie* to the U.S.A. and Canada. My time was spent mainly in Canada, where I lectured on antisemitism and refugees to various types of Christian audience, and tried to persuade the Canadian authorities to open their doors more widely to professional refugees from Nazi Germany. It was a very interesting, but very exhausting, tour. An interesting sidelight on the Canadian situation, was the open sesame in Montreal and Ottawa created by an ability to converse fluently in French.

In the continuous discussions of 1939 about the future of Palestine, I found that Malcolm Macdonald was of my generation at Oxford, and that we had met through my work in the League of Nations Union. He kindly made it easy for me to meet himself and others in the Colonial Office of which he was then Secretary of State. For the record I would like to

assert with all the force at my disposal that Macdonald did
not have sufficient antisemitism or antizionism in his make up
to fill his little finger. The ill repute in which he has been held
for his two White Papers is quite unmerited. They were inevitable in view of the British situation in 1939, the imminent
fear of war, and the position and proposals which he had inherited in Whitehall and Jerusalem. The White Papers were
intended to be only the formal opening of a policy of seeking
direct agreement with Arab rulers and the Arab leaders in
Palestine on a development which would be fair to both Arabs
and Jews.

Though chronologically it belongs to the next chapter, I
insert here an incident in which Malcolm Macdonald's true
colours are shown. I was in London for discussions with members of the Board of Deputies at the moment when the Germans
invaded Norway. I.M.S. was in America, and Lady Reading
was giving me hospitality. She was deeply concerned with the
many German Jewish youngsters training in Scandinavia for
life in the kibbutzim, and was afraid that they would fall into
the hands of the Nazis. She went to see Macdonald, who could
give her no definite answer on the spot. It was a highly emotional period, and she came back blaming me for having anything to do with a man who was in her view nothing better
than a murderer.

I had no direct concern with the matter, but I felt it would
be worth while finding out what Macdonald was doing, so I
asked him to see me the following day. In less than forty-eight
hours he had the whole situation at his finger-tips. He knew
where the youngsters were, which could be taken along with
the British to Narvik, which could find their own way across
the Swedish frontier, and which would have to be rescued by
others. For these he had already made arrangements with a
neutral ambassador who could contact them and see them safely
into Sweden.

At that time I was seeing a great deal of Tom Martin, and
he knew Macdonald better than I did. He persuaded Simon
Marks to meet him privately early in 1940, and we four had
dinner together, in Martin's house in Westminster. Simon
heard, and promised co-operation with, some of Macdonald's

plans for action once the war was over. Unfortunately he left
the Colonial Office shortly afterwards. The evening news in
those days was at nine, and Martin had an expiring battery
on his radio set. We all four lay on the floor at nine o'clock,
with the dying battery-set in the middle, and heard it dramatically telling in the faintest tones of the final fall of France.

In addition to writing, lecturing and travelling, I took what
part I could in village life. Quite early I became a manager
of the Church Primary School—being at the time the youngest
manager by a century or so—and its Correspondent. I became
also a member of the Parish Council, of which Redcliffe Salaman was Chairman. When Munich came, I became Vice-
Chairman and was responsible both for organising A.R.P. and
for making plans for the evacuation of adults, and especially
children, from London. Being a countryman, and knowing that
a village feud can last a thousand years, I made solemn village
treaties with all the villages which had a common boundary
with Barley to define the support which each could give and
ask in case any one of us were subject to air attack. In each case
the treaty was ratified by a joint meeting of the two parish
councils. I think they worked very well in the war, though I was
not a member of A.R.P. at that time. I had had two unsuccessful operations on my Dupuytren's contractions since I returned
to England, but my fingers would have made me a liability
more than a help in any rescue operation.

For the evacuation of school children I formed a committee
of village women which I named *The Cats' Club* since, as I
explained to the women who came from each section of the
village, we had to be completely frank among ourselves as to
whether a villager was a suitable foster mother or not. I did not
know them all personally, and had to rely on their advice. As
will be told later, the Cats' Club did a first class job.

Ecclesiastically I became a licensed preacher of the Diocese
of St. Albans, and did what I could in helping either in Barley
or in the surrounding district. But I was too often host at week-
ends to scholars who came down to discuss their or my work
to be able to undertake any regular clerical responsibility. My
most interesting engagement was to preach at Oxford a university sermon, endowed by a Principal of my College (when it was

Magdalen Hall) to be devoted to "the application of the pro-
phecies in Holy Scripture respecting the Messiah to our Lord
and Saviour Jesus Christ, with an especial view to confute the
arguments of Jewish commentators and to promote the conversion to Christianity of the ancient people of God". I don't know
whether I ought to have refused the invitation, for I preached
on the subject, but with intentions opposite to that of the pious
giver of the endowment. As it was the first positive formulation
of my attitude to missions to the Jews, it is appropriate to close
the chapter with a quotation from the concluding paragraphs
of the sermon. After detailing the tragic and disastrous story of
Jewish-Christian relations over the whole period I asked the
basic question:

"What, then, are we to do about it?

"To many the answer is simply that we should try the old
methods, but in a spirit of love and repentance, admitting,
when convenient, our past sins, but maintaining unaltered
our historic conception of the relations of Christianity to
Judaism.

"I think that they are wrong.

"To me at least the challenge goes much deeper, and
affects our whole attitude to Judaism. The men of the historic church were no less Christian, no less sincere, no less
filled with missionary zeal than those who would set out
today along the paths they trod to retrieve the consequences
of their errors. They were not wicked men, filled with hatred
and a lust for cruelty, but men who set out to do the will of
God. They failed, and did incredible harm because what
they set out to do was not the will of God. They believed
themselves possessed of the whole truth, setting out to convert
those who wholly lacked it. In both beliefs they were in
error. The Gentile Church to which we belong does not
possess the whole truth; the synagogue of rabbinic Judaism
does not wholly lack it. Gentile Christianity and rabbinic
Judaism are two parts of one whole; the separation of the
Church from the Synagogue was the first and most tragic
of all the schisms in our history, and like all schisms, it left
truth divided. We have retained the person of Jesus, Judaism

his religion; we have retained His teaching; Judaism the setting in which that teaching is coherent. And the same is true as we look to the developments of the two religions. While we have developed a theology far richer than anything to be found in the synagogue, they have shewn the same diligence, and, at times extravagance, in the understanding of the life of the holy community; we have too often been pessimistic about this world, Judaism too often indifferent to the next; we have preached charity, Judaism has insisted on justice; to us the mystics alone with the infinite, to them the social reformers busy in the crowded life of men; to us the emotional power which can raise up them that fall, to them the intellectual democracy which can strengthen such as do stand. And, if both of our religions are facing critical times today, an analysis of the causes often reveals that it is just for the lack of that in which the other faith is strong.

We have failed to convert the Jews, and we shall always fail, because it is not the will of God that they shall become Gentile Christians; antisemitism has failed to destroy the Jews, because it is not the will of God that essential parts of His Revelation should perish. Our immediate duty to the Jew is to do all in our power to make the world safe for him to be a Jew."

VIII

JOHN HADHAM: PART I

IN THE SPRING of 1940 there appeared a Penguin Special entitled *Good God* by John Hadham, but the story of its genesis belongs wholly to the period before the war, and dates back even to my times as a secretary of the S.C.M. What sparked it off was one of those delightful evenings with I.M.S. in the spring of 1939. We had been discussing religion, and one of us— I forget which—had spoken of the difficulty of the ordinary man seeing a real God in the now archaic language and thought of both our religions. I then told him that I had long wanted to write a book called *Sketches of the Character of God* in which I did not theologise or seek to prove that God existed, but simply described his activities as I would those of the prime minister or the Archbishop of Canterbury. Writing about such people one would not begin by seeking to prove their existence, and I wanted to assume the existence of God in the same way. "But James," said I.M.S., "you must write it. Go and do it." I then told him of my failure to convince colleagues, for whom I had the greatest affection and respect, that it was a right and proper thing to do.

In fact I had once approached Hugh Martin, who was director of the Student Movement Press, with the idea, and had said that the book would be called something like *Sketches of the Character of God*. Hugh's reply was: "Well, Jimmie, I cannot prevent you from writing such a book. But do not insult the Student Movement Press by asking them to publish it." When I found that Eric Fenn, probably the colleague whose views I respected most, took the same view, I perforce dropped any thought of trying to produce it. But the desire to do so, and the conviction that it was a book which needed writing, remained constant, waiting for a fresh opportunity or a change in attitude of my colleagues.

In the summer of 1939 I set out to write it. It was not an easy book to write, because one is so apt to introduce proofs, or at least argument and evidence, when one is dealing with religion, and the essential thing about this book was that at no point was argument to be allowed entrance. As soon as I began to argue for anything I wanted to say, I stopped writing, until I had reformulated it in my mind in such a way that I could simply set it down descriptively, in exactly the same way as I would set down the plans, purposes or activities of the Arch-bishop of Canterbury. I had completed two-thirds of it when the war came, and left me, as I shall describe in the next chapter, with neither the peace of mind nor the time to continue.

It was not until the early spring of 1940 that I saw my way to completing the manuscript, and by that time I was without any secretarial help. So I asked I.M.S. if he would lend me a typist. He agreed, and I came up to London and dictated the last third of the book direct to the typewriter in an afternoon. I was staying with I.M.S. as usual and he was in bed with a bad cold. I came back in the evening, threw the mss on to his bed, just as it had been typed. "There it is," I said, "and if it is to get to the people we were talking about, it will have to be a Penguin Special." Then I returned to Barley to get on with my many war-time jobs.

The rest of the story I was told later. I.M.S. rang up Leonard Elmhirst of Dartington Hall, an old friend and colleague of his in P.E.P., and said that he was sending him a manuscript to read. If he thought well of it, he was to send it to Allen Lane. Elmhirst protested that he did not know Lane, whereon I.M.S. replied that he was ill in bed, and not to be argued with. Though he considered himself an agnostic, Elmhirst was sufficiently impressed with it to ring Allen Lane. Lane told him to send it along, and gave it to his regular readers. They were enthusiastic, so Lane read it himself, and protested to them that one could not write about religion without producing evidence and proofs. The readers replied that their absence was what gave the book its appeal. Lane was unimpressed, and sent it to what he called to me his 'court of appeal'. The 'court' sup-ported the readers, so Lane rang up Elmhirst and asked who the author was. It was not until that point that I came again into the story.

The book by now had its familiar title of *Good God*, which had been a sudden inspiration one evening. As to the author, I wanted a *nom de plume* because I did not want it confused with the already controversial books I was writing on the Jewish question. But I wanted one which was not an existing name of someone else. So I went through the names of all the neighbouring villages in the London Telephone Directory until I found one which was euphonious but not in that collection of surnames which must surely cover every family name in the country. So I came to be *Hadham*, which had also the advantage that supposing a bishop bore down on me in full sail in the Athenaeum, to which I had just been elected, and said: "I suppose you think you are Much Hadham," I could reply: "No, My Lord, I'm Little Hadham." So much for 'Hadham'. The Christian name *John* was for family reasons. It is a forbidden name for a Parkes, for the last John Parkes sold the land on which we had lived for generations near Dudley because, so family legend goes, he disliked his relations. But he, and he alone, knew that every inch of it was coal, and the purchase of it started the fortunes of I forget which earl. I had no ambition to be a coal-owning millionnaire, so, as soon as I ceased to be a Parkes, I became a *John*.

Good God came out during the 'sitz-krieg'. It was the first Penguin Special on religion, and it was the first by a completely unknown author. It sold well, but in the first week of June it fell below a hundred, and that was then the sign for a Special to be marked as finished. But in the next week France fell. Its sale rose at once. By July it was selling at the rate of 300 a week. In August the Blitz started on London, and it rose above 100 a day. From then until it stopped for lack of paper its sale provided a perfect graph of the seriousness of the situation. If God does not know by now that people turn to him when things go wrong, he will never learn!

The book completely bewildered the reviewers. Some, of course, were violently abusive. But it was difficult to accuse the author of heresy, because what I was 'sketching' was traditional christo-centric Christianity untraditionally expressed. On the other hand, the fan mail it produced astonished both me and the Penguins. In fact it continued for about five years after the book had gone out of print, coming from the remotest corners of the earth. Even after that, from time to time a letter would come from the wilds of the Antipodes or some other remote corner of the world asking for a copy of it or discussing its contents. Practically none of the fan mail was abusive, little of it from cranks. It came from genuine enquirers, and was the beginning of a number of friendships. William Temple, to whom I had, of course, sent a copy, told I forget whom, but it was not me, that he considered it the most important contribution to theology for the past fifty years.

From the autumn of 1940 *Good God* was accompanied by *God in a World at War*, whose sales fell only a little short of those of its elder brother. Each of them was still selling over a hundred a day when circulation stopped because of the paper shortage. *Good God* had sold 100,000, its successor 75,000. Lest anyone think I became wealthy from such sales, I would add that my total royalties were £175. *God in a World at War* added to my experience of the dangers which beset an author. I sent it to the Penguins, but received no acknowledgement of its arrival, and was too busy to make enquiries. Three or four months later the postman delivered an envelope with a scrap of paper attached which bore the Penguin imprint—and nothing else. I rang them up to ask what it had once contained, and was told that it contained my mss of *God in a World at War*, together with proofs which they asked me to return within two days! This was the first I heard that it had been accepted! I asked them if they had another copy of the proofs, and then went up to Harmondsworth the next morning and corrected them. But the original mss and proofs never reappeared.

The circulation of the Hadhams led to a regular series of articles in the *St. Martin's Review*, (published by St. Martin's in the Fields), and also to a number of broadcasts, and the latter were not without unexpected incidents. Broadcasts during the war had to be delivered from an approved text, and one was warned that at the slightest variation from that text one would at once be automatically struck off the air. An unseen censor followed every word with the approved text before him and a button by his side which he could press. The button automatically ensured an immediate 'technical hitch' until the broadcaster returned to his text. I still have a number of my war-time texts with their huge red rubber stamping PASSED FOR POLICY and PASSED FOR SECURITY.

Religious broadcasting was then at Bristol, and it was quite a journey from Barley. But Eric Fenn was now assistant to Jimmy Welch, Director of Religious Broadcasting, so that I always had somewhere to stay a night or two. Trouble started when I was broadcasting a series of intercessions, and prayed for those countries which had been deprived of their liberty by the war. It was correct to pray for Poland and Czechoslovakia overrun by the Nazis, but I included Esthonia, Latvia and Lithuania, quietly absorbed by the Soviet Union. I nearly caused an international incident thereby; for we were just seeking to wean the U.S.S.R. from her alliance with the Nazis.

The next trouble came—very unexpectedly for me—when I was Lifting up Hearts in a week's early morning broadcasts, which were then given live (but of course from an approved typescript), and meant my staying in Bristol for a whole week. I stayed with Mary Somerville, creator of school broadcasting. She had taken a pleasant house, which she shared with Nancy Hussey, at Iron Acton. Nancy Hussey was the inventor of the first family history to be created by the B.B.C. 'The Armstrongs' were designed to get involved in all the new regulations which were constantly being promulgated, and the series was devised in reply to a government request for help in putting these regulations before the public, and explaining them in such a way that the public would understand what they were about. It was an extremely successful invention. Besides getting involved in all the new regulations, the Armstrongs used to meet interesting people, and John Hadham, who had been lecturing in their town, was brought along one evening to have supper with them. Mary Somerville also made me do some work for her in school programmes, and I later did her a whole series on Jewish history.

These, however, caused no problems. The upset was caused by my uplifting hearts. It was the period of the brilliant and moving weekly broadcasts by J. B. Priestley, in which he frequently spoke of the need for radical reconstruction after the fighting was over. Reconstruction was a word much in discus-

sion, so I took six parables of the Kingdom of Heaven and used
the word 'Reconstruction' instead.

On the Friday the Ministry of Information discovered that
I was mixing religion and politics, and the fat was in the fire.
The whole of my Saturday morning broadcast was telephoned
to London. Fenn told me what to expect when Welch summoned
me to his office. I met him on the way up, and asked him whether
he wanted me to find a compromise or dig in my heels. But he
had already become the bureaucrat.

"If you dig in your heels," he replied, "there will be no
broadcast tomorrow morning."

Arrived in his office, he continued with the same severity:

"You have been making use," he accused me, "of the
facilities placed at your disposal by the British Broadcasting
Corporation (mentioned each time in full) to express what is
entirely your personal opinion."

"But," I asked mildly, "except for the secretaries of companies
who rise to read the minutes of the previous meeting, don't we
all speak in public to express our personal opinions?"

"You have been saying," he continued, "Reconstruction, said
Jesus. Now it is a simple matter of fact that he did not say
'reconstruction', he said 'the Kingdom of Heaven'."

"Excuse me, but what evidence have you that Jesus ever
spoke English?"

"I do not see that that has anything to do with it."

"It has everything to do with it. I will broadcast it in Aramaic
if you like, though I don't suppose many hearts would be up-
lifted, but when Jesus said 'the Kingdom of Heaven' his hearers
thought of an event which was going to happen very soon, and
in the world they were living in, which was going to be basically
changed thereby. When we say it now, we think of the next
world, and a remote future. But in fact we are all talking of
fundamental changes in the near future, and we call it reconstruction."

"The British Broadcasting Corporation cannot permit you
to mention Jesus and reconstruction in the same sentence."

"May I mention them in succeeding sentences?"

"I have no instructions on that head."

Welch then became human again, and the interview termi-

6

nated. Those who knew of this conversation enjoyed Saturday morning. I managed never to get 'Jesus' and 'Reconstruction' the same side of a single full stop. But by a little grammatical adjustment, the broadcast was able to proceed with its sentiments unaltered.

For about a year my incognito remained and John and James were known to the public as two people. This occasionally caused amusing complications, as when, John having refused an engagement, the organisers then asked James. I always used to hope that the same book or article would quote both authors in support of each other, and this actually happened with an article which was written in Jerusalem and appeared in the United States. The first part was headed by a quotation from James, and the second part by one from John. Incidentally, when we arrived in Jerusalem in 1946, I found Hadham almost as well known as Parkes. For the last batch of Penguins which got through before the Mediterranean was closed had contained the two Hadhams, and they had apparently been a tonic to Jews as well as to Christians.

In 1941 I was approached by Longmans Green for another Hadham. I was told that the success of my two Penguins made the success of another Hadham certain, and the royalties on such a book would really help my housekeeping. There was much I wanted to say about the necessity of theological reform, and this seemed an opportunity for doing so. Today reform means almost entirely the negative abandonment of some doctrine once dearly held. The Bishop of Woolwich, and his school of demolishers, assume that traditional Christianity had, as it were, reached a doctrinal and metaphysical maximum, so that each doctrine abandoned as unacceptable involved a diminution in the total. I had assumed the opposite. When a formulation had to be abandoned it was because our increase in knowledge and sensitivity had made it an inadequate description of the truth or experience it was meant to convey.

Punishment in the New Testament offers an obvious example of what I mean. Writers of that period thought of punishment as purely a penal deterrent, and consequently saw nothing wrong in eternal punishment as a final reward for sin. But we have grown to realise that punishment should be mainly remedial, and that it is usually a poor deterrent. Hence eternal punishment in hell has become a disgusting and unworthy doctrine. But we still recognise that the insistence on the contrast between right and wrong needs adequate expression. Abandoning hell, we have not just become pantheists, to whom right and wrong have no permanent distinction.

In the Longmans Green book, *Between God and Man*, I tried to show the gradual development of religion, the creativity of its forms in each age, and then the tremendous need for a reformulation in the idiom of our own day. The book fell as flat as a pancake, and had practically no sales.

I wrote the opening pages of *Between God and Man* while I was staying with Mary Somerville in Iron Acton, and my conviction of the need for really drastic reformation was accentuated by a leading article which Dr. Garbett, then Bishop of Winchester, published in April in the *Daily Telegraph*. The article dismissed with contempt all those who complained that there was anything deeply wrong with the Church of England. It was astonishingly complacent even for a bishop. As I had been invited to preach a university sermon at Cambridge on the first Sunday in May, it seemed to me a suitable text for a sermon of dignified but profound protest. While Charles Raven wrote and told me it was the first university sermon for some time which had kept him awake, it aroused no such sympathetic response in other quarters. Published, as is usual, in *The Cambridge Review*, it resulted in a torrent of abuse from the bishop. Otherwise it produced no visible result.

At the Malvern conference which William Temple brought into being early in the war, the entire inability of the Church of England to face its own need for reform was conspicuous. It was as miserable a failure as had been, nearly twenty years earlier, the conference on Politics, Economics and Citizenship (COPEC) which had been brilliantly prepared and was left with no follow up. I was at both conferences, and they were most disheartening experiences.

At the beginning of the war J. H. Oldham and Eleanora Iredale brought into existence *The Christian News Letter*, which ultimately became *The Christian Frontier Movement*. While Oldham readily invited James Parkes to write on Palestine or the Jews, he had no place for John Hadham. A profound scholar, Oldham was soaked in continental theology, though I must admit that he quoted Buber as readily as Barth! But he would never allow the entrance into the *News Letter* of the basic metaphysical challenge which I believed to be fundamental to any renewal of religion. I wrote pages and pages of appeal and protest to him without any effect, though we remained always very good friends. I did, however, once succeed in provoking him to a defence in print when I invented two lovely new words in the English language to describe his policy. I said in the *St. Martin's Review* that he 'oombled and wivered with dispassionate gentility amidst the fundamentals of every inessential issue'. In a footnote I explained that *to oomble* was "to boom humbly" and *to wiver* was "to quiver with righteous hesitation". I still feel that the English language would be enriched by these two charming words. The basis of my charge I can describe from the letter which I wrote in reply to his protest. "This generation," I wrote to him in February 1945, "is called upon to face two fundamental problems. Everything else falls into place, or takes on a new character, according as we deal, or fail to deal, with these two.

    a. How can we discover a sense of community and common purpose which will give personality, meaning and dignity to the lives of ordinary men?

    b. What is to be the shape of our society, an issue presented— whether we like it or not, and with innumerable varieties in detail—by the choice between capitalism and socialism?

"For Christians these two questions are naturally resolved into another form: (a) How can we get men to believe in God? and (b) How can we bring the forces of Christianity into the political struggle? To be silent on these two points is to avoid the fundamental issue."

In 1943 my career in religious broadcasting came to an end. I was asked by Eric Fenn to open a series entitled *Worship and Life*, and I began to saying that "I do not believe that those who have ceased to worship in the churches or chapels of this country will ever return to take part in the normal services offered today." I continued with the statement that "they will not be brought back by the kind of tinkering with the services that is all that progressive elements in the churches have attempted so far." I also closed the series, and used my concluding broadcast to repeat the same warning, and to call for more urgent consideration of the needs of worship. These remarks so offended Dr. Garbett, who by then was Archbishop of York, and was Chairman of the Committee on Religious Broadcasting, that Fenn was told I was not to be invited again.

In 1944 my final 'Hadhamism of the first period' appeared as a third Penguin Special entitled *God and Human Progress*. In some way it covered the ground of *Between God and Man*, for it was a historical sketch of human development, of the first Christian civilisation whose death pangs in the agony of war we were then witnessing, and of the challenge of a new age in the reconstruction after the war. Today its main interest to me is that, while it was still an expression of orthodox traditional Christianity, I was provoked by the constant denunciation of humanism by Oldham in the *Christian News Letter* and Visser t'Hooft in the incipient World Council of Churches to end the book with an insistence that if there would not be real spiritual renewal after the war without religion, it would be a very amateurish affair if Christians did not recognise that in many fields they had to sit at the feet of those they denounced as humanists.

IX

BARLEY IN WARTIME

JOHN HADHAM WAS only one of my wartime activities. In fact all through the war I had far more activities than income. I.M.S., facing both war-time taxation and the immense need of Jewry in Europe and Palestine, was unable to continue his assistance, and my private income of three pounds ten a years proved inadequate as a basis for research! Fortunately the house could be very easily adapted for evacuees, as it had two staircases and two bath rooms (an estate agent's definition, I believe, of a 'mansion'). I moved my bed down to my work room, kept my bedroom for a secretary (if I was ever able to have one), and was able to turn a sitting room, with three bedrooms and a bath room reached by their own staircase, over to various people from London. At first it was three school mistresses; when the one who had the largest room left, Mr. and Mrs. Zoellner, a charming couple of German refugees whose house had been destroyed in London, occupied it for a considerable period, in fact until I got married. That still left us with a large kitchen and a common dining room.

The rents for my rooms, together with odd payments for literary work or cabbages, kept the wolf from the door, but I never reached an income during the war which rose to the minimum level of income tax! Fortunately I had two acres of land, with a very large number of fruit trees, and I kept a part time gardener for the modest sum of one pound a week. We grew all our vegetables for the whole household, and sold quite a lot as well. The vegetable garden was scattered in patches all over the two acres, so that it could not be all destroyed by one 'incident'. This was quite fortunate when one of our own fighters emptied its spare petrol tank all over one corner of the estate.

We were surrounded by aerodromes, and we had nightly visitants, both on their way to London and on their return.

Those who funked going into London, where the ack-ack fire was fierce, dropped their bombs in our neighbourhood; but we had no casualties in the village, and the village treaties worked very well. The A.R.P. was called out to nearly a hundred 'incidents' in our own area or in our neighbours'. As it was evident from the very beginning that we were likely to be lively in the air, I appealed to the fathers of the school children to come in their spare time and dig enough trenches through my orchard for the school to take cover. The school projected into my land on three sides, and on two sides—those nearest the trees—I took down the fence between us. I explained to the children that I had done this so that, wherever they were, they could quickly make straight for the cover of my fruit trees; and I told them that, in return, they were on their honour not to steal my fruit. I don't believe I lost a single plum from them, or from the London evacuees when they came, during the whole of the war. For the first time I was glad that my predecessor had planted his trees so closely that they offered admirable cover.

We did not have an immediate inrush of children, but had a delayed 're-evacuation' from a Hertfordshire town which had received more than it could house. When they came they overwhelmed our school numbers, both of teachers and of children. My 'Cats' Club' worked admirably. The buses arrived at 12.40 at the entrance to the village. At 1.15 I sat down to lunch with the headmistress, Miss Waters, and her two colleagues all of whom I had billeted on myself, and the headmistress and I had seen every child on his or her way to her home under the care of the appropriate 'Cat'. This was largely due to the headmistress. I had gone over and kidnapped her three days before, and made her bring a list of her children—about 120 of them. Then we spent a whole evening with the Cats' Club, while she described each child in turn, and we discussed which home would best fit. Dr. Salaman took twenty five in his big house, and Miss Gardiner at the Rectory took a dozen. Afterwards we only had to rehouse one child, and the reaction of the Cats was typical of any village committee: "Oh, Mrs. X, she's not local; she's a Londoner." One of the evacuees is now a churchwarden and secretary of the Barley Parish Council.

Of course large numbers of the children almost immediately developed impetigo. Mrs. McHugh, our very competent village nurse, came and told me that she had been round the village and found a shed which, if I could get it commandeered and then persuade a team from my Cats' Club to clean it up, could make a possible clinic. But I told her that I had already commandeered a much better one—my own scullery. I had just built it. It had a W.C. attached and hot and cold water. John used it up to a certain time in the morning, washed it with disinfectant, and handed it over to the clinic 'staff'. They dealt with the children, washed it over again, and handed it back to me in time for the evening cooking and washing up. This was not our only contribution to evacuated life whether for children or adults. Baths were almost non-existent in our corner of the village, so on one or two days a week we had a succession of bathers to our two bath rooms. We never had any trouble with them, and they never left the bath rooms dirty and wet. "What, never? Well, hardly ever."

By agreement with both the London and the Barley teachers, we ran the school as a single entity, mixing the children, and opening our village prizes to the Londoners. We had adequate accommodation, including our historic Town House which was built in 1532 with charming statutes. It was for the meetings of the town elders, the keeping of the town arms, *and for poor maids' marriages*. Whenever a Barley youngster wanted to get married, I used to explain to the children that they would study botany that afternoon—in other words, be taken for a walk—as one could not abandon a four hundred year old custom. When I got married myself, our party was in the town house, and our joint incomes certainly justified our having it!

The joint school worked extremely well, and the Londoners brought quite a number of modernisations to our more traditional practice. Only once was the peace threatened. There was then no secondary school to which Barley children could go; but the Londoners profited from an arrangement between the L.C.C. and the County which allowed them to go to the new secondary school at Buntingford, in another division of Hertfordshire. The first time this was to happen, the London boy was billeted with a Barley boy of exactly his age, and the two youngsters were great friends. Now the London boy could go to Buntingford and the Barley boy could not.

Fortunately there had been a change in County Education direction. The previous Director, good though he was, was a perfect bureaucrat. Now John Newsom, with whom I had been at Oxford, was at the wheel. I rang him up, and said that I could not accept this. Either both boys went or neither; if one was favoured more than the other, all our work for harmony would be destroyed. John's answer was typical of him.

"Have you got, or can you get, a car?"

"Yes."

"Go over and see the Headmaster. If he will take both, I am perfectly satisfied."

I went over. The headmaster said that he had room to take these two boys, and the other Barley or London children as they reached the age. In that way Barley children had a secondary school right through to the time when we had one in our own division at Royston. After the war, I became in due course Chairman of both schools.

Royston had a very unsatisfactory market for anyone who was trying to eke out a living by selling surplus fruit and vegetables. The seller paid the auctioneer a fixed sum, so that the latter was in no way out of pocket if he sold your produce for less than you had to pay him. The first market after war broke out I sent a quarter of a ton of perfect apples to be sold. The whole lot made one shilling and six pence, and I paid the auctioneer more than ten shillings to sell them! And I had to pay the same amount for carriage to the market. So I stored what I could until the new year. Then I tried the market again. I sent a quarter of a ton of perfect fruit (Newton Wonders and Bramleys) to the auction, and history was exactly repeated. My fruit was sold for one shilling and sixpence, and I had more than a pound of expenses. The rest of my harvest rotted where it was. Incidentally until Churchill became Prime Minister I was bound by a fantastic war-time regulation, introduced by the Chamberlain government, which made it an offence for me to sell my produce to anyone *except* the Royston market. So I could sell nothing to friends who came down, or neighbours who lacked something. How the regulation was supposed to

6*

help the war effort none of us ever discovered. Anyhow, R. S. Hudson, the new Minister of Agriculture, quickly abolished it.

I told this story one evening to I.M.S., and he reproached me, saying: "But, James, why don't you sell it to us?" I did not then know that Marks and Spencer had started a produce department, but thereafter I sold everything to them. The change was fantastic. They bought the fruit at the gate, and I sent in a separate bill for any carriage they asked me to pay. They told me to what store to send it, and asked me, whenever possible, to send not less than a quarter of a ton, as that justified a locked container and avoided pilfering in transit. While neighbours gloated over me while, for a very brief spell, they were getting black market prices at the beginning of a season, they soon discovered the advantages of my method. I met one of them one day, when I had had a very nice advice note from the store I had sent the last lot to; for I always received a note saying how much each skip had been sold for, and crediting me with two-thirds of that sum. I asked him how he was doing.

"I took half a ton of apples, pears and plums to market today, and brought every pound of them back. I didn't sell a single skip."

"Give them to me. I'll sell them for you. Only you must promise they are sound fruit to the bottom of the skip. I haven't time to reweigh and repack."

I sold them all for him, and continued to do so for the rest of the season. Gradually more and more of my neighbours came to me to sell for them. When the accounts were settled at the end of the season, I went to the first and asked him how much he expected. He worked it out as best he could, and said that he would be very disappointed if it was not in the neighbourhood of five pounds. I gave him a cheque for nearly twenty. We were all, of course, very small village producers, but M & S would buy everything which we grew.

One of my biggest regrets is that I had to abandon, almost before I started it, my original intention to keep a diary and produce at the end of the war *A Village in Wartime*. I think it would have been a best seller, for I was involved in every aspect of the life of the village. I was involved in the affairs of both the

parish church and the Congregationalists, for I used frequently
to take the services for the minister, who was air raid warden
for his village. I preached at most of the Congregational
churches round Barley. I was, of course, involved in the whole
educational life, in evacuation and billeting. I knew all the
farmers and watched the agricultural changes. I was also in
touch with A.R.P. I knew Redcliffe Salaman, Chairman of the
Parish Council, intimately, and could have received after the
war all the secret information about plans for evacuation and
emergency feeding had there been an invasion. Barley was in
the area where on the fall of France we expected it from the air.
Its fields were huge cornfields where aeroplanes could land;
the main railway line and road to the north were ten miles
to the west of us, and those to the north-east ten miles to the
east of us, while London was less than forty miles away. It was
a perfect area for a parachute or airborne landing. But I was
perpetually too busy, and at the end of the day, far too tired
to make the necessary effort to write up a diary.

The desperate days of the spring of 1940 are brought back
to me above all by one quite unexpected incident. Before the
war I had met an entertaining Frenchman, a member of the
Chambre des Députés, who was spending some time in England
gathering material for a book on the English. P. O. Lapie had
been *enregimenté pour le week-end* at Barley, and had included an
amusing sketch of me, John, my hound *Rassenschaende*, and the
parish council in *Certitudes Anglaises* which he published in 1938.
Lapie arrived one evening, clothed in the strangest assortment
of garments, and promptly went to sleep for twenty-four hours.

He had been evacuated from Narvik with his company on a
boat which had no wireless. He arrived at Cherbourg, and
discovered to his horror that the Germans were only an hour
away and that the government was in flight at Bordeaux.
Loading his men onto a lorry he made his way through
Brittany to Brest. He had previously evacuated his mother to a
Breton village, so he passed through it and offered to take her
with him to England. But she would not move without her pet
dog, and a pet dog was more than he could cope with! He had
been a member of the *Commission de Guerre* so that, when he
arrived in Brest, he assumed command of the port, ordered all

available ships to get up stean and make for an English port, and then himself embarked with his men on the last, made for England and found that de Gaulle had already arrived. Fitting himself out at a Portsmouth slop shop, for his clothes were falling off him, he 'regimented' himself down to Barley once more, to sleep off his adventures before he joined de Gaulle, who very shortly after sent him out to Chad as Governor.

In the autumn of 1940 we had a second largish batch of children, this time from the East End. Their coming involved me in the only refusal of help which occurred during the war. I needed extra accommodation and asked the Rector if we might use the very suitable large choir vestry. This was refused on the grounds that the children might have nails in their shoes, and scratch the Victorian red tiles.

The children and their teachers were in a pitiable condition when they arrived. The teacher whom I had billeted on myself was an unattractive yellowy greenish colour, and could hardly speak. I forget how many nights it was since she had been able to sleep. We could not start either teachers or children at school for some time. My Mrs. Wadsworth sat in the garden, practically without moving, for three days before she began to resemble a human being and gradually became her own bubbling and loquacious self. About this time I handed over the problems of billeting to Mrs. Salaman as I had become so busy with my own work. Incidentally we had no adult evacuees except a few parents and relations. Some had come at the beginning, and Redcliffe Salaman and I had fitted out an empty house for them. The first ones stayed a week, and decamped in the night taking with them all the furniture and carpets with which we had tried to make the house nice.

Very shortly after the outbreak of the war, I was rung up by A. G. Brotman, the secretary of the Board of Deputies of British Jews, who asked me if I still had the car running. When I said I had, he asked me if I would go down to Bishop's Stortford, as the Board had had vehement complaints that all the expectant mothers evacuated to that pleasant town had turned out to be Jewish prostitutes, who immediately put on their war paint and began the very next morning to seduce the innocent countrymen of Hertfordshire. Wondering what on earth could be the matter, for professional prostitutes are usually sufficiently experienced not to become expectant mothers, and the morning is, anyhow, a bad time to seduce innocent countrymen, I made straight for the vicar of Bishop's Stortford. I learned from him that Bishop's Stortford had received no evacuees, adult or children, but that there was a crying scandal, to which I must be referring, in the neighbouring village of Ugley. I got him to ring up the vicar of Ugley and tell him I would be coming straight over on an important matter. I may get my villages mixed, but approximately I pursued that story for the best part of the day from Ugley to Stansted Mountfichet, from thence to Manuden, from Manuden to Widdington, from Widdington to Newport, and so on. In every case the scandal was firmly believed in, but it had never happened in the actual village to which I was referred or, still more, the actual village in which I was making enquiries. I would love to know who started the story.

I had a similar case nearer home. Lady Graham Kerr, whose husband was M.P. for the Scottish Universities and who lived in Barley, rang me up to tell me that a large number of Jewish pawnbrokers had evacuated themselves to Royston the previous afternoon, that they had all put out their signs by nine o'clock that morning, and had begun to ruin the local inhabitants—this was by lunch time on the same day!

My two secretaries left when war was declared, but John McNeilage stayed on for a bit, and then went to help in the running of the Y.M.C.A. at Ipswich. There he stayed until his health gave out, and he came back to us for the last part of the war. Meanwhile my household was run for me by Grace Gardiner, the excellent sister of our very unsatisfactory rector. His combination of selfishness and incompetence amounted almost to genius. At first Grace ran both households, but in due course she came to live with us, and allowed her brother to hand his affairs over to a villager. Until the early spring of 1940 I had no secretarial help whatever; but affairs became so impossible that I begged Mrs. Sieff (I.M.S. was doing national jobs in the U.S.A. at that period) to give me enough money to get some kind of secretary. What came varied from the youthful but first-class William Lynch and the loyal Elmes to the other extreme who shall be nameless. In November 1941, when I had a decent room spare in the house which I could give her, I had for the first time to abandon masculine secretaries; and the result runs through all the subsequent pages of the story. When Dorothy Wickings came, it still left a small bedroom available on my side of the house, and Grace installed in it a 'houseboy' of great wit and humour, Keith Tye— he always referred to himself as 'evaporated'—who had been billeted on an aunt in the village. Dorothy had the room which had been occupied by the Zoellner's, and Grace that of a teacher who had returned to London. Mrs. Wadsworth completed the household.

The first autumn Grace and I turned every fallen or unmarketable plum and greengage into hundreds of pounds of jam for a Shaftesbury Home at Royston, which had wisely laid in a good supply of sugar when war seemed threatening. We would have done the same thing the following year, but could find no sugar.

My activities during the war were amazingly varied and involved a quite fantastic amount of travel. I lectured or preached all over the country, sometimes as John Hadham, more often as James Parkes. In addition I was constantly meeting people in London for every kind of serious discussion. The first steps to the formation of the Council of Christians and Jews were taken under a pear tree at Barley, through the instrumentality of Mrs. Freeman who did almost all the preliminary visiting of possible supporters. She was a lady of considerable experience and ability who had become interested in the relations of Jews and Christians, and had been to see Dr. Mattuck to ask him where she could help. Dr. Mattuck sent her down to me. It was she who prepared the inaugural meeting with William Temple, the Roman Catholic Bishop Matthew, the Chief Rabbi, and a very representative group of Jewish and Christian elders.

One of the pleasures resulting from both being a pioneer and growing old is that one sees things and people develop. Just as the discussions under the pear tree have led, not to a mere partridge, but to a substantial national institution with the Queen as patron, so I have seen its incomparable secretary,

W. W. Simpson, grow from an idealistic theological student whom I met at Swanwick, first to a young Methodist minister who had asked to begin his ministry at Stamford Hill in a deeply orthodox Jewish quarter, then to the secretary of the Christian Council for Refugees when that was established, and finally to be the first secretary of the new Council of Christians and Jews, and an acceptable broadcaster on all aspects of Jewish-Christian relations. His twenty-one years of service with the C.C.J. was worthily recognised by his O.B.E. in 1967.

I was often asked in its early days whether I did not think that *I* should have been invited to fill that post which I had done so much to bring into existence. My reply always was that I would have wrecked the Council in a month. Nor can I disagree with those who consider this estimate of my patience and diplomacy rather exaggerated, and who consider that a week is the maximum I would have borne the frustrations, the necessary compromises, the dilatory verbosity, which W.W. has surmounted with unruffled patience for a generation—and still looks relatively young in spite of it!

One effort in 1942 which led unhappily to no immediate result was the attempt, at the request of Captain Halpern, to persuade the authorities to constitute a Jewish force under its own flag. Captain Halpern was a sailor, and was most anxious also to extend Jewish interest in the sea. I was also a member of Eleanor Rathbone's Parliamentary Committee which tried against a very obdurate Home Secretary (Herbert Morrison) to rescue individual refugees with whom we had somehow got into contact. As the war developed, and as more and more American airmen were stationed in eastern England, we also became a kind of headquarters for American chaplains, especially Jewish ones, and two of them, Rabbi Morton Fierman and his—we should call it 'batman', for a chaplain's batman was not a servant but a secretarial aide—Haskell Lazere, were constant visitors. They used to amuse Dorothy by bringing us toothsome American food one week, and turning up starving a week later and asking naively whether there was any of it left! Incidentally we received admirable parcels from American friends, which greatly helped out our economy.

The war did not bring to an end the stream of visitors who

wanted to consult my books, though we sometimes had difficulties in putting them up. Walter Zander came down constantly while he was working on his book on Soviet Jewry. Towards the end of the war, John Bowman came down while he was trying to get the great manuscript on Disputations of Dr. Samuel Krauss into a state where it could be published in English. Finally we had constant visits from Rab, then Jewish chaplain for the greater part of eastern England. I had lent him my car, since I found that the army did not provide him with any transport of his own. Rab might turn up with any kind of problem, at any hour of day or night. For at least one Passover we provided from the garden the entire supply of horseradish required for the Seder! In 1944 an Australian cousin, Barrie Parkes, came with the Australian air force, and used Barley as his home address while he was in England.

All that I have so far described were the *hors d'oevres* of my war time activities. It remains to chronicle the three main dishes. The most important is that in August 1942 Dorothy Wickings and I got married, and started a most happy partnership which is still prospering while I write this. To marry a scholar of 45 with a reputation (well deserved) for being difficult requires considerable courage, courage which it naturally took some time to turn into pleasure—and custom! We had to arrange to be married either in her home, Hildenborough outside Sevenoaks, or Barley, depending on the blitz. In the event, I got down to Hildenborough, with John as my best man, to be greeted on the platform by Dorothy's small nephew with a laborious reading from the most prominent poster on the station:

IS YOUR JOURNEY REALLY NECESSARY?

Dorothy Wickings was not a stranger either to James or John —she naughtily told her vicar that she wished to bring along her 'two fiancés' to make arrangements! On the advice of John she had introduced a cat fish into the pond in her mother's rockery, and for some years she had been working in the Christian Council for Refugees. She had been one of the founders of the 'Thursday Group' of Jews and Christians at Bloomsbury House where all the refugee organisations had their offices. It was Laura Livingstone, sister-in-law of George Bell of Chichester, who introduced us at a meeting at which I was speaking at Chatham House. I told them both that I was desperately looking for secretarial help. Now the refugee work was gradually shutting down, and Dorothy had had full measure of the blitz from the beginning. She had either travelled up and down between London and Hildenborough daily, or she had slept in London, and often spent evenings at Phyllis Gershom's club in Stepney for Jewish girls in the East End. So she offered herself as a possible 'stop gap', and came down to Barley in November 1941.

When Dorothy and I were married it was with a silver wedding ring because I had no money to buy a gold one. Moshe Oved made it for us from a Georgian teaspoon—he only later discovered he was not allowed to convert hall-marked teaspoons to this pleasant purpose. Moshe also made John Hadham's engagement ring—Dorothy had required one from each of her fiancés!—out of a 13th century Pehlevi seal which had been given by Layard of Nineveh to an old lady in Guernsey who had later given it to me. When we were in London we often spent time in the little office behind his shop, looking at his lovely things and discussing everything under the sun. The prices he charged us when we wanted some memento bore no relation to what he gave us.

Shortly after we got married John came back to us and took over the main charge of the house, no easy matter in the later days of the war. When with new housewifely pride Dorothy telephoned Mr. Offord, our magnificent Royston fishmonger, and carefully ordered haddock and plaice, she was a little dashed to meet the reply: "Yes, Madam, one wet one dry." It was not until we were living in Stephen and Louise Wise's flat in New York that she could really let herself go. But there also there were pitfalls. When she asked the butcher for "a nice *joint* for Sunday" she was given the name of a night club. She should have asked for a *roast*! Incidentally, she always insists that this story is apocryphal. It is a nice warning for a scholar to be careful in his judgments of what is authentic, that I am bothered if I can now say whether it is apocryphal or not! *L'appétit vient en mangeant* and it is a good story to repeat.

Quite early in the war I was asked by Chatham House to join their team which was to prepare material for a hypothetical peace conference. This involved three subjects, each involving a considerable measure of research. Two concerned the Jews of Europe—there was no rumour of the 'final solution' then. One was obviously antisemitism. The other was the issue of the Minority Treaties of the twenties. Could they be revived? Was their ineffectiveness inevitable? What could replace them? The third question involved the National Home and its future. The collection of material and its translation meant the help of a number of people. My Polish material was translated for me by a young scholar in Cambridge who was at the moment somewhat penniless and glad to do the job. His name was Flajszer—if that is the way the Poles spell Fleischer. Some years later I was lecturing in Jerusalem and was told there would be a small reception for me after the meeting at Professor Talmon's. Talmon had just become famouse for his brilliant *Totalitarian Democracy*, and I was keen to meet him. It was a small room, and I knew most of the people in it. After some time I went over to the Professor who had brought me there.

"What has happened," I asked, "to Talmon?"

"That's Talmon there."

"No, it isn't. It's Flajszer. I knew him at Cambridge."

I had forgotten that so many had, so reasonably, changed their names to Hebrew names when they settled permanently in Israel. After that I was careful to find out, when going to meet apparently a stranger, whether I knew him under another name.

The work involved frequent visits to Oxford, made delightful by the hospitality of Sir John Hope Simpson, with whom I usually stayed, and each section of each chapter was examined with a microscope and discussed with Sir John, and with Harold Beeley (who was then pure economist without pro-Arab or pro-Jewish leanings). The Palestinian part was likewise discussed with Albert Hourani and Professor (later Sir Hamilton) Gibbs. From time to time Arnold Toynbee, whom I had known since the early days of Chatham House, paid us a visit. Curiously my discussions with him involved John Hadham more often than James Parkes.

During my study of the Mandate I tried to meet as many as I could of those who had been concerned with the Middle East during the vital period of the first world war. In this way I met Sir Hubert Young, Sir Ronald Storrs, and, especially, Leopold Amery. He was in the cabinet office in November 1917, when Lord Milner asked him to try and put together the different texts of the declaration on the National Home which the cabinet were to discuss that morning. In this way the ministers would have a single text before them. Knowing that one of the most curiously unexpected problems was that the Balfour Declaration promised to safeguard the 'civil and religious rights' of the non-Jewish population, and that Commander Hogarth, on the instructions of the same government, told the Sharif Husayn that their 'political and economic' rights would be safeguarded, I asked Amery whether he had chosen the words 'civil and religious' and, if he had done so, what particularly was in his mind. He replied that he had, indeed, chosen them but that nothing particular was in his mind except to find a euphonious phrase!

It is this delightfully—or infuriatingly—casual and typically British way of doing things which is most incomprehensible to others. In this context, it is apposite to remark that it was completely incomprehensible and unconvincing to Berl Locker and to others at 77 Great Russell Street, the Zionist headquarters in London. Again and again I found that Berl Locker had 'proved' an elaborate plot by a series of what I was quite sure were unconvincing coincidences. Through my own contacts, and through the help of Tom Martin, I was often able to discover exactly what had happened, but I imagine that Berl Locker merely decided that I also, being British, had become party to another anti-Zionist plot. Yet he was a humorous and most intelligent man when he was not discovering plots.

Just at the time of Macdonald's ill-fated Land Regulations, I was lunching with Sir Arthur Wauchope, once High Commissioner for Palestine and admitted by Zionists to have been the most friendly of all the holders of that office. I made some remark about the Regulations, and Sir Arthur at once replied that "the fellow's merely carrying out the promises I made publicly to the Arabs".

In spite of all its midwives, *The Emergence of the Jewish Problem* was not Chatham House's 'cup of tea'. I wish I had the original typescripts, which had all to be officially examined, a condition which was not unnatural if they were to be the accepted material for the hypothetical Peace Conference. While the section on the Nazis was being written, news was filtering in of the reality of the 'final solution'. In the first draft I had written that there had been 50,000 Jews murdered in cold blood. The Foreign Office crossed off a nought. More news came in. In the second draft it was half a million—and the Foreign Office crossed off a nought. When they did the same to five million, I gave it up, and no figure is mentioned in the book.

For a considerable part of the book I never corrected the proofs. Paper was scarce; it was the 'doodle bug' period. All sorts of things were difficult. The proofs had been sent from the London warehouse of the Oxford Press to Chatham House in St. James's Square. When next heard of, they were scattered in the gutter of a street in the East End, where an intelligent policeman collected all he could and sent them to Chatham House. But large sections of the copy which should have been sent on by Chatham House to me were missing and I could get no replacement.

The book came out in December 1946 while we were in the States. Its American agent was the Oxford Press Inc., who had signed me up for a *History of Palestine*. When they showed me a copy, I asked them if they could let me have some. They were unwilling to do so, as they had only seventy-five copies for distribution in the States. As soon as I got back to England in March I asked for a dozen copies, but was told it was out of print. I asked when a reprint would be ready, but the answer was that there was no intention to reprint as there was clearly no demand for the book!

It is no part of my intention in this record to moan over the number of times I found myself 'on the wrong side of the fence' for failing to live up to the attitudes expected of a Christian cleric or 'non-Jewish' scholar. I was naturally accused of being a partisan, or being in the pocket of the Jews, and so on. But I started the work itself with my eyes open, and the original title I chose for this story was *A Life Enjoyed*. Moreover, I have never written on any aspect of the question without doing my very best first to understand all the issues and both of the sides involved. It is pleasurably typical of the actual situation that the war-time book, which was too 'pro-Jewish' for Chatham House, was dismissed by a very prominent Zionist with the bitter comment that "it was as good as could be expected from a notorious pro-Arab"!

Now, twenty years after the book became out of print, it is pleasant to record that its chapters on Poland and Rumania are mimeographed and used as text books in some of the schools of Israel, and that the book as a whole has its place in the same schools as an example of literary English.

In addition to the big book for Chatham House, I did two in the series of *Oxford Pamphlets on World Affairs*. That on *The Jewish Question* caused no special problem, but the other was on the thornier issue of the Palestine Mandate. Not surprisingly, the Colonial Office, learning that there was to be an Oxford Pamphlet on Palestine, demanded to see the text. Indeed they might well have insisted on their authority, as it was written during the darkest period of the war. What happened was slightly different. I was rung up one day by one of the syndics who said to me: "Tomorrow you will receive a letter from me, requesting you to make a number of changes in your manuscript. I want you to know that this letter has been dictated to me by the Colonial Office. But we asked *you*, and not the Colonial Office, to write the pamphlet; and if you tell me that you do not agree to any of the changes I suggest, the pamphlet will be published exactly as you wrote it." So I refused to make any changes, and the pamphlet was published exactly as I wrote it. Incidentally our American Embassy did not find it as unwelcome as the Colonial Office, for when I was in Washington after the war, I forget how many thousand copies they told me that they had distributed.

Towards the end of the war James Parkes joined John Hadham as a writer of Penguin Specials. *An Enemy of the People: Antisemitism* had also an American edition, and, after the war, a German edition. The American edition was actually profitable. It sold 50,000 copies.

That I should be involved in literary activity was not surprising, but it was completely unexpected that I found myself succeeding J. B. Priestley as chairman of the new political group, *Common Wealth*. I first met Sir Richard Acland at the Malvern Conference, and in my capacity as John Hadham. We had, in fact, been following each other round England, he commending *Good God*, and I appealing for a sense of Christian responsibility in politics. But this was the theme of his manifesto *It Must be Christianity*, and of the organisation *Forward March*, which he had created to implement it. Richard asked me to join it, which I did. Then in the summer of 1942 *Forward March* united with the *1941 Committee* created by Priestley, with Tom Wintringham as its most prominent supporter. This group was non- and in some cases anti-religious, and arose primarily out of the brilliant Saturday evening broadcasts of Priestley during the dark days of 1940 to which I have already referred. I believe these broadcasts had as much influence as the occasional speeches of Churchill in rallying the nation during the long-drawn out crisis of 1940, so that, whatever its religious complexion, I personally welcomed the merger.

In September 1942 I was asked by Tom Sargant, whose book *These Things Shall Be* was a deeper analysis of the needs of the time but along similar lines to the ideals of Acland, to let my name go forward for the national committee of the new organisation. I agreed. Shortly afterwards Priestley resigned from his post as Chairman, leaving a great deal of muddle and resentment behind him. An emergency conference was called in October to straighten things out, and to try and allay the mutual suspicions between the two somewhat disparate bodies, as well as an amount of personal malaise. I attended the meeting, and to my intense surprise was asked, with the agreement of the two vice-chairmen, Acland and Wintringham, to take the chair. My only qualification was that, as a completely new member, I was not involved in any of the suspicions and intrigues which had bedevilled the situation. It was not an enviable position. All I knew was that the meeting was called in order to wash dirty linen in public—and my main qualification was that I alone of those present did not know what the dirty linen was, or round which corner I should suddenly find it. The fact that several hours later Common Wealth was once more a relatively united body with some understanding of its purpose, was taken as evidence that, while I did not pretend to know anything of practical politics, I did know how to take the chair, and I remained as temporary chairman for a number of months.

They were not easy months, for Common Wealth was supposed to be working for a new democratic society, and none of its leaders had any idea of what democracy involved. Richard was a typical prophet, impetuous, impatient, always ready to class men at once into black and white, and better at generating ideas than working them out. But, after all, one does not expect a prophet to be democratic. Elijah seems to have been entirely unaware of the seven thousand in Israel who had not bowed the knee to Baal! Tom was in a quite different category, an intensely logical and doctrinaire Marxist. He rarely came to committee meetings himself, but sent his wife, whose constant intervention of "Tom says", when Tom was never there to explain or defend his sayings, was one of the standing irritations of committee meetings.

The third leading personality was R. W. Mackay, ambitious, autocratic, unscrupulous, who intended to dominate Common Wealth, and who had a complete contempt for its amateurish committee, ideas, and intentions, and made no secret of it. But he also had much more knowledge of the practical working of party politics than anyone else. He came into office as general secretary, but intended from the first to copy big business technique rather than that of political tradition. He was determined to be both chairman and managing director. I was perfectly willing to hand over the chairmanship to him, and told him that he had only to ask me to resign when he was ready to take over, and I would do so. But that was not his method, and instead I was subjected to a series of false accusations, intrigues and plots which did no good to the movement. In the end I was deliberately 'framed', and had either to split the movement by defending myself or allow the false charges and what not to stand. It was less than a year after the trouble with Priestley's resignation, and I was sure that another internal conflict within the leadership would be fatal to the movement, especially as Mackay and Tom were prepared to inject quite an amount of anti-religious fervour into the issue. So I retired without saying a word in my defence, or making any explanation to the membership to account for my disappearance. This was not easy, for many of the members in the field were old members of the Auxiliary who had come in through Richard's *Forward March*, who had known me for many years, and who distrusted and disliked the autocracy introduced by Mackay.

One of the interesting personalities I met through Common Wealth was Norman Glaister, psycho-analyst but also political thinker of considerable originality. He was particularly interested in the psychology of those who ran organisations, official or unofficial. From this point of view men were divided into two types, executive and sensitive. The first type tended to get on to the direction of organisations, with the result that any question of basic principle got put low on the agenda, on the grounds that this or that decision had to be taken before next Wednesday. Thus quite fundamental questions came up at the end of the meeting, when people were tired and in a hurry to get away. The result was that they were shelved from meeting to meeting, or hastily consigned to a sub-committee—whose report, when delivered, would like-wise find a place low on the agenda. Norman's solution was to give an official place to the 'sensitive' type concerned with fundamental principles. He wanted to experiment in Common Wealth with a dual committee system, neither in automatic superiority to the other. On the one hand would be the usual executive, but on the other would be a 'sensory committee' which could demand re-examination or postponement of a decision, if it believed it necessary. Such an idea interested a number of us, and we were prepared to try the experiment. It had no place in the plans of a man of the type of Mackay.

The other interest of Norman was in what he called 'multi-mental' activity. The world had become so complex, and decisions were so interdependent, that one man could no longer weigh up all the evidence himself, and take a fully considered decision. On the other hand, the relegation of the decision to a committee, meeting only for a fixed amount of time, and consisting of people already busy with other executive tasks, was no better. What was wanted was a new kind of corporate relationship, permanent, intensive, and with time for reflection. No decision would come from such a group until it was unanimous, and so had the full contribution of many minds. This was very much what Zoë Fairfield and I had discussed years earlier. To experiment with this idea was impossible in Common Wealth as it then was. After the war, Dorothy and I still kept a very friendly relation with Norman and watched with sympathy and interest his attempt at Braziers Park to put some of his ideas into practice. So far as I know, Norman was the only member who spotted all that was going on at the headquarters of Common Wealth. When I suddenly disappeared, he came down spontaneously to Barley to see if there was anything he could do. He made me write out a full account of all my experiences since I joined the movement, while it was still fresh in my mind. But it is not yet time to say more than I have.

Just when we were at our busiest, new regulations controlling women's service were introduced, and affected Dorothy's position. She had become an out and out pacifist some years earlier as a result of strange experiences in the City more fitting James Bond than a respectable insurance firm. There were mysterious tie-ups with the sale of armaments in various parts of the world; large quantities of 'paint' were being insured at Lloyds for export from a country which manufactured no paint, and of 'wheat' from a country which exported no wheat; finally a letter was dictated for her to type which concerned a huge amount of arms to be purchased through an Austrian ex-archduke. Having thought it over, she went in to the director and said: "Had I been interested in the sale of arms, I would be working in an arsenal. I am here to do insurance work, not to sell arms." She then deliberately tore up her notes.

Three weeks later she resigned entirely, and it is quite surprising, considering that she knew much too much of what was going on, that the James Bond parallel did not result in her being quietly bumped off! The City might have been more efficient than the Nazi thugs in Geneva! Dorothy went to Max Plowman for advice, and he sent her to Kingsley Martin, who was just starting the China Campaign Committee. So she worked with that for a time, but found that was mixed up with Communism, which she did not find much more *sympathique* than the arms racket. After various other stages she ended with the Fellowship of Reconciliation, where she stayed until she joined the Christian Council for Refugees from Germany and Central Europe.

Under the new regulations, which were for the purpose of directing women into munitions, Dorothy explained her pacifism to the woman who interviewed her, and was then asked what she was doing. When she gave a picture of the mass of work in which we were together involved, the admirable interviewer told her that she appeared to be doing most exemplary work, and advised her not to work herself to a breakdown.

The intense life which we lived throughout the war years, a life more difficult for Dorothy than for me since so much of it (including myself) was new to her, would have been quite impossible had we not had a secure retreat to which we could fly at any time, and for any length of time, at Kilmarth, between Par and Fowey in Cornwall, the home of Charles and Dorothea Singer. Their hospitality was boundless. Not only was Kilmarth itself a delightful house, delightfully situated above Polkerris, with its superb view across St. Austell's Bay, but it was always a centre of wisdom and knowledge and of true spiritual refreshment for both of us. My debt to Charles crops up again and again in these pages, and is still inadequately expressed.

The doodle bugs in the last stages of the war brought us again to the situation where total strangers came to the door and asked us if they could stay with us for a week or a fortnight. The oddest of them were two sisters whom we christened "the bitch and the beldame". The 'bitch' found us as odd as we found her, but she added an immortal phrase to our repertoire. Because of the shortage of fuel, baths were fairly strictly rationed at the time, and it was her turn to have one. I asked her if she would like one and she replied: "May as well, mayn't I. Saves the trouble of washing, huh?"

POST-WAR TRAVELS

As soon as Guernsey was liberated I received from Mrs.
Crocker, where my father had lodged for the last ten years of
his life, a copy of the *Guernsey Evening Press* devoted to a full
and fascinating report of the government of the island during
the German occupation. It had been prepared by the Rev. John
Leale, who had for the greater part of the period been Chairman
of the Emergency Committee which had taken over the function of the States; and it gave in the fullest detail a survey of the
problems of an occupied country. Just at the same time members of Chatham House decided that they wanted to know more
about these problems, and were fishing around to find someone from some corner of Europe who could enlighten them. I
suggested to them that they need not go outside the King's
subjects to get an adequate description of the problems of
occupation, and sent them my copy of the *Press*. This entranced
them, and they telephoned and asked me for permission to make
a photographic copy of it for their archives. I graciously gave
permission. Two days later the Foreign Office rang me up,
and begged for the same permission. Carefully avoiding pointing out to them that they could telephone or write to the island
and get as many copies as they wanted, I renewed my gracious
permission! I was regarded as the keeper of a unique document
for about a fortnight!

As soon as I could I went over to Guernsey to settle up my
father's affairs. He had died peacefully, and the Germans had
never troubled him, presumably having never discovered his
link with me. He had buried his copies of my books, and told
Mrs. Crocker never to try and communicate with me. I had
kept in touch with him through the Red Cross, simply by
attaching myself to the family of Mrs. Crocker's daughter in
England, none of whose own children were, fortunately,
called either Jim or Dorothy. Pathetic evidence of the

enfeebled state of the island at the time of his death was given by
the position of the granite tombstone over my mother's grave
where he had been buried. The grave was on a steep slope
in Foulon cemetery and the undertaker had been able to
dislodge the stone, which had then rolled down the hill, but
the men were too weak to pick it up or roll it uphill again.

The island was an unhappy place, full of mutual suspicions
aroused by the fact that what appeared to neighbour A to be
proper acceptance of their state under occupying authorities,
appeared to neighbour B to be collaboration with the enemy.
The result had been that, once the Germans had gone, floods
of complaints poured in to the authorities, all of which had to
be carefully sifted before the courage of the islanders could be rewarded in the usual way when the King and Queen visited them.

I stayed in a guest house which had been made an officers'
club by the Germans. All that my hostess was allowed as a
private sitting room was a curtained recess in the passage to the
dining room. There she had listened to B.B.C. news on a crystal
set made in a Cherry Blossom boot polish tin (the B.B.C. had
explained how to make it, and many islanders had got them),
and linked *via* her sleeve to an earphone concealed under
plaits of her hair.

My first literary task after the end of the war was to produce
a new edition of *The Jewish Problem in the Modern World*. The
Home University Library had gone bankrupt and its books had
been bought by the Oxford University Press. It was the Oxford
Press Inc. of America which asked me for it, and it involved
naturally the writing of a whole new section of the book. The
real situation of Soviet Jewry was still unknown, the Palestine
Mandate was drawing to its tragic end, the whole future was
uncertain. No new edition of the book was produced in England,
but the Allied governments in Germany asked for German
translations both of my Penguin, *An Enemy of the People: Antisemitism*, and of this book. Neither had enormous sales, because it was still too soon for the German people to face the
terrible realities of the Final Solution, and these books were the
first objective studies of the whole issue of Jewry to appear in
Germany since 1933.

In 1949 an Italian publisher asked the Oxford Press for per-

mission to translate *The Jewish Problem* into Italian, and thereby
produced the third act of my unexpected relations with that
distinguished press. The Italians reasonably wanted the book
carried up to the establishment of the state of Israel, which I
agreed to do. I wrote of Bevin's policy with great moderation,
but without concealing my disagreement and regret. The
Oxford Press was seriously upset, insisted that I rewrite the
chapter because I was 'fouling the British nest abroad'. As on a
previous occasion, I refused to alter my text, whereon the Press
told me that they would apply to the Italian publisher for permission to publish a disclaimer of any responsibility for the
author's views in the final chapter! I replied that I never
expected a publisher to approve all an author's views. Nevertheless a pompous disclaimer appears on the back of the title
page in the Italian edition! Finally in 1965 it appeared in
Spanish in Buenos Aires, the only one of my books to have five
editions in four languages.

The Emergence of the Jewish Problem 1878–1939 was, in theory,
meant to be followed by a similar work describing the changes
resulting from the war in the Middle East. I told Chatham
House that it would be absolutely essential for me to visit
Palestine for myself if I was to undertake this second volume.
In actual fact the book never came under serious consideration,
but it was through Chatham House pulling the appropriate
strings that Dorothy and I were able to set out in March 1946
on the *Strathnaver* for a visit to Palestine which lasted nearly
three months. This visit was preceded by a trip to all the centres
where Jewish youngsters were training for kibbutz life. This we
were given petrol enough to make, and the car was taken out of
the dust sheets in which it had been wrapped ever since Rab
had gone abroad to North Africa and Italy. It was Dorothy's
first of many long trips by car. Our route took us through
Bedfordshire and Warwickshire up to St. Asaph in North
Wales; and we took advantage of it to visit Mary, one of John
Hadham's most interested correspondents.

On the *Strathnaver* we were the only passengers not on some
government service. And we were scarcely 'pilgrims' visiting
the 'holy land'. It was not a visit to arouse religious memories,
for it was wholly involved in a contemporary political problem.

Most of the accommodation was taken up by the Sixth Airborne Division, going out to Palestine, and the result of their presence was that the 'intercom' was going all day long repeating their not very large selection of popular songs. As intercom is designed to be heard in every corner of the ship there was no escaping it anywhere. Dorothy shared a cabin with another woman, but I had more primitive accommodation with thirty or forty other men. We landed at Port Said in a terrific sandstorm, and went on to Jerusalem by train. The long wait at Qantara was enlivened by our eating too many fried eggs and tangerines. At Rehovoth station we were welcomed by Weizmann, who was meeting Simon Marks. We saw something of him and Harry Sacher in Jerusalem, and Simon was kind enough to say he would pay my book-bills! In consequence they came to several hundred pounds, for the second-hand book shops were filled with books which had accumulated during the war.

During our stay in Palestine we were guests of the Jewish Agency. This fact, together with the fact that I.M.S. had paid our passage, so offended the Anglican Bishop in Jerusalem that we received even less welcome from St. George's than I had previously had from the Anglican Church in Geneva. Though we were regular attendants whenever we were in Jerusalem we left three months later knowing precisely as many members of the congregation as we did on arrival. The one exception was Canon Witton-Davies, the bishop's 'adviser' on Jewish matters, Hebrew scholar, friend and translator of Buber and Klausner, who showed us every courtesy and gave us all the assistance he could, and was rather embarrassed by the whole situation. He has remained a friend, and indeed colleague, ever since, for he was for a period chairman of the Parkes Library, and is still in the same office in the Council of Christians and Jews.

I have never been embarrassed by the fact that I have been financially dependent for most of my life, nor have I felt restricted by this dependence. I suppose that trouble would have arisen, either in I.S.S. or later, had there been an attempt by my benefactors to say you shall do this, and you shall not do that, and on this issue this is your opinion. But, in fact, such a situation has never arisen. That a rich friend should help me financially to do something we both want to see done, has always seemed to me similar to a busy friend giving me his time to help in the understanding of some problem of concern to both of us. I am a debtor to my parents, my teachers, my contemporaries, and to my whole community and its history. I have no desire to set upon my tombstone

HIS MONEY AT LEAST WAS HIS OWN

As a matter of fact, for a year or two after we came back from Israel we were financially independent. My father had left me a certain amount, and enough of it was in realisable form for us to live on it for that length of time. We both felt that the calls upon anyone like I.M.S. were so enormous, both in Europe and Palestine, that it would have been shameful for two Christians to keep a nice safe nest egg to themselves and live on Jewish funds when they did not need to.

The Jewish Agency lodged us in the *Pension* of Grete Ascher in the modern suburb of Rehavia. It was an excellent place to be, for British officials used to come in for lunch or stayed there, the Agency H.Q. was near and its members used it; and it was also a place where university scholars used to entertain their friends.

The first thing I wanted to do was to get a general sense of the country as a whole, and here Gershon Agronsky of *The Jerusalem Post* helped us. On our first Sunday he made us meet him down town at 7 a.m. gave us coffee and rolls, and set out with us for the most northerly point in the country, Metullah. We went through Nablus and Jenin to Tiberias and the Sea of Galilee, thence by the Jordan valley to Metullah, back to Safed, where we had lunch, then down to Nazareth and Hadera, and home by Ramleh and the maritime plain. We covered over three hundred miles, and as a result I had a feel for the layout of the country which greatly helped my understanding. The most outstanding memory is the complete treelessness of the hill country between Jerusalem and Jenin. There was just one giant pine, though there were, of course, olives and fruit trees. But centuries of Turkish rule and peasant neglect had destroyed any trace of the well-wooded landscape of the Bible.

In our first week we met Dr. Judah Magnes, the Chancellor
of the university, and many of the professors, had meals and
walks with them, and long talks on every aspect of the religious
and political situation. These conversations continued all
through our visit, especially after the lectures which I had been
invited to give in the Hebrew University. These dealt with
*The Foundation of the Church, The Traditional Attitude of the two
Religions to each other, The Recognition of Judaism as a living
Religion and the Jews as a People,* and *Judaism,' Christianity and
the Future.* A surprising sidelight on Israeli society came on my
visit five years later. I was travelling on the new road through
the Jerusalem corridor and, since the track was only wide
enough for a single car, my car had to back off the road to let a
lorry full of workmen pass. While I was waiting, the foreman
came up to me and said: "I am sorry to keep you waiting, Dr.
Parkes." I asked him how he knew my name, and he replied:
"You lectured in Jerusalem five years ago and I came up from
Tel Aviv each night to hear your lecture."

These lectures marked another stage in the development of
my theology, a stage which was first adumbrated in a lecture
which I gave to a conference of American chaplains in the last
year of the war. In this lecture, as in my lectures at Jerusalem
and in their further development delivered later in the year in
New York, I affirmed the equality of the two religions, their
need of each other, and the impossibility of either absorbing
the other. But while I could see clearly the different characters
of each, and their relevance to some fundamental aspect of the
human situation, I was not prepared to go beyond saying that
their future, or divine, relationship was beyond our present
understanding. It was this position, so new and yet so tanta-
lising to the deeply religious Jews we met at the university,
Professors Bergmann and Guttmann in particular, that made
discussions with them, as with Buber, so interesting.

We spent a day with Buber down at his flat in the Arab
quarter of Deir Abu Tor, whence Campbell MacInnes, later
Anglican archbishop, then archdeacon in Jerusalem, was to
rescue him heroically in the middle of the fighting in 1948. I
was asked afterwards by one of his colleagues which language
he had been using. I said that most of the discussion was in

English. "You were lucky," was the reply, "Buber can make himself incomprehensible in five languages; but he does not yet know English well enough to be incomprehensible in it." An agreeable witticism, but one which contains the truth that Buber's thought is nearly always most penetrating at its briefest. After all, one of the trick writers who inscribe the Lord's Prayer on a grain of wheat could easily include the whole of *I and Thou* on a postcard; and, as Jo Oldham used always to maintain, it was in *I and Thou* that Buber had created a new epoch in philosophical thinking of universal significance.

Through Chatham House I had letters of introduction to the British administration, and I must record of that much maligned group of fellow-countrymen my admiration for their understanding and their integrity. The failure of the mandate did not arise from the inadequacy of their ability to administer it. I paid several visits to Sir John Shaw, the chief secretary, and Sir John Gutch, his deputy, neither of whom had yet received knighthood and the K.C.M.G. I also met most of the heads of departments and some of the district commissioners. Following their careers in *Who's Who* one is at once struck by the fact that to belong to the Palestine administration was but one phase of a typical—and distinguished—career in the colonial service. It was one of the misfortunes of the Palestine mandate that its staff was recruited from that service, where it was an asset to know Arabic and useless to know Hebrew or Yiddish, and where dealing with men and women of the general level of the Palestinian Arab came more easily than arguing with a sophisticated European Jew. Again and again I found myself describing inter-war conditions in eastern Europe in order to help them to understand the why and wherefore of the Jewish desire to immigrate into the National Home. From the Jewish point of view, a few men taken from the consular service and with experience in central and eastern Europe would have been an immense asset.

Nevertheless I do not think that any body of men could have better fulfilled an impossible task than those we had sent out to administer the Palestine mandate; from the High Commissioner, Sir Alan Cunningham, right through his administration we did not encounter one obvious failure, though we found many stretched to the point where it was amazing that they could keep going at all.

When we got back to England I went to see Mr. Creech Jones, Colonial Secretary, and told him that I had not come to talk about either Jews or Arabs, but about the British who, I was convinced, would crack first. In fact, the arrest of all the leaders of the Jewish Agency just after we had left, marked the beginning of the mental collapse. For it must surely be almost rule number one of such an administration never to arrest and detain persons whom one cannot afford to bring to trial, to retain in detention, or to release unjudged, without serious loss of face and authority. The blowing up of the King David took place while all the responsible leaders were under arrest. It was a building I frequently visited to see members of the administration, and it also housed high ranking officers of both security and army. The building was cocooned in barbed wire, one had a stengun pointing at one's midriff from a hundred yards away till one was actually in the office of the man one had come to see, and yet nobody seems to have thought it necessary to close the cellars beneath the wing where all these people were housed. The terrorists came in with their explosive in milk churns which they pretended to be delivering in the normal way to the hotel store rooms. This would not have been a conceivable omission in a situation where men's minds were functioning normally.

I would have liked to meet the Arab members of the secretariat, but I found it to be quite useless. The Director of the Department of Agriculture, having just told me that the Arab farmers were out of debt for the first time for centuries owing to the enormous demand for agricultural produce by the armies and others in the country, introduced me to his chief Arab assistant who, he said, could tell me more. The Arab then explained to me that it was impossible to buy much from the Jews as they insisted on an enormous profit from everything they sold, but that the Arab fellaheen, being passionately loyal to the English, were selling the whole time at a loss, because Britain needed the food they could grow. I felt unworthy to meet such nobility, and found that I could get much more reliable information either from the British, or from Jews like

Moshe Shertok (Sharett) outside whose office door in the Agency building were always several Arabs waiting to ask his advice. We also met Ezra Danin in Hadera, who was the court of appeal for Arabs for twenty miles round and who had a school to teach kibbutz *mukhtars* (chairmen) the courtesies which would make possible friendly relations with their Arab neighbours. Abba Eban was still in the British army and could enlighten us on many war-time relationships. Finally independent Jewish farmers such as one found in the older villages where Arab labour was employed side by side with Jewish completed the local picture. We were fortunate in having as friends the Stiassny's, a delightful family from Germany who were farming at Gedera.

We had several meetings with Chaim and Vera Weizmann at Rehovoth, and met most of the outstanding members of the Yishub. The two who impressed us most were two women, Hannah Chissuk in her school outside Tel Aviv, and Helena Kagan, in her clinic in Jerusalem. Dr. Chissuk had opened an agricultural school for girls before the war. After the war she saw, as the greatest need, the rehabilitation of the orphan children who had finally been brought, or struggled of themselves, to Palestine after unbelievable wanderings over half the world. It was immensely moving to see her with these waifs, scarcely human when they arrived, hating and fearing the whole world, and gradually being changed by love into normal happy children. We had a similar experience in the children's village of Ben Shemen, where we met its creator, Dr. Lehmann. I would add that we found kibbutzim accepting the same task of rehabilitation for survivors from the concentration camps. Dr. Kagan was a Russian Jewess who had opened a clinic for children of all the communities in Jerusalem long before the British Mandate, and was one of the best loved figures in that city.

We spent some time with different departments of the Histadruth, meeting Ben Zvi and Golda Myerson (Meir) in Tel Aviv, David Hacohen in Haifa, and the leaders of various co-operative enterprises; but our main travels outside Jerusalem were to visit the kibbutzim, moshavim, and independent villages. We spent Seder at Degania and Ashdod Yaakob, meeting the whole Baratz family at the former; and we spent a day with the Dayan family at Nahalal. In all these visits my being a countryman was a great help, since I could really appreciate their experiments and achievements in many fields. Dorothy was not so lucky. At one kibbutz she asked to be shown the specifically woman's sphere—and was introduced to an endless row of babies being 'potted' after their midday meal, and to a laundry. She felt that neither really expressed 'the heart of woman speaking to the heart of woman' as her guide poetically expressed it.

I was particularly interested in kibbutz accountancy, since I had so often met the unfriendly criticism that the whole movement was artificially sustained by the immense financial aid which came from America, and could never have survived on its own. Having learned early on to ask about its 'investments' not its 'debts', I discovered a great deal from these accounts. Kibbutzim were just beginning industries at that time—many of them tentative experiments to meet wartime shortages—and in subsequent visits one witnessed the immense and stable transformation which we then saw in its pioneer stages.

To list all the kibbutzim we visited would be pointless. They extended from Kfar Giladi and Honita in the north to Revivim in the south, and I refused to be hurried from one to another, so that we spent most of a day in those we did visit. This sometimes puzzled, and even annoyed, our guides, some of whom would have had difficulty in distinguishing a carrot from a carob. We met a certain number of *kibbutzniks* whom we had first met on our trip round England or at the orthodox farm near Thaxted which was less than twenty miles from us. We paid a long visit to the group of orthodox kibbutzim, first around Tirat Zvi near Beth Shan, then in the Kfar Etsion group between Bethlehem and Hebron.

Linking this visit to our subsequent stays in the country, we have been enabled to realise the splendour and determination of the planning and its realization. In 1946 we saw Holon being built, and watched with amazement, almost amusement, the dwellers bringing in barrow loads of earth to make their gardens in that absolute waste of sand. But we shall always remember the thrill when, on a subsequent visit to Tel Aviv, a lady who had met us at Holon ran up to Dorothy, reminded her of our first meeting some years previously, and exclaimed: "My dear, the birds have come to Holon!"

We did extraordinarily little sight-seeing, though we did enjoy several visits to the Old City with L. A. Mayer, and, of course, our visits to the settlements involved seeing the Dead Sea, the sea and the mountains of Galilee, and much of the coast. We saw surprisingly little evidence of the breakdown of the mandate and of law and order throughout the country. I was given permission to drive right along the northern frontier near "Teggart's Wall" of barbed wire. The Arab military police were quite unable to read my passport or my special permission but we had fortunately a Yemenite driver who spoke Arabic, and were waved through. We were amused to hear, on our return to Jerusalem, that the chief secretary himself, trying to take an afternoon drive along the same scenic road, was stopped by a similar policeman, and was quite unable to persuade him of his right to pass.

One night in Jerusalem we were dining in the outskirts of a suburb, and our normal route home would have involved our going a couple of miles towards the centre and then out again to our lodging in Rehavia. It was brilliant moonlight, and I said to Dorothy that I was quite capable of taking her home direct across the hills. Suddenly it seemed that every searchlight in the country was focused on us. I had quite overlooked the fact that a ceaseless patrol against marauders and terrorists was a normal part of life. However we established our innocence, were suitably rebuked for our folly, and were escorted home!

We had considerable difficulty in getting a return passage. There was nothing to be secured by boat, and all depended on air transport. I had flown a fair amount, but Dorothy had never done so. Finally we were told that a plane from India had a certain number of unused kilos, and were sent to get weighed. Unhappily either of us alone would have absorbed most of the kilos, so the official said meditatively that he would send me home first as it would be easier to get a seat for Dorothy on compassionate grounds as a forsaken wife, and he would look for 'a light woman' to travel with me! Our amusement at his phraseology was increased when, on returning to the Grete Ascher, we learned that Dorothy's unused kilos had been offered to Walter Zander, secretary of the English Friends of the Hebrew University! Finally Dorothy was allowed to come with me, but we were not allowed to bring any luggage, and luggage provided an unexpected irritation for several months.

I had asked so many historical questions during our visit that my main desire on our return was to get down to writing the history of the country and of the Jewish, Christian and Muslim communities in it during the unknown centuries between the New Testament and modern times. Palestine during those centuries merely provided an occasional isolated episode in other histories—Christian at the time of the crusades, Jewish in sixteenth century Safed, Napoleonic at Acre, and so on. But before I could get down to this work I was asked by the Bureau of Current Affairs, which was primarily responsible for the army's educational programme, to write them one of their pamphlets on Palestine. I did so, and submitted it to people like Sir Hubert Young to check that it expressed fairly the Arab point of view, even though it approved of the Balfour Declaration and the achievements of the Jews in the country.

In September the editor of *Current Affairs* turned my manuscript down as one 'espousing the Zionist cause', which was regarded as undesirable in 'a pamphlet which would circulate widely among troops in the Middle East'. What I had tried to do was to make the soldier understand both causes, and I would willingly have developed the Arab side further, had I seemed at any point to be unfair. But my offence was not that I had expressed the Arab side unfairly, but that I had expressed the Jewish side too fairly. The Bureau seemed mainly concerned that the whole description of Zionism should at every point arouse either hostility or contempt. This they certainly obtained to their satisfaction from their alternative author.

The most incredible passage in the pamphlet as it finally appeared seemed to me one dealing with the origin of Christianity. Jesus and the apostles, being Jews, were not mentioned at all, and the *whole* passage read:

"At the end of their history as a nation they [the Jews] rebelled against Rome, and in A.D. 70 the Temple was burned, and the Diaspora, the scattering of the Jews, began; in 135 Rome completed the destruction of Jerusalem.

"The Jews had far too much vitality to disappear. Some, no doubt, were converts to Christianity, and their descendants must form part of the Apostolic Arab church of Palestine".

When I protested against this passage, and its implication that Christianity was founded by Arabs, I was met by the reply that the Bureau did not think this was implied at all. The Church of England also claimed to be apostolic, and nobody thought that Christianity was founded by Englishmen.

At that I gave up. But, at least, I secured that the pamphlet was *not* distributed in Palestine. Lord Nathan was then at the War Office, and I knew he was a friend of Leonard Stein. I rang up Stein, begged him to get Nathan to ask for a copy of the pamphlet, read it, and take what action he thought wise.

During our last days in Palestine we had met Rabbi Stephen Wise, whom I knew from Geneva days. It was just after I had written *The Jew and His Neighbour* that I called on him in his hotel. He came into the room with a copy of the book under his arm, though the porter had merely announced that 'un jeune homme désire vous parler'. Though I often called him Stephen Unwise in despair at his one-sidedness, I had a great affection for him and for Louise, his wife. Both his gifts and his limitations were manifest in those visits to Geneva in the early thirties, when the World Jewish Congress was coming into existence with two conferences, largely under his inspiration.

Wise invited me to give the Charles William Eliot lectures at his Jewish Institute of Religion in the winter of 1946, and invited Dorothy to come over with me, I had been in America twice, Dorothy never. The six lectures were to be an expansion of those I gave in Jerusalem, still developing the general theme of the relations of Judaism and Christianity. I was able to devote separate lectures to Jesus and to Paul, and I considerably extended that on 'the rediscovery of Judaism', largely out of the books which the generosity of Simon Marks had enabled me to buy in Jerusalem. The lectures developed my dual conviction of the equality and of the different individuality of the two religions. In the introduction to them as finally published (p. 19) I wrote: "Both Religions are true. Neither is simply an incomplete form of the other; and I do not desire to see either disappear, even by conversion to the other." I elaborated this further by saying that "I can only recognise in Sinai and Calvary two closely interlocked and complementary stages of a single divine plan. I cannot carry our present separation from history back to God. The two religions are a historic fact. Their separation is not a divine intention." I ended the introduction with the words: "In Judaism and Christianity together the 'I-Thou' relationship of a free creation is ultimately fulfilled. But in each is an essential part of the fulfilment, and until there appears the way by which they can fulfil the two together without losing their own essential nature, each must fulfil its own part. But the better the Jew or the Christian understands the reality of the religion of the other the better his own task can be fulfilled."

I think that it was in preparing these lectures that I first realised that Judaism was just as much a missionary religion as Christianity. True, it did not attempt to make converts of individual Christians, but in every society in which Jews were admitted to citizenship they sought to mould the life of the community one stage nearer to the messianic ideal. Likewise in preparing them I made contact with a fascinating by-path of post-reformation Christian history, the Christian Hebraists, who flourished roughly from the sixteenth to the middle of the eighteenth century. Men of amazing learning and still more amazing verbosity, they were well represented on my shelves, though I did not meet the greatest of them, William Surenhuis, until Professor Sandmel introduced me to his work when I was repeating the lectures at Cincinnati.

We had immense difficulties in getting transport, for Wise's formal invitation came only in July, and he wanted us to arrive in time to start the lectures in the beginning of December. Finally, with the help of the American ambassador, we sailed on an American transport, the *John Ericsson*. Instead of paratroopers, the ship was full of British G.I. brides. How on earth—

or rather *at sea*—they managed to prance about sloping decks with an immense baby and a feeding bottle occupying both arms and the highest heels on their feet, we never understood.

The *John Ericsson* was delayed outside her pier, with the result that she came up the river very slowly, and Dorothy saw the whole panorama of Manhattan Island with its sky-scrapers unfolding against a perfect sunset. Usually everybody is herded down below just as one passes the Statue of Liberty for the most ridiculous examination of passports I have met with in any country, and one never sees the sky line of New York from the river.

In New York we found that the Wise's had lent us their delightful home overlooking Central Park from the 12th floor, and with a view downtown of serried ranks of skyscrapers. It was amazingly beautiful in the dimpsey light, when outlines were lost in the evening haze and all the offices were still illuminated. Our location meant that we could often take a walk in Central Park, which is an excellently planned urban park. It is an interesting reflection that we often walked back across it from an evening party in 1946, but that, when we were again in New York in 1954, we were warned never to go into the park at night because of the danger of thugs.

As soon as we had settled in we set out to find an episcopealian church, and found one in the next block. We went to the early service on Sunday, and as we came out into the aisle after the service a lady stopped us and said: "I think you are new, aren't you? Will you come and have breakfast with us all?" There was a common breakfast after the service every Sunday, and we got to know several of the congregation as well as the Rector, Dr. Sutton, who showed us every courtesy. He invited me to celebrate at Christmas, he came to some of the lectures and to my reception of an honorary doctorate, and made us feel completely at home. In fact we were happy all through the district. We had only to mention in a shop that we were friends of Stephen Wise and staying in his apartment, for them all to go out of their way to help us.

We did not do much travelling on this trip, though some of the lectures were given at the Hebrew Union College at Cincinnati. It was there that I discovered for the first time that

7*

my library was beginning to be of real value. The lecture on the period from the Renaissance onwards dealt with printed books. I suggested to the Librarian that we used their admirable show cases by showing the books I was mentioning, all of which were on my own shelves. I found there were quite a number they had not got—and the College possesses the largest collection in the world of printed Judaica. I had already come to realise I had one or two rare books when I was accused of dishonesty in quoting from an antisemitic work which, said the accuser, was so rare that I must know my quotation could not be verified. As the book was published in 1869 I had no idea it was at all rare. But, as we were just setting out for New York, I said to myself that I would verify my quotation at the library of the Jewish Theological Seminary. They had not got it! I was not worried, because I knew I was going to Cincinnati. They had not got it either!

From Cincinnati we went on to Chicago, where Haskell Lazere was working with the Anti-Defamation League. We had some very useful discussions with them, but my main memory of that windy and freezing city is of full sized trees along the lake blown by the wind right over till their topmost branches were bent down to the earth, where they were frozen stiff to the ground. Chicago was also the city in which Dorothy had her first experience of commercial broadcasting. I was one in a series of interviews; I talked to a very intelligent and well-informed interviewer for thirteen minutes—quite Third Programme level—and then I was moved aside, presented with a small packet, and looked round for Dorothy whom I found in a state of collapse with mirth.

"Did you hear the end of your broadcast?"

"No, I was moved away from the chap who talked to me, and could hear nothing."

"Well, the end of your broadcast was this: 'You hear what a kick I got out of talking to Dr. James Parkes. I get just the same kick out of X's shaving cream, the whisker-wilting shaving cream.' That's some of it you're holding."

And, sure enough, it was!

From Chicago we went to stay with friends at Buffalo, and saw the Niagara frozen, then back to New York, when I ful-

filled a number of preaching engagements in and around the
city. But our main job was preparing the lectures for publication, as Chicago University Press had asked for the right to
publish them as soon as possible.

When the Wise's returned to New York, we remained their
guests, but moved to a hostel next to the Jewish Institute of
Religion, which Wise had founded, and of which he was the
active President. There we worked like beavers. Every moment
that we had not a lecture, preaching or other engagements I
was working in the library of the Institute, and Dorothy was
correcting and typing the manuscript, which was considerably
enlarged from the lectures, both by incorporating criticisms,
and by adding the long introductory chapter from which I have
already quoted. I used to return to the hostel around midnight,
and we then used to walk up to a Viennese cafe on 72nd St.
where we had Viennese coffee and the delightful cream cakes
which we had not seen since before the war.

On one of our visits to the members of the Oxford Press Inc.
they learned that my desire as soon as we got back to Europe
was to do research into the history of Palestine from A.D. 135.
This interested them, and I signed a contract with them for the
American edition of the book before we left the States. Both
they and the Chicago University Press asked me to try and get
a publisher for an English edition as soon as I could. I hoped
that Jack Davidson, of the Soncino Press, would be interested,
but Jack's one ambition was to get me back on to the History
of Antisemitism, of which I had produced two volumes before
the war. Alas, it was never possible to return to this work, and
now there are thousands of cards in Southampton waiting for
someone to use them. However, Victor Gollancz, whom I had
met over Common Wealth, was at that time interested in
publishing books of Jewish interest, and he took both of them.

We returned home over a stormy Atlantic in the *America*, the
new flagship of the American Line. What a tinny ship she was
compared with the solidity of the older French and British
vessels. Everything was terribly 'posh' and chromium, but she
shuddered and shook in seas which would scarcely have been
noticed on the *Ile de France* or a comparable British liner. I kept
Dorothy awake with annoyance one stormy night by casually

remarking that the ship would probably break her back before morning—and then taking a sleeping tablet and going to sleep. It was, after all, Dorothy's first experience of Atlantic gales, for we had been lucky on the *John Ericsson*.

XI

LEAN AND BUSY YEARS 1947–1957

THROUGH THE PATERNAL benevolence of an American Income Tax official, Dorothy and I returned from America with a few more dollars than we had expected. The Jewish Institute of Religion sent me to a lawyer to make out my tax return, telling me the issue was rather complicated and that this man was an expert who would do his very best for us. We had not earned a great deal, and he finally 'reduced' my tax obligations to something over three hundred dollars, which, he said, I had to take in cash to the Tax Office. I did so, and produced the form with all its unintelligible calculations. The official gave it one look and said: "This is all rubbish," tore it up, produced another form which he began to fill in on the spot. I was alarmed, as anyone might be, but his questions seemed designed to increase rather than diminish such privileges as I was allowed. Then silence fell between us while he made calculations and filled in figures, and I waited wondering whether I could produce enough cash to meet my obligations.

"There you are: that's it," he finally said.

He had reduced my tax to three dollars ninety three cents.

So on our return we had at least enough to do up the house, where nothing had been done since 1939, and where a number of ceilings had lost bits from the constant vibration of bombers passing low overhead. We quickly settled in to build up the work again and remake our many contacts. Innumerable people came to stay with us, or took a meal as they passed through Barley, but unfortunately we kept no visitor's book. Two memorable visitors were Dr. and Mrs. Rosenfeld. Dr. Rosenfeld had looked me up in *Who's Who*, because he was interested in my medieval volume. Finding I was just approaching my fiftieth birthday, he wrote and congratulated me on it. We got the letter in New York, but I invited him to visit us when we returned.

As I always did, I said that, if there was a Mrs. Rosenfeld, she should come with him. There was. She did. Dorothy had been summoned to Hildenborough that week-end because her mother was ill, so she missed our first meeting. Rosenfeld was a shy and scholarly civil servant, who had been expelled from a high post in the Prussian ministry because he was Jewish. Else, his wife, was a non-Aryan Christian and a person of quite exceptional quality. They became regular visitors to Barley, where the library was of perpetual service to them and they to it. After her husband's death in 1947, Else spent long periods at Barley, helping with the garden, with the cataloguing of books, and in many other ways. In 1952 she was able to return to Germany, built herself a pleasant cottage at Icking in Bavaria, and spent half the year there and half with her married children in England.

Another visitor, who had indeed known Barley since the first weeks after I bought the house, was Kathleen Wood-Legh and her shrewd and humorous father. They were great walkers, and thought nothing of the fourteen miles from Cambridge. Kay was a great standby while I was working on *The Jew in the Medieval Community*, since she was a learned medieval historian with a special knowledge of the activities of the medieval Church. In fact, she is *the* authority on the medieval chantry. We were able to help her in return by reading the proofs of a most revealing record of a small chantry which she had discovered at Bridport, and by providing a rural retreat near Cambridge, for she is a Canadian with few relations in this country.

My first literary task after our return from America was the very considerable research necessary for the projected history of Palestine, and I plunged into this with pleasure. It was a new field, whereas the straight Jewish-Christian relationship had reached a point where I had said most of what I wanted to. There existed two works on the subject already, but both were written from a strongly Zionist standpoint, and paid little attention to the Christian and Muslim contributions to the history of the country. I was determined to steer a course which would give a balanced view of the whole complex story. During the nearly two thousand years that I was covering Palestine had never been a defined or separate country (except for the brief crusader kingdom), nor had it ever been ruled by one of its own inhabitants. It was always an unimportant province of an empire which had its centre elsewhere.

As my researches progressed the contours of the post-crusading Christian story became more and more heroic, in the courage with which pilgrims braved the terrors of Mediterranean pirates and rapacious bedouins, and the Franciscans maintained their rights of residence and possession of holy places; the Muslim story became fascinatingly entangled with long pre-Muslim, pre-Christian, and even pre-Jewish memories among the fellaheen; but the Jewish story out-topped both in its hidden splendour. Having learned my Jewish history from historians in the great tradition of Heinrich Graetz, I had seen Europe as the overwhelmingly most important element in Jewish development since the time of Maimonides—that is, since the end of the twelfth century, and I had regarded Palestine as of minor and entirely episodic importance. It is one of the examples of the failure of communication which one finds so often in Jewish affairs, that still today Israeli propaganda and ideology are largely based on this European myth.

In actual fact, as I discovered, Jewish life in Palestine was not merely continuous, but was maintained with a courage and determination which outbid that of the Christians. During most of the story Christian interests could turn to some great Christian power which had political or commercial influence with the successive Muslim rulers. Charlemagne and Haroun al-Rashid had corresponded as equals. Frederick II was more at home with Islamic than with Christian culture. The French in the sixteenth century had commercial interests in the Levant which gained the favour of the Turks, and so on. But nobody between the fourth and the nineteenth century had lifted a finger to give even basic security to the Jews. In spite of this, if one Jewish community was massacred or starved out, its place was immediately taken by immigrants from East or West; and on four occasions in Jewish history, when the Jewish future was really in peril, it was from the struggling Palestinian community that new life and new opportunities had come. All this is explored and told in my *History of Palestine* which was published in 1949 in Britain and America.

The book was, like all my books, built up on long card indices. When Israel became a state in 1948, it 'borrowed' all my
cards dealing with the Holy Places; and, even today, my history
is, I am told, the only continuous and comprehensive account
of the country which there is, and it is used by ministries, truce
officials, and educators, though it has never been translated
into Hebrew, and has been out of print for ten years.

While I was working on the book we were building up what
was, in effect, a small institution, though it had no institutional
status, and Mr. Westmore, who manfully dealt all through the
years with our income tax, had a perpetual struggle to convince
the authorities that money which came in from various sources
was used for the work and not to enable us to live in personal
luxury. I would add that, though there were constant arguments with tax authorities, we had the great benefit from Mr.
Westmore's work that we never had to argue for our personal
integrity, or prove that we were doing the work we claimed.
The arguments were technical not moral.

The Barley 'institute' was a tripod. While I wrote books and
articles, and was frequently away for conferences, lectures and
committee meetings, John McNeilage ran the house and exer-
cised a general control of the vegetable garden, surrendering
the reins to Dorothy for the evening meal. Dorothy was responsible for the whole secretarial and filing work, as well as
being hostess to a continual series of guests. It was only by the
competence and generosity of these two 'legs of the tripod'
that Barley remained upright until the mid-'fifties. Financially
we spent all that was realisable from my inheritance, and then
relied on I.M.S.

It was a difficult situation, made possible only by the complete intellectual freedom which dominated our relations with
I.M.S. But it was unnatural that work which was largely
concerned with Gentile responsibility for past and present
antisemitism should have to be financed by a Jewish friend.
It meant that we never asked for twopence if we could just
manage with a penny-halfpenny. For we always knew we were
but one of the many causes I.M.S. supported, and the more I
uncovered of the past relations of Jews and Judaism with
Christians and Christianity, the more I realised the total re-

sponsibility of the Christian tradition and its manipulation for tragedies of Jewish life. Even the ill-treatment which Jews received as second class citizens under Islam was taken over from their second class status under Byzantium. But the more I emphasized the Christian responsibility, the more difficult it became for us to augment our resources from Christian contributions, for the conventional attitude of Christians who are interested in Jews is to support efforts for their conversion to Christianity, and the missionary societies, the Anglican *Church Mission to Jews*, and the relevant department of the *International Missionary Council*, regarded me (quite rightly) as their increasingly dangerous opponent. But I knew from the beginning that pioneering to reverse a verdict with nearly two thousand years behind it would not be easy, and Dorothy was generously willing to share its substantial but inevitable burden.

In March 1949 I was actually invited to present my views to a study conference organised at Bossey by the Committee on the Christian Approach to the Jews of the International Missionary Council. I did so, but I really had no common ground on which to base a discussion with the almost wholly Barthian assembly and its biblical fundamentalism. Condemnation was divided between myself and W. W. Simpson. For the Councils of Christians and Jews which were then emerging in various countries were regarded as serious impediments to direct missionary activity, and Simpson was invited to Bossey to justify their existence. In fact the Councils had a much easier time than I had, for human activity, unlike scholarly research, is not ruled by logic, and it was generally agreed that all that a Christian council member was expected to do was to leave his missionary opinions and commitments, with his coat and hat, in the vestibule. This was a very sensible decision, for it made possible a great deal of work in circumstances in which my approach would have been quite sterile.

I have never actually had a reasoned debate with those who regard the missionary approach as the only approach loyal to Christian principles. I cannot argue with a constant "how do you reconcile that with this or the other verse of St. Paul". In all fairness I must record that William Temple, while willing to regard the break between the two religions as leaving truth on both sides, still refused to agree that Judaism was so special a case that it justified special treatment in relation to Christian missionary activity.

A good deal of my literary activity will be dealt with in the following chapter. In the Jewish field I was almost wholly concerned with Zionism and then with the State of Israel. Nevertheless in 1949 I was greatly honoured by being invited to become President of the Jewish Historical Society. In its more than fifty years of existence I was only the second Christian to be invited to fill that post. When in 1950 the Hebrew University celebrated its twenty-fifth anniversary, I went out as official representative of the only Jewish learned society which had survived the war on this side of the Atlantic. In the procession I was paired off with an American rabbi of quite incredible orthodoxy. He looked at me curiously and asked who I was.

"I am the President of the Jewish Historical Society of England."

"But are you a Jew?"

"No. I am an Anglican clergyman."

He was then entirely uninhibited by the presence of the victim in expressing his opinion (a) of an Anglican clergyman who became president of a Jewish learned society; (b) of a Jewish learned society which could so far forget itself as to elect an Anglican clergyman to be its president; (c) of the whole of Anglo-Jewry which allowed such license to its learned society that so appalling a calamity could happen. He was just passing to the fourth point when the procession reached its destination.

As soon as the *History of Palestine* was published, Bertha Urdang, who was temporarily working with the Zionists at Great Russell Street, came down to Barley and asked me to do a short book on Jerusalem. Bertha was a Jerusalem Jewess, whose husband had been killed in the siege of 1948, and who was almost unique in the field of Jewish public relations in that she realised that, if one wants to present a case to the Gentile, one should get a Gentile to do it! On her own initiative she did what hours of argument with dear Sidney Salomon had never achieved—gave me a free hand to present the facts about Jerusalem which, in this case, were the best argument for the Jewish interest. *The Story of Jerusalem* which resulted from our

discussions went into two editions and was extensively used in
the new Israel embassies. But it was never favoured by the
Zionist organisations. In fact they produced a rival publication.
That it was a conscious rival was shown by their using the same
unusual *format* that we had adopted because so much of the
book consisted of maps excellently drawn by Leslie Thurston,
who refused to take a penny for his work, because it was an
honour to work for Jerusalem. The rival work was a piece of
pure propaganda, unjust to Christian and Muslim interests.
It had only one map—which was taken from a British project
for the building of a scenic road round the city. The project
was never realised, so that the map was of an imaginary
Jerusalem; a fact which made it less important that it was
printed upside down! Truly Zionist organisations are often
their own worst enemies.

By the summer of 1950 the debate as to whether there ought
to have been a Jewish state at all was in full spate. So I prepared
a mimeographed document of 26 pages entitled *Israel: Intrusion
or Fulfilment?* which we sent to some two hundred people who
had political, commercial, or other interests in the Middle
East. In every case I got the names from people I knew personally, and wrote a letter telling the recipient who had suggested that he might be interested. The document itself was
discussed with experts like Ronald Storrs and Leopold Amery
before it was mimeographed. It produced a very interesting
correspondence, a great deal of reasoned agreement, some disagreement, and only one letter of pro-Arab abuse. That came
from a quite prominent Scottish Presbyterian.

The document and the letters of criticism formed the basis
of my next book, which dealt with the case for a Jewish state,
the nature of such a state, and its relations with the Jewries
dispersed throughout the world. I had hoped that V.G. would
publish it, but he had at that time lost interest in his 'Jewish
list'. Then I met David Kessler at a party, told him about the
book, and he said that Vallentine Mitchell would gladly
publish it. This they did, and the name *End of an Exile* was
their suggestion. It should have had a question mark, but we
thought of that too late. It went out of print almost immediately,
and in 1964 it appeared in French, translated by Michel

Leitner, and its first part, *The Five Roots of Israel*, was republished from a fund which was given us to commemorate the life of Rosa Eisendrath, wife of Maurice and one of my first Jewish friends.

I had planned to follow *Intrusion or Fulfilment* with a careful study of the Arab refugees and the causes of their plight. For it was evident that it was quite inaccurate to blame any one cause for all the fugitives, even though Jewish military commanders were clearly responsible for some expulsions. Just when I had assembled most of my facts, the refugee section of the World Council of Churches called a conference on the subject at Beirut. They had apparently had some difficulty in getting co-operation from the refugees themselves, and I received an earnest appeal through Simpson not to publish anything on the subject until they had established satisfactory relations. Of course I agreed. There was a solemn promise that they would keep in touch with me so that the delay should not be unduly prolonged. Needless to say the promise was not kept, and the opportunity was lost, for I got involved in other things. But all the cards are at Southampton University, though such a treatment of the subject is now basically out of date. Yet I have not seen anywhere an attempt to explain why, when every advantage of numbers, terrain, and support was with the Palestine Arabs, when they would have been able completely to sabotage the new Jewish state simply by staying put, their whole behaviour was so inexplicably foolish. My reading of the history of the country suggests one possible explanation. In conditions of Arab warfare, both between bedouin of different tribes, and between fellaheen and bedouin, the weaker party never stayed to fight. It 'retired', knowing that the raid would soon be over, and then it would be possible to return and rebuild. With such a tradition behind them the Palestinian Arabs did not take into account, either before 1947 or during 1948, that this policy could only mean that they lost that from which they retired. For those on whom they had declared war in November 1947 were not bedouin who intended to go back with their loot to the desert.

In the years after the war it was a pleasure to watch the development of the Council of Christians and Jews. In 1946 there was a very valuable international conference at Oxford which Dorothy and I attended. Then followed Seelisberg, and its famous 'Ten Points', and in the following year Fribourg, where Everett Clinchy, founder of the National Conference of Christians and Jews in the States, and the main mover in the two previous international conferences, dumped the whole problem in Simpson's lap. This was probably fortunate, for the British shared more common ideas with Europe than the Americans, and Simpson and his colleagues have steadily developed contacts with Europe, effectively culminating in the well attended conference at Cambridge in 1966. Until our retirement I remained a member of the Executive of the C.C.J. and their meetings were one of the occasions I tried not to miss.

Besides my 'professional' work we were involved in many local activities, some of which are more appropriately treated in the next chapter. Because of various rectorial problems, I became chairman of the village school during the war, and piloted the managers through the application of the new Education Act. This was quite interesting; for I refused to accept a majority decision as to whether we should change from church to controlled status, and I insisted on a full parish meeting in order to discuss it with the parents of children. In the end, in spite of fervent moves from the diocese, which was given every chance to state its case, we voted unanimously for controlled status. This provoked a grin from the county educational authorities later, when one of them visited me and explained that they proposed to have an acre of my orchard for a proper playground which the Church could never have afforded. I replied that, as owner of the property, I entirely agreed that the school should have it, but that, as chairman of the managers, I insisted that the owner of the property must modernise his sewage system, otherwise various accidents (frozen ground or all the emptiers of cesspools having simultaneous influenza) precipitated a large amount of sewage on to the proposed playground. The county was able to satisfy both the chairman and the owner, and the acre passed to the school, giving it room for additional buildings, better sanitation, and a reasonable playground.

The inauguration of the secondary modern system under an adventurous County Director like John Newsom was extremely interesting, and I was lucky to be governor, later chairman, of the two schools involved in our neighbourhood. One of the things I set out to do (but did not get very far in doing!) was to bring the staff and governors together. Both sides regarded it as an unprecedented, and not quite proper, activity.

The one black spot in our life at Barley was the parish church. After the rector who had been there when I originally came to the village had retired in disgrace, but as a very effective poison pen, the bishop planted on us a retired missionary to the Jews, who had never been in charge of a parish in his life, had never lived in the country, and who announced from the very beginning that he regarded the parish as a pension, not as a field in which to work. This to a village shocked and humiliated beyond measure by the disgrace of its previous rector, and in desperate need of the healing touch which has, at last, come to it! I was, in fact, completely excommunicated by him, as even a desire to take a mid-weekly communion service was at once claimed by him to be a desire to create "a clique". Fortunately at that time I was fit enough to take duty at a distance, and almost every Sunday we were at one or another of the vacant parishes within a dozen miles of us.

I had never really been enthusiastic about the Anglican diocesan system, and I always considered ridiculous the embroidered hats and cloaks in which bishops had become obliged to prance about. Almost all my S.C.M. contemporaries who were in Anglican orders had become bishops, and in most cases I felt that they had been much more useful before the change. An affair in the neighbourhood acted, I grieve to say, to increase my prejudices. We heard by accident that a bachelor parson, whom we did not know personally, had been convicted of homosexual intentions. I went to see him. I found him alone in a vast rectory. Nobody had been near him for nearly a week (he was from one of the dominions and had no relatives in England), and he possessed five pounds in the world. I took him home. We sent him off to Belgium for a holiday with friends, and he then came back to us. He was too hurt and shocked to let me tell any of the authorities he was with us, and it was six weeks before diocesan or suffragan bishop, archdeacon or rural dean made any enquiry as to what had happened to him. A diocese so big that such a thing could happen is, to me, an intolerable outrage.

Politically I agreed with most of my colleagues in accepting that Common Wealth had done its job during the war, but that now the place in which to work was the Labour Party. It is an enormous, and still unaccomplished, task to organise the Labour Party in the villages and we were much too occupied with other tasks to accept responsibility for the Barley branch. All we could do was to give up time at elections for speaking in the constituency, and help with the car on polling day. But here we proved to have a genius for picking up people who wanted a car ride, but had neglected to see that their names were on the register.

One of the pleasures of local life was membership of a society called the Duodecimos. It was small enough for us to entertain each other at our own houses. We met once a month, heard a paper, and continued discussion on it till near midnight. The membership consisted of business, professional and academic dwellers in the general neighbourhood of Saffron Walden. Redcliffe Salaman brought me into it, and I enjoyed producing papers on subjects quite outside my own field—from ghosts to Talleyrand! The Duos was a peculiarly English institution, and foreign visitors whom we brought to our meetings were usually amazed that a country area could produce such distinguished and learned discussion on such a variety of themes.

Among our post-war visitors was one unusual guest, known to us as The Old Man of the Road. Some tragedy early in life had turned him into a 'tramp', and he had been on the road since the first world war. He took great pride in keeping himself clean; he knew that he could have a bed in our 'garden house' when he wanted, that he could come to us when he felt ill, and that there would always be a meal for him. Once or twice we sent him to hospital, where he never stayed long. He loved the country, would tell us of its beauty and bring Dorothy some offering of flowers or fruit culled on his way. His visits continued till we knew he was too old for the road, and we found a place for him where he died peacefully and well loved in an old people's home.

Once or twice we managed to get over to the islands, and I took Dorothy for an unforgettable spring holiday in Sark.

But for holidays we went mainly towards the east coast, exploring in turn all the estuaries and ancient ports from Maldon to Overy Staithe. Our favourite became Walberswick, where we could walk straight from *The Anchor* to the beach and harbour. Our holidays were short, and we rarely went away in the summer, as visitors constantly turned up unannounced at Barley. Occasionally conferences took us away for a few days. But on the whole people came to us, not we to them, and Barley was a peaceful spot for quiet discussion and reading.

In 1951 we were both so tired that we took advantage of the falling in of an insurance policy of Dorothy's to take a long holiday in my beloved Provence. There we spent some time with the Cru's, and listened to their extraordinary war-time activities. Theodore Vogel, who had married Helène Cru, had been in the *Resistance*, and for much of the time Alice was living alone at La Rolane, on the outskirts of Marseilles just at the level where the Germans were fixing battalion h.q.'s. A German officer with a squad of soldiers visited her, found her living alone in this large farm house and announced that soldiers would be billeted on her. Every statement he made she capped with a more generous one. Did he say that a room would hold five, she said they often slept seven hikers in it, and so on. But there was always a slight disadvantage which she was sure they would be able to overcome. The rain came in here, the drains were a little smelly there, the black out was defective somewhere else. The climax came in their largest bed-room. The German officer announced that he would place eight men in it. "No," said Alice "you can place more here. It is the best room in the house. My invalid sister lived here for many years until she died of tuberculosis last month." At that the German officer fled—and Alice, with a German battalion h.q. on each side of her, opened a perfectly safe dormitory for the *Resistance*!

Our holiday ended with a pleasant visit to Strasbourg, where one of our most learned French friends, Marcel Simon, was Dean of the Humanities. There, in my capacity of President of the Jewish Historical Society of England, I opened the *Année Culturelle* of the Jewish community, speaking in French with discussion in French to follow. It was a translation of one of my presidential lectures and Theodore had helped me to render it into good French; but I was able to sustain a long discussion afterwards. We stayed in that lovely city for a week as the guests of the Jewish community.

Early in 1953 Maurice Eisendrath invited us to join him in Israel during the time that the Union of American Hebrew Congregations, the liberal Jewish organisation, was making a study of the religious situation there. That country paradoxically guaranteed and practised complete religious freedom for Christians and Muslims, but the only form of Judaism tolerated was an extremely rigid orthodoxy. For a religious Jew who was not traditionally minded the position was often almost intolerable, for the rabbis possessed considerable authority in personal matters, could refuse to recognise a person as a Jew, and were a quite unscrupulous political pressure group. The fact that every government in Israel was automatically a coalition gave them very unjustified power.

We accepted with pleasure, but a month or two before we were due to go I was taken ill at a conference and had an emergency operation in Charing Cross Hospital. However we went out by sea, and that acted as a convalescence. It was a very interesting trip, though the Union decided, rightly I think, that at that time it would be a mistake to press for a change in the Israeli situation. Now, in 1968, I am glad to say there is a chance that things will become different, and the rigidly orthodox will no longer be seen as the only representatives of religion in Israel. There is to be a move to develop further, and more publicly, progressive synagogues in the community. While we were in Israel Maurice asked me to make an extended lecture tour in the States in the winter of 1953–54, in which I would speak to audiences of Christian clergy, under the auspices of the Union, on the relations of the two religions.

This invitation brought to a head the impossibility of continuing indefinitely with no secretarial help, no room for files and archives except, metaphorically, under the bed, and no certainty from one day to another. The library was by now a very valuable and unusual collection since, apart from the good middle-eastern section I had built up while I was able to pay my own book bills, we had for some years had the advantage that Maurice Blinken, an American friend, paid our American

book bills. We often had the only copy available in England of
the latest American publications in our field, a matter of increasing importance as the standard and range of American
literature on Jewish themes steadily increased. When I met
Bishop Burgess of Canberra, and he told me of the founding
of St. Mark's theological library in that city, I was able to
promise him a collection of the basic essentials for the understanding of Judaism, not only from sources I could tap in
England, but, through Maurice Blinken's generosity, also
from basic works published in America. Knowing what the
average theological library possesses on Judaism, I could
ensure Canberra having an almost unique collection which we
continued to augment until our retirement.

In addition to books, the collections of both pamphlets and
periodicals continued to grow and to demand substantial space,
and the mere record of my activities in the field of Jewish-
Christian relations covered twenty-five years.

We still could not get any definite action from I.M.S. which
would have turned us into an institution and solved many of
our financial problems. We did, however, get enough to build an
office and to engage a secretary. This was the more necessary
as we by then had Dorothy's eighty year old mother living
with us, and it would have been more than John could cope
with unaided in our absence. Mrs. Wickings had a very pleasant
'toy house' in the orchard, made from two caravans joined by a
substantial 'lobby', with its own telephone, and its own garden.
The old lady could be as independent as she wanted, but also
could be looked after from the house when necessary.

In preparation for our visit I made a flying trip to the States
in September 1953, staying most of my time with Maurice in
his 'shack' fifty miles from New York in a beautiful country
of woods and lakes. The purpose of my visit was to explore
the possibility of combining the programme envisaged by
Maurice with any lectures in the field made possible by my
History of Palestine and my memorandum *Intrusion or Fulfilment*.
This visit was discussed at length with Eliahu Elath, then Israeli
Ambassador in London. The value of including lectures on
Israel depended on the extent to which American Christian
interest in the Middle East was tied up with support and identi-

fication with the Palestinian Arab refugees. If it was, then only a fully prepared and whole-time campaign would be any good, and that could not be combined with my theological lecturing.

I went with personal introductions to all the Christian agencies, academic like the *Near East Foundation*, or religious, whether Catholic, Protestant or Quaker. The experience was horrifying. The ignorance of Israel was as complete as identification with the refugees. A Quaker lady, whose views would have pleased Goebbels, explained to me that, if they did not identify their opinions completely with those of the refugees, they would not be allowed to work in the camps. This hideous and destructive moral cowardice was common to Catholics, Protestants and Quakers. It is a curious fact that I have never met a pro-Israel Christian with whom one could not discuss in a rational and friendly way any question concerning the Arab world. Every Christian I have met who is "pro-Arab" is not merely anti-Israel but both ignorant and mildly or virulently anti-semitic. It is a most tragic problem, and does immense harm to the unfortunate Palestinian Arabs whom it encourages to live in a world of fantasy, where none of the limitations which apply to the rest of humanity apply to them, and where they have no responsibility for any sins they have committed.

In January we set out for our main tour, which was due to last four months. It involved lecturing right across the continent, going by the southern route, returning by the northern, and speaking—though I have not put them in their right order—at Orange, Philadelphia, Washington, Nashville, Dallas, Los Angeles, San Francisco, Kansas, Milwaukee, Chicago, Detroit, Cincinnati, Buffalo, Rochester, Boston, and so returning to New York. The trip was much more exhausting than Maurice had reckoned when he invited me, or his deputy, Jay Kaufmann, realised when he made the day to day arrangements. The physical side was, of course, tiring. The whole journey was made by air; we were often only three days in a city; we were continually meeting new people; we were living in very changing climates on very scanty luggage, and so on—but it was not these factors which were the main problem.

It was a very heavy strain for a Christian theologian to be constantly explaining to his Christian brethren that their views of Judaism, however benevolent in intention, were theologically an intolerable offence to their Jewish neighbours, though these would be too polite or nervous to show it. In almost every discussion I had to explain that Judaism was *not* an incomplete form of Christianity, that it was *not* an unchanged 'Old Testament religion' any more than Christianity was an unchanged 'New Testament religion', that it had not ceased to be creative when B.C. changed to A.D., and that it had to be treated as an equal in any discussion between Jews and Christians. I can say quite objectively that there was then no other Christian theologian in existence who would even have tried to perform such a task. Though I was talking all the time on the same basic subject, I did not have a written text which I just read out to successive audiences. I sought in each city to understand the situation in that city, and to adjust my subject to meet their particular needs and interests.

We had a somewhat longer stay in Chicago than elsewhere, and there I began to be really ill. I lost my voice, my hatred of hotels became obsessive, and we were most generously rescued by the deeply spiritual rabbi of the free synagogue, Dr. Eric Friedland and his wife Pearl. They not only took us into their own home, but gave us their own room, because it was the quietest and most comfortable. At some stage before our stay in Chicago we went for a few days to the holiday centre that the U.A.H.C. possessed on a lake (which was quite frozen) at Oconomowoc. There we had the only touch of real country during our whole trip, and could really relax amidst the smell of cows—most homely for a born Guernseyman. Yet even there we had a youth conference, and I spent a good deal of time preparing my most important lecture in the whole trip, the Gilkey Lecture to the University of Chicago. The U.A.H.C. subsequently published it under the title of *The Concept of a Chosen People in Judaism and Christianity*, and it became the model for the subsequent series of pamphlets of the Parkes Library.

From the cold and windy city of Chicago we went on to Cincinnati. I had another collapse there, and was completely exhausted when I arrived back in New York. In fact my very efficient New York doctor, who would not take a penny from me, calling me his 'National Health Service patient', refused to allow me to give another lecture, and told Maurice to ship me home as soon as he could!

Though the voyage was marred at the end by the news of the death of Dorothy's mother, it was a most pleasant convalescence. We were given first class passages on my favourite boat, the *Ile de France*, and the voyage was a gastronomic *tour de force*. Eating but little at breakfast and lunch, we had at the latter meal a solemn assembly to decide the evening meal. There was our table waiter, the wine waiter, various chefs, and the head waiter usually managed to attend. We first chose the wine, so that Dorothy might taste the main different wines of France. It was not an expensive bottle, but it was one they all considered typical of that *région*. The wine chosen, they then debated what local dish would set it off to perfection. Every meal was a poem; and, at the end, when I apologised for my modest tips and thanked them for making the voyage so pleasant, I met the charming reply: "Others can give us the dollars quite easily; you, Monsieur, have given us the pleasure."

We returned with some eight thousand dollars, to find that nothing had been done in our absence to turn us into some kind of institute to which we could hand over the money. In spite of the efforts of Mr. Westmore, we lost a large part of it in super-tax. Then followed an agonising time. I.M.S. was really too busy to give sufficient thought to our problems to make a sensible decision possible. He was also involved in too many demands to give us the minimum financial help we needed. We struggled on for a year, not knowing from month to month whether we would have to close. In June 1955 I collapsed with what, so to speak, should have been a stroke, but fortunately was not. The doctors, wondering why against all convention, it was not one, decided to call it a 'cerebral spasm'. In any case it was extremely painful and lasted a long time. I.M.S. sent us on holiday to Crans in Switzerland. On the way back I showed Dorothy Geneva, but found that nothing was left of my flat except the outside walls. The whole inside of the house with its dignified eighteenth century interiors, and its sixteenth century servants' quarters (my flat) had been swept away and replaced by three beastly little boxes (with all mod. cons.) on each floor.

Of the next two years there is little pleasant to say. Late in 1955 there were signs that I.M.S. was at last having steps taken to put the work in institutional form, but it looked less and less likely that I would be able to profit from this decision, which we had hoped for more than ten years earlier. For on three occasions Dorothy accompanied me in the ambulance to hospital, being warned by the doctors that I had a bare fifty percent chance of reaching the hospital alive. But I must record one incident because of its spontaneous and unexpected generosity. Some years earlier I had written for Mrs. Bryce-Salomons a pamphlet describing the life of her distinguished forbears in her old home, which she had handed over to the County as a convalescent home. From time to time she sent me a large and unexpected cheque, explaining that it was royalties from the pamphlet. After one of my illnesses Dorothy was told that she must get me south, as I should not survive the winter in England. It was a moment when we were quite penniless and I.M.S. too pre-occupied to help. Suddenly there arrived a letter for Dorothy from Mrs. Salomons saying that she had heard that I was ill, that she knew what expense a serious illness entailed, and enclosing a cheque for two hundred pounds. We spent the winter at Menton, in the diocese of my old S.C.M. colleague, Tom Craske, then bishop of Gibraltar; and I received from him the laying-on-of hands. It was not until late spring that, much restored, I returned to England by easy stages, one naturally being with our old friends at Marseilles, another at Lyons, a third at Dijon, neither of which cities Dorothy knew, and a final one at Paris. I was still to have another serious illness, but of this whole sorry period I will add only one thing for the benefit of any possible readers. For a married couple a serious and prolonged illness is far worse for the partner who is *not* ill, than for the patient. For the patient everything that can be done is done. All the anxiety, all the uncertainty, all the long hours of waiting, all the strain of convalescence falls on the partner. My poor Dorothy had a far worse time than I did.

In the middle of these distresses, on August 9, 1956, a week after I had started having coronary thromboses, we at last became *The Parkes Library Limited*, a company created for charitable purposes, and registered under the Board of Trade.

XII

JOHN HADHAM: PART II

I HAVE SAID earlier that this story partakes inevitably of the character of a theological whodunit, for the concern to relate what we really believe with what we say in church dates back to my childhood. While we were still at Les Fauconnaires and I shared a bedroom with my elder brother, David, I remember coming back from church full of rage at the meaningless and unacceptable psalms which we had been singing. David was always a good conservative, and at once defended the psalms on the grounds that we had always had them, and I replied that we had had the psalms of David long enough, and it was time we had the psalms of James! It is only due to lack of time that I have not attempted to fit our liturgical use of the psalms to intelligent twentieth century beliefs, but at least I can applaud my friend, Canon Richardson, for having attempted to do so.

During the period of 'lean and busy years', when my main Jewish interest was focused on Palestine and Israel, the religious puzzles and experiences of many decades began to fall into place. The American tour of 1946 helped; the growing intimacy with Charles Singer helped; my deepening studies of Judaism helped; my anger at the abominable heresy of Barth helped; until I realised that what had come to express my basic and most profound convictions was a restatement of the doctrine which had always fascinated me, the doctrine of the Trinity. The Trinity as a description of the nature of Deity itself always seemed to me as meaningless as the logical positivists and other linguistic philosophers maintained. But, if we substitute 'channels' for 'persons', and if we confine the sphere of our definition to the activity of the Deity as creator of this particular world in which we live, then an intelligible doctrine emerges which claims for *Judaism* the flow of the divine purpose into the life of the community, for *Christianity* the flow of the same purpose into the life of man as person, and for the kind of scientific *Humanism* which Charles Singer represented, the divine response to man as seeker. Moreover we have a doctrine of divine activity which can be tested by history and experience, which explains why man in his three capacities of social being, person and seeker, subjects himself to distinguishable and not interchangeable disciplines, and which yet emphasises that none of these disciplines or human capacities is sufficient in itself to control and direct the whole of life. For the unity is as important as the diversity. So, incidentally, is the equality.

Just at this period when I was arguing for the equality of Judaism and Humanism with Christianity, and proclaiming the inadequacy of a Christocentric religion, we were thrust into a series of experiences which compelled us to recognise that it was a larger view of God, not a smaller view of Christianity, which had to be put forward. For there came to us both, through the effect which *Good God* had had on Mary, an experience of the unique power of Christ the healer. Mary had had one leg amputated because of bone tuberculosis; she also had cancer, and she was full of psychological tensions. With it all she was a most lovable and delightful human. She became convinced that, if she could put herself in the hands of John Hadham, God would give her healing. It was her faith, not mine or Dorothy's, which effected the cure, but the cure was effected. She came down repeatedly over several years to Barley, sometimes well, sometimes extremely ill. There was a period when we did not know from day to day what age we would encounter when she spoke to us as all her childhood troubles poured out in chaotic confusion. She is now a happy grandmother.

This experience, and others like it, sent us to books like Rebecca Beard's *Everyman's Search* and Agnes Sandford's *Healing Light*. We met Brother Bill and Christopher Woodward, both leaders in the healing movement within the Church of England. We also met Americans of the same experience, especially in the dynamic and refreshing movement, *Camps Farthest Out*. There was no doubt in our minds that, if the Jewish work were to collapse, we would go with a sense of gratitude for the past and excitement for the future, into some aspect of this pioneering renewal of the twentieth century. Dorothy and I both agreed at the end that the Jewish work could and should go on, and must be my main preoccupation, but that left her free to give a good deal of her time, and to identify herself more fully, with the healing movement. She became a member of the international and interdenominational Order of St. Luke the Physician, and has found continual refreshment in the contacts thus made; I would add that it brought down to Barley another group of visitors whose presence enriched our lives and also, from time to time, illuminated and puzzled the scholars who were our normal guests.

The elation which I felt at my long theological pilgrimage having reached so fruitful a goal expressed itself in the publication in 1952 of *God at Work*—a title suggested by David Edwards, a not infrequent visitor to Barley at that period, whom I had known since he was a schoolboy evacuated to Cornwall. It was published by Putnam's and they insisted on it being a Parkes and not a Hadham, which was, I am convinced, a mistake. In any case, like *Between God and Man*, my previous effort to plead for a revolution in theological thinking, it was, so far as sales went, a complete flop.

It is, I expect, a temptation of the devil to attribute these two failures to the publishers! When in 1966 a Trinitarian *Good God* was issued by David Edwards just before he left the S.C.M. Press, it also was a failure. It sold two thousand copies, while an American edition of the original (somewhat bowdlerised) sold in the same period twenty thousand. But I suspect that the real reason is not the machinations of the devil but just that the two Trinitarian books were not written on the right wavelength for the readers whom I hoped to attract. Few of us can reach the public with equal success on a variety of media. While *Good God* was averaging over a hundred a day as a book, John Hadham as a preacher or lecturer was most disappointingly ineffective. So, while details undoubtedly do affect sales, I am sure that there are deeper reasons why I cannot convey to others the satisfaction and excitement that it is to me to see the vision of God in terms of the restatement of the Trinity. That this is the inevitable and only possible way forward I am still convinced, but it will probably be someone else who finds

8

the right way in which to express it. Not but what I shall go on trying whenever opportunity seems to open.

The next opportunity to create a new 'John Hadham' came in 1960, when Victor Gollancz asked me to contribute to his *Common Sense* series by writing *Common Sense about Religion*. In it I absorbed the trinitarian doctrine which had been the central theme of *God at Work*, but without drawing any special attention to it. I simply emphasised the debt we owed to Judaism, its justified survival, and its independent contribution to contemporary life. The new element which this book brought into my theology was the conception of 'creative tension' between the three channels (or 'persons') as being the essential fuel with which the Creator ensured the development of his creation. In *God at Work* I had indeed emphasised the different techniques which needed to be followed if a community, a person, and a seeker were to fulfil the role designed for them. The pursuit of *love*, which is naturally spoken of as the supreme Christian virtue in the relations of one man with another, becomes the pursuit of *righteousness* or justice in the relations between whole communities, and that in turn becomes the pursuit of *truth* with man the seeker. In *God at Work* I emphasised that it was evident that love, righteousness, and truth were neither in opposition to each other, nor identical. In *Common Sense about Religion* I saw the relationship as creative tension, and that has since been fundamental to my theology. It is, as I said above, the fuel which 'makes the wheels go round'.

Common Sense about Religion also allowed me to say more than I had previously done about other religions, and I just adumbrated there, what has since been a developing interest, the amazing variety of the contributions of the different races and peoples, *and their irreplaceability*. No eastern people has done so much as the peoples of the three monotheisms to define and develop a systematic metaphysic about the *Divinity* behind the manifestations of creation. But the eastern peoples have done much more than the western to understand the physical, psychic and spiritual resources of *man*, whether we think of Japanese Judo and Karate, Chinese acupuncture or Buddhist meditation. No lesser unity than the whole of mankind would provide all the elements which would be absolutely necessary before man could claim to be 'adult'. At present he is best described as a rather dangerous 'infant prodigy', and there is no more foolish or superficial theology than that which has proclaimed that man is now adult, and needs no God to help him.

John Hadham was again dormant for some years until Dr. Kennedy, director of the Forward Movement Press of the American Episcopal Church, asked an English representative at an executive meeting of some committee of the World Council of Churches whether he could get into touch with John Hadham as he wanted to get permission to issue *Good God* in the States. With great discretion she told him that James Parkes would know, so Dr. Kennedy rang me up and asked me to put him in touch with John Hadham! The result I have already described.

What I hope is that the time will soon come when the contemporary theological approach will pass from the negative to the positive. Books like those by the Bishop of Woolwich assume that there was in the past a static maximum understanding of God. That maximum contains elements we cannot accept, so that we are constantly reducing the picture by having to abandon now this now that once treasured belief. I believe this approach to be upside down. The famous *Observer* article which launched *Honest to God* had the heading: *Our Image of God must go*. The real heading for any generation is:

OUR IMAGE OF GOD MUST GROW

I have no desire to denounce the thirteenth century or the sixteenth for holding beliefs I cannot share. Those beliefs expressed in contemporary terms real experience which I can share. My job therefore is to explore the experience and to relate it to my own time in my own terms. The result is almost always to find that the old terms were too small, not too large. And I trust that I shall go on enlarging them as long as life lasts.

XIII

THE PARKES LIBRARY LIMITED

THE PARKES LIBRARY LIMITED was registered in August
1956, largely through the persistent efforts of J. C. Parry, legal
adviser to I.M.S.; but it was more than a year before I was
well enough to resume an active life, and it was the same time
before I.M.S. was at last able to secure the basic stability of a
covenant income which our corporate existence made possible.
The intervening period was very lean indeed.

I.M.S. was connected with a number of other causes,
causes which issued appeals and raised considerable sums. Miss
Rosefield, his private secretary, was a genius at knowing which
wealthy man or woman to invite to support which cause, and
it was 'Rosie' who compiled a list of invitations to a dinner at
the Savoy at which I.M.S. launched the project of the Parkes
Library with a brilliant speech, not merely on my work, but
on the long term necessity for it.

The income produced did indeed guarantee us a modest
security and the continuation of the work for the next seven
years, but it made no allowance for expansion, and, just over a
year later, another dinner was held at which it was proposed
to join together the Parkes and the Wiener Libraries. This was
not really a very sensible project, because I had somewhat
doubtful strength to run my own work, and certainly could not
in addition spend several days a week in London running the
Wiener Library. Dr. Wiener was several years older than I
was and had in effect retired; his assistant, C. C. Aronsfeld, was
much more concerned with accurate research into the whole
of contemporary antisemitism than with administration. Both
were good friends of ours, and the two institutions fitted admirably into each other. But I was not the right leader for both.
Nevertheless, as soon as we could get funds for Else Rosenfeld
to make it, she copied our library catalogue so that it could be
accessible in the Wiener Library in London.

When the project itself proved unrealisable, Leonard Montefiore, president of the Wiener Library, insisted that all the work
and preparation of the dinner had been organised by I.M.S.,
and that it was his supporters who had contributed the cove-
nants. It was, in his opinion, the Parkes Library which should
benefit from the result, and he refused to have the income
divided between the two institutions.

This meant that at last we were able to have adequate
secretarial help, adequate room for the books, pamphlets,
periodicals and archives. We were lucky also in getting a
voluntary part-time librarian in Colonel Geoffrey Stevens.
What we were not able to persuade I.M.S. to bring into existence was a competent finance committee which could also
plan expansion and look after the succession when I was ready
to retire. We did make two unsuccessful attempts to employ
an organising secretary, but we had not the right setting for
his work. Though we had no administrative and finance
committee, we did have a valuable list of governors, both
Jewish and Christian, both British and foreign. They included
Professors Alexander Altmann of Brandeis, David Daube of
Oxford, Marcel Simon of Strasbourg and Zwi Werblowski of
Jerusalem. Lady Stansgate was full of both political and religious experience and prevented it from being a purely masculine
body, Eliahu Elath linked us with the political as well as the
academic world, David Kessler was a publisher, Maurice
Eisendrath was my oldest Jewish friend and life president of
the progressive Jewish organisation in America, and Carlisle
Witton-Davies was not only an old friend from our first visit
to Jerusalem, but also chairman of the Council of Christians
and Jews. Charles Singer was a governor until his death.

Apart from a visit to Jerusalem we did little travel during
these years, but I had a very full literary programme. During
the period of my illnesses I had started to put my trinitarian
convictions into scholarly form by a book which traced the
growth of rabbinic Judaism and of traditional Christianity from
the time of Ezra onwards, showing how each was a natural,
indeed inevitable, outcome of that dynamic period so much
misrepresented in conventional Christian scholarship. In fact
there is no argument for the divine guidance of Jewry which

is not an equally valid argument for Christendom, and there is no argument for a divine guidance of Christendom which is not equally valid for Judaism. Dorothy may well be right in saying that it was the fact that the book was unfinished when I started having coronaries and what-not which kept me alive because of my determination to complete it, which I did in 1959. It was published by Kessler (Vallentine Mitchell) the following year with the title *The Foundations of Judaism and Christianity*.

Its publication had the unusual accompaniment of my being made an *Observer Profile* in September. The *Profile* ended by quoting me as saying that the part of the world in which I feared most that antisemitism might break out again was Latin America. Various friends took me to task at the time for making such an improbable suggestion, but it was not long before my expectations were tragically fulfilled in the Argentine. Just at that time we met Henry Levy, the brilliant representative in Latin America of the American Joint Distribution Committee (the largest and best organised Jewish charity in the world). Through this contact I got both my next books translated into Spanish and published in Buenos Aires, the first scholarly works to be published in the Argentine dealing with antisemitism and with the post-biblical history of the Jews.

My Gilkey lecture of 1954 had been published as a pamphlet by the Union of American Hebrew Congregations, and they generously supplied us with as many copies as we wanted. The eagerness with which these were asked for by our visitors or in places where I was speaking made me begin a series of *Parkes Library Pamphlets*, with an admirable and distinctive format and presentation, devised in co-operation with Kingham's of King's Langley who printed them. Many of them were my own lectures or articles, but we also published work by Jules Isaac, Raphael Loewe, I. K. Cosgrove and Maurice Eisendrath. We published David Astor's moving leader in *The Observer* on *The Meaning of Eichmann*, a leader which set in train a whole series of events culminating in the creation, linked with Sussex University, of an institute on *The Psychopathology of Politics*. This was headed by Norman Cohn who took over, and completed with a comprehensiveness I could never have achieved, the material I had collected on *The Protocols of the Elders of Zion*.

The signs of a resurgence of antisemitism made me ask Sir Allen Lane whether he would publish a revision of my Penguin Special on the subject. Lane was unconvinced about this, but asked me whether I would do a *Pelican* for him on Jewish history. This was an invitation which I received with the utmost pleasure; and he gave me eighty thousand words to cover the period from Abraham to Ben Gurion, with fifteen hundred words extra if needed! The result was 'an essay in the art of omission'. I took as my model of what *not* to do Dr. Epstein's Pelican on *Judaism*, a superb and exhaustive encyclopaedia article and a totally unreadable book!

My objective was to produce a leisurely and unhurried survey. I was determined never to mention a name unless I had time to say something about the man concerned, never to produce a list or to make use of the phrase which I regard as a writer's last confession of incompetence: 'there is no time here to . . .' or, alternatively: 'this is no place to . . .' If it's not the time or place to, then don't! To achieve the desired result I first planned the titles of the chapters, then considered whether they told a simple or complex story, allotted them so many words, and juggled with the words until the total came to eighty thousand. Each chapter was then divided into a dozen or less sub-headings, each heading was allotted its quota, and the names to be introduced were sketched. Thus, before a word was written, I could have told you the subjects I should be treating between word seventeen thousand two hundred and five and word eighteen thousand. My secretary, as she took each section, counted it and came back to me reporting 'you are seven words in hand' or 'you are five words over'. It sounds laborious, but it was worth it. I was no more hurried at the end of a chapter than I was at the beginning.

I have gone into this detail because it was not merely an important book to be asked to write, but it was a rewarding one. It gave a sense of fulfilment to the whole work. It enabled me to put before the reader a perspective which could only be achieved by decades of more detailed study and writing. In particular it gave me the opportunity of breaking with the Graetz-Roth tradition of treating the history of Jews in the

Middle East as episodic, and concentrating attention on Europe. In relation to the length of the book, I paid much more attention to Palestine and neighbouring countries than my predecessors. It was also a delightful book to write because I was only the fourth Christian to write an original history of the Jewish people in close on three hundred years. The father of post-biblical Jewish history was himself a Christian—the Huguenot Jean Jacques Basnage. His work appeared in five volumes at the beginning of the eighteenth century. It has an interesting history. It was almost immediately re-issued in a subtly altered edition by the Jesuits, with a wonderful introduction, claiming that Mr. Basnage should be very flattered by their improvements, and not at all angry since the public could still buy his edition if they preferred. Basnage replied with an exposure of the plagiarism of which apparently only four copies survive—one in the Parkes Library. Then in the early nineteenth century came Dean Milman, who wrote a remarkably learned history, but from a conventional Christian point of view. Finally at the end of the century came E. A. Abbott, famous headmaster of the City of London School.

The *History* has appeared in Dutch, Italian and Spanish editions, as well as in hard and paper covers. I am told it is used in Israeli schools though it has not been translated into Hebrew. It was due to appear in German, but the publisher was dissatisfied with the translation.

When I had finished writing the *History* I discussed with David Kessler the preparation of a hard back successor to the Penguin on antisemitism. It was not merely out of print, but had become out of date; and it meant that there was no book immediately available should there be a new danger of antisemitism in the English speaking world. So a completely rewritten study of the subject was published by Vallentine, Mitchell, in 1963. As events have turned out, it has become more dangerous to be a West Indian, Indian or Pakistani than to be a Jew, and the public cannot concentrate its hatred or fear on more than one minority at a time. Nevertheless, there is no security for any minority while group prejudice remains one of the little understood and little combatted diseases of public life.

While I was in Addenbrooke's hospital, and Dorothy was staying in Cambridge with K. Wood-Legh, she became a member of the congregation of St. Edward's, a 'peculiar', and a church which was intimately connected with Latimer and the reformers at Cambridge. When I returned to Barley we both became members of St. Edward's and remained so till we retired. It had a 'chaplain', not a vicar, and the Chaplain during this period was Arthur Dowle, a genius at binding his congregation into a unity of friendship and worship. We found there all the fellowship which we had lacked at Barley. I used to preach for him and usually read the lessons. When we brought one of our visitors with us, he used to introduce them to the congregation with a natural and overflowing affection which bubbled from him, whether he was praying, preaching or just being himself. When *Common Sense about Religion* was published I dedicated it to him and to his congregation. He died, while still young, in 1968.

One of the most encouraging facts which emerged during this period was the growing involvement of Roman Catholic scholars in the revision of the traditional Christian attitude to Judaism. In 1945 it was possible for an English Roman Catholic scholar to write a pamphlet on *The Pope and the Jews* which was full of the grossest mis-statements, and made the wildest claims for the Vatican and Catholic clergy, and for such a pamphlet to be issued under the imprint of that great movement *The Sword of the Spirit*, and to be circulated and defended by the Council of Christians and Jews. I have just been looking through the appropriate file. Charles Singer and I threatened to resign from the Council. I reviewed it in scathing terms in the *Jewish Chronicle*, on which Charles indignantly commented that the review had the merit of being short, but would have been improved by being reduced to vanishing point as such an outrage should be given no publicity. My correspondence to establish the truth or falsehood of his statements involved the Wiener Library, and letters to France, Germany and the States, not to mention various persons who were wrongly quoted in the pamphlet.

As late as 1961 an Irish Roman Catholic priest could find a publisher to print, and a distinguished Catholic scholar to

8*

introduce, another outrageous work in which Jews are made subtly responsible for the whole history of antisemitism. However, that work provided a good example of good growing out of evil. It brought us into contact with the Order of Our Lady of Sion. The story of the Order is interesting. Early in the 19th century two Alsatian Jews, the brothers Ratisbonne, underwent an experience which led to their genuine conversion to Catholicism. They were an early example of Jewish converts who retained affection and respect for their Judaism, and they founded two Orders of Sion, one for men and one for women, which should have a special concern for helping Catholics to understand Jewry, while they were not to seek proselytes.

The *Pères de Sion* had, with one exception, come to be a general diocesan factotum, but the Sisters, together with their world-wide educational work for girls, were developing their responsibility towards Jewry and Judaism. The one *Père de Sion* who was seeking to maintain the special function of the Order was Father Paul Demann, who edited an extremely valuable, but rather irregularly appearing, periodical, *Les Cahiers Sioniens*. He had been to Barley, and I had met him in Paris. Now there were added to our friends Mother Edmund and Sister-Louis Gabriel, as well as other Sisters of our Lady of Sion. Mother Edmund was at that time either at their House at Worthing, or else at Holloway. Sister Louis Gabriel came to lead their work from 17 Chepstow Villas in West London, where she created a real centre for Biblical and Jewish scholarship. At the time of writing, she is going to a Catholic University in Washington as a professor, and Mother Edmund is Mother Superior of the Convent at Ein Karem, Jerusalem. When first we met Sister Louis Gabriel she was working on a thesis dealing with Jews in the French and German literature of the nineteenth century, and she naturally found much to help her on our shelves. She became a regular visitor, and a regular borrower of books, while I became a lecturer on Palestine and other subjects at convents to which she introduced me.

It is much more difficult for members of a strongly hierarchical Church, which also has strict doctrinal orthodoxies, to face the appalling challenge set by the basic Christian responsibility for turning a normal 'dislike of the like for the unlike'

into the abominable sin of antisemitism. But in the last decade
the changes that have been made are enormous and encouraging. At the centre is undoubtedly that remarkable personage,
John XXIII—(As a scholar I am puzzled how historians will
cope with him. Will he be John XXIII the second, since John
XXIII the first legitimately summoned a church council before
he was expelled from his office for crimes in which Gibbon
delights?)—but the Order of Our Lady of Sion has had an
honourable place in the change. Tribute must also be paid to
the Dominican Order in England which initiated a Catholic-
Jewish conference which has now become an annual event,
bringing in other Christians and held under the auspices of
the Council of Christians and Jews. Through Mother Paul
Baring of the Convent of the Assumption, Hengrave Hall, we
added yet another Catholic educational order to our contacts.
Mother Paul was an enthusiastic pilgrim to Israel and the
Middle East, a subject on which she has become no mean
expert.

Today it would be unthinkable to plan any Jewish-Christian
encounter in which one did not expect full Catholic co-operation.

This does not mean that there are not still difficulties before
them. I know from my own experience how deeply a contemp-
tuous and hostile attitude to post-Christian Judaism has eaten
into our Christian consciousness, and we are capable of inno-
cently making remarks which are actually deeply offensive to
our patient Jewish friends. It is only a few of us who have
reached the stage where we ourselves produce an inner warning light against such calamities. Roman Catholic scholars,
men such as Cardinal Bea or Father Flannery, may still drop
bricks. The change is that nobody, Jew or Christian, doubts
their integrity and the sincerity of their determination to write
a new page in the relations of the two religions.

At the beginning of the sixties I was increasingly concerned
with the change in Israeli demography created by the flight
of large numbers of Jews from the Arab world. Internally it
set the Israeli, with their strong east-European tradition, a
considerable social and educational problem; but in the presentation of Israel both to the world at large and to the Middle

East in particular, the dwindling presence of Europe seemed to me a factor of immense importance, and one on which a new and positive relationship with the Arab world might be created. For if more than half the Jews in Israel were in their family background and tradition even more deeply rooted in the countries of the Middle East and North Africa than the Arabs themselves—who only erupted from the peninsula in the seventh Christian century—it was increasingly absurd to maintain that Israel was a totally inacceptable foreign intrusion.

When Kenneth Lindsay, of the Anglo-Israel Association, asked me to give them a lecture in the autumn of 1963, I chose as my title *The Continuity of Jewish Life in the Middle East.* Six months later I was asked to give the Brodetsky Memorial Lecture at Leeds University, and developed the subject still more fully in *The New Face of Israel.* It is one of my great regrets that the Israeli government will never make use—not of 'this argument' but of this basic fact—in its presentation of the case for Israel on every possible international occasion, and especially in the United Nations.

The beginning of the sixties also added a new—and very acceptable—reason for scholars to visit Barley. Some came, not to consult my books and archives, but to learn more about what I had myself written on the Jewish-Christian relationship. In 1962 Malcolm L. Diamond, at present Professor of Religion at Princeton, spent the summer staying in a nearby village with his family so that he might go through all our files, pamphlets and books, and draw a coherent picture of the development of my thought over thirty years. This is to be part of a larger work covering the whole field, but a preliminary study entitled *James Parkes: Honesty in the Jewish-Christian Interchange* was published by Roy Eckardt in the April 1965 number of the quarterly he edits: *The Journal of Bible and Religion,* a number entirely devoted to the scholars involved in this particular encounter.

The following year Roy Eckardt himself, Professor at Lehigh University, Pennsylvania, spent a still longer period at Barley. He and his family lived in Cambridge where the two children could go to school, and both Roy and Alice spent most of their time, Roy delving in our archives, Alice helping Dorothy in a number of ways. His visit produced its result in 1968 in a long section in his book *Elder and Younger Brothers*. Nor was it only from America that we received visitors. Peter Schneider, once of Cambridge and at that time adviser on Israeli affairs to the archbishop in Jerusalem, used the library extensively, both to work on my own writings and to obtain material for his book on Judaism in the 'Christian Presence' series of the Student Movement Press. *Sweeter than Honey* appeared in 1967.

To complete the picture of our activities in what was to be our last whole summer in Barley, I cannot do better than quote a paragraph from our Christmas Letter of 1963. We wrote:

"While we are drafting this letter, we have one scholar— from America—working in the Hall on material from our periodicals; another in the Garden House—from Jerusalem —writing a book on the present confrontation between Judaism and Christianity; a third—from Germany—in the South Room preparing for publication by Gollancz her wonderful broadcasts on her life before, through, and after the Nazi period. A fourth is occupying a corner of my work-room checking rabbinic references to a German work which he is translating for an English publisher. Dorothy is correcting the galley proofs of two publications due to appear this winter. And I am busy on my next book! We are also busy making preparations to spend March in Israel studying the new situation caused by the unexpected fact that it has become statistically a middle-eastern country. You will see I refer to *the Hall* and the *Garden House*. The Hall is the big Club house next door which was idle and which we lease. We have all our periodicals there as well as three offices. The Garden House is the old granary which we restored in 1961 with sitting room, bedroom and utility room."

The occupant of the South Room was Else Rosenfeld. As we learned more of her life under the Nazis, and how she, a 'non-Aryan' Christian, had deliberately identified herself with the Jews, and donned the yellow star (which actual star is now one of the Library's treasures), we felt that she had a story to tell if we could find the right way to tell it. Her married daughter lived in Birmingham, centre for Midland Broadcasting, where we knew that producing genius, Charles Parker. We told Charles to look Else up. He did so, and was so entranced by her story and her way of telling it, that he introduced a microphone into the room, almost but not quite without her knowledge. The result was broadcast every evening for a whole month.

So many people wrote in to him asking whether the broadcasts would be published, that Charles sent them to me, saying that I knew more about publishers than he did. I sent them to V.G., and received back from him a typical letter which went approximately in these terms: "My dear Jimmy, you know that stories about the Nazi period are as dead as mutton, and have no interest for the public. But I cannot resist the spirit of these broadcasts and will publish them. Bring Dr. Rosenfeld to see me." We wired to Else in Germany, and the wire itself caused a ripple of excitement in Icking. For it was not only that Else's experience was to be published in England, but also that V.G.—Victor Gollancz—a name revered throughout the country for the stand he had made immediately after the war for the feeding of Germans, was to be their publisher.

We saw V.G. who explained that the one essential was that we doubled the length of the material, since it was quite uneconomic to produce as short a book as the broadcasts would be by themselves. Else came to Barley to produce the additional material—of which there was no lack in her amazing life. Alice Eckardt became assistant producer, and I was editor, for Else broadcasting, and Else carefully writing out or dictating her experiences to Alice, had two quite different styles.

The *Four Lives of Elsbeth Rosenfeld* justified V.G.'s flair, and the edition sold out. Few who read it were unmoved by her experience with its courage, its tragedy and its triumphant conclusion. In 1966 we were able to visit her in her charming cottage in Icking, and every year she still spends some time with us while she is visiting England and her growing family. It is one of life's perfect evenings after the storms of the day.

In the autumn of 1963 John McNeilage told us that he would not be able to carry on much longer. This did no more than bring to the surface a conviction which had been growing in my own mind that we ought to be planning for the future of the Parkes Library, and for ourselves to retire while our own contribution was still 'in full sail'. As I have said earlier, Barley was a tripod with three equal legs, and the removal of any of the three legs would be bound to be definitive. For it would be impossible to replace, when the other two would also need to be replaced within, at most, a couple of years.

It was very difficult to decide what to do. It depended largely on whether one should consider the material which I had collected to be a permanent reference library, or to be tools of permanent research. A reference library would be best situated in London; research, in my strong opinion, was best conducted outside London. Our first thought, of course, was that both positions would be satisfied if it were possible for the Library to be associated in some way with Cambridge University. But this, on the advice of Professor Butterfield, Master of Peterhouse, we had to reject as impossible.

We went through a very difficult period, because I.M.S. started negotiations with Sir Ifor Evans, who was a close friend of his, for the library to be accepted by University College, London, of which Sir Ifor was Provost. I was not party to the negotiations, but late in 1963 he told Dorothy that all was arranged, and that I had only to settle the details of the transfer with Sir Ifor. I went to see him, and discovered to my horror that it was to be the complete termination of the *work*, and that the books, I suppose with such of the archives as they found interesting, would be in a locked room with my name on the door, to be used for reference by any graduate who was concerned with the subject. I had not previously clearly distinguished in my own mind the two quite contrasting possibilities, and University College had a long tradition of association with Anglo-Jewry, and indeed with members of my own family. For of two distinguished cousins of a previous generation, one had been Professor of Clinical Medicine, and the other had deposited all his papers with the college, so that the name 'Parkes' was already on a door.

The insistence of Sir Ifor that the College could accept no responsibility for any continuation of the work made me feel that I could not risk the continuation of a situation where I.M.S., genuine as was our affection for him, could settle the future of the Library without my knowing what was being arranged. It was a grief to both of us that I felt obliged to ask him to resign the chairmanship he had assumed when first the institution was established, and it was a great happiness to us that we could forget the past and renew our previous relations before we actually left Barley.

Meanwhile I was determined to put the whole library into packing cases, and to retire, if no satisfactory solution could be found. We had already decided that our retirement would have to be to the south of England, since our beloved Suffolk was proving too bitterly cold for me in winter. With the experience of Barley behind us, we had only two absolutes in our search for a place to retire to: a bishop whom I respected as I did the then Bishop of St. Albans and whose churchmanship I could accept, and a parish priest in whose village I wanted to live.

Just at this moment we were invited to be the guests of Southampton University at its big annual event, the Montefiore Lecture. I had been Montefiore Lecturer in London the previous year, and I thought it was a graceful acknowledgement of that connection which led to us being invited. We would not normally go over a hundred miles to attend a lecture—of which we did not expect to understand one word (an expectation amply fulfilled)—but Southampton was well on the way to the part of England we wanted to retire to. So I easily persuaded Dorothy that we should accept. There was a reception in a long common room for the guests before the lecture. We were at one end of it, but when the Vice-Chancellor appeared at the other end, he exclaimed across the room: "I thought it would be Jimmy," came across to us with his wife and explained that they had both been students at Aberystwyth when I was a secretary of the S.C.M. They even told me the title of a lecture I had given there in 1924. We were staying with Dr. Ellis Tavener, a geographer who was interested in Israel, and who had visited Barley. When he came home and told us the Vice Chancellor would like to see us after breakfast, I thought it was to reminisce on Student Movement days. But when we went into his room, he started straight off with "I hear you are very troubled as to where to place your library. Would you consider Southampton?"

It was an adventure to set such work in the ambience of a modern university which had no particular traditions associated with the subject—except that Claude Montefiore had once been its President when it was still a college, and that it had received a considerable part of his library. But after discussions with our own governors, and with Southampton personalities, a decision was taken, the library was removed together with all the archives which we did not take with us. And it had at once this reward— that the range of books *as books* greatly enriched the university, which would not have been the case in London or Cambridge. The oldest book we gave them was printed in 1475, the oldest pamphlet in 1493. Should they want to give an exhibition of bindings, of book illustrations, or works in some particular language, the Parkes Library was an acquisition to a modern university on all such occasions. Moreover, while University College would have taken, giving nothing in return, Southampton University set aside the funds for a Parkes Research Fellowship in some aspect of the vast field of relations between the Jewish and non-Jewish worlds.

Excited by the unexpected possibility of a solution to our problem, we then spent a few days exploring the diocese of Salisbury—that is, the counties of Wiltshire and Dorset. For we had picked on Joe Fison as our bishop. He was an old friend, and had been a chaplain in Jerusalem during the second war. We then set out to find a parish, and by gradual elimination came to ask Rex Wells, Vicar of Iwerne Minster, if we could call on him. But at the time we proposed he was taking a communion service. We went to it; we greatly liked the way he brought parish problems and personal needs into the service. We met him afterwards, and asked him if he knew of a cottage for sale in his parish. "My churchwarden is trying to sell one," he replied. And it is in that cottage that this book is being written.

XIV

A LIFE ENJOYED: RETIREMENT

IN MID-VICTORIAN TIMES Mr. Glyn, the banker, bought the manor of Iwerne. When he decided to become a Lord he wisely bought another village called Wolverton. For it would be painful to a newly created peer always to be mispronounced, and Iwerne is pronounced approximately Yeurn. The village follows the pleasant Dorset habit of calling itself after a river. The river Iwerne actually rises in Rex Wells' cellar, and flows down Watery Lane through the village. It names two more villages before it flows into the Stour. Its neighbour, the Tarrant, names eight. So to find one Tarrant village from another, just follow the valley. But beware of a Winterbourne! For Winterbourne simply means a stream (bourne) on the chalk that flows visibly only in winter, and there are several such in the chalk hills of Dorset and Wilts. So Winterbourne Stepleton, Winterbourne Abbas, and Winterbourne Bassett have no relations with each other. Iwerne Minster is a pleasant village, nestling under the western heights of Cranborne Chase, a village of cows and pigs and their attendants in the first and second degree, of Clayesmore School—and of retired persons like ourselves.

We bought the cottage in March, 1964, and in August we settled in. In the meantime Beresford Bland, the University Librarian, visited Barley and calculated how he would deal with the problem of removing the books and archives. It took some days to pack the library up, as it took some days for us to demobilise and reassemble ourselves. But I deliberately left all the final clearance to John, so that the memories which Dorothy has of the house are of it in a relatively normal state, with all its beauty of floors, beams and furnishings.

Once the books got on to their shelves in Southampton, I undertook to put them back in the order indicated in our subject catalogue, whence Geoffrey Hampson, the Librarian in charge of 'special collections', could create a simplified order for the purpose of reference and cataloguing. The greater part of our archives we also left at Southampton, for the cottage had not room for more than what we expected to find necessary in what we imagined would be a simpler and more leisured life.

The autumn of 1964 was fortunately very dry, for the garden of the cottage had been desolate for at least five years, and, on top of that, was covered with the muck that the builders who transformed it are accustomed to leave behind them. Garden making has always been one of my pleasures, and here I re-designed it completely, altered its levels and its main axis, and made a garden that should be visually effective from the kitchen when we are washing up, and from the one window which looks over the whole of our vast estate. We are Dorset landowners to the extent of one-fourteenth of an acre, just a convenient size to retire to.

There is a sense in which one whose life has been devoted to scholarship never need retire. He can go on writing and lecturing, even if his capacity for work grows smaller and the range of his activity becomes less. In that sense this need be no concluding chapter, for the last sentence might truthfully be "and in the autumn we hope to go to Canada, and it is quite possible that next year will see us in Jerusalem". We have indeed been much busier since we came to Dorset than we expected. We have been to Israel; I have lectured there and in various conferences in England. At the time of writing we are expecting proofs of a collection of my lectures and articles which Vallentine, Mitchell are publishing under the title *Prelude to Dialogue*. And I hope that my lectures in Israel will be published in Hebrew. They would have appeared already had not the Six Day War centred all interest in current events, and made it an inopportune moment for such a publication.

Since those amazing six days I have been a kind of backroom boy to press, film, and broadcasting, being constantly asked for information and being equally constantly unable to get a platform for what I myself want to say. The star of my 'backroom boyhood' was to be rung up by a great national newspaper during the sacred hour of the siesta of septuagenarians, and asked to explain the psychological significance of living under Islam! In other words, why did I say that Nasser's greatest problem was not Israel, but the appalling difficulty of coping with the fatalism of Islam, a fatalism which married itself so tragically with the Arab tendency to see things in a static black and white.

The press, the B.B.C. and all mass media have insisted throughout in giving first one side of the story, then the other, indifferent to the fact that the general public have no means of knowing or judging between the different statements. "What I myself want to say" is a statement which attempts to be fair to *both* sides. To expect the Arab world to accept the Balfour Declaration is absurd. To expect them to recognise, first that Jews have never been absent from their Holy Land, and have been present in the maximum numbers which could gain any livelihood is reasonable. For Jews to expect Arabs to be indifferent to that kind of Zionism which is always demanding unlimited Jewish immigration is unrealistic; to ask them to see in Jewry an element in world culture akin to Islam, but rooted in Jerusalem rather than Mecca, is not. In the same way it is unreasonable to expect the Jewish world to ignore the fact that it was the Arabs who went to war in 1947 and created the refugee problem. It is easy for those who look at the situation from the Israeli angle to overlook that there is a definite nobility in the willingness of Arab states to espouse a cause, at tremendous cost, in which no personal advantage to themselves is involved, but in which an injustice to a 'fellow Arab' appears intolerable. The existence of Israel has infringed the rights of no single Egyptian citizen, no Algerian, no Iraqi.

At the same time the desire to be fair to both sides is no guarantee of infallibility; but debate by those who were setting out from such a position would contribute far more to the possibility of a peaceful Middle East than the present policy of the press and of broadcasting to put out exclusively one-sided statements which the public cannot weigh.

In January 1968 I tried unsuccessfully to persuade the Council of Christians and Jews to establish an "Autonomous Committee for Peace in the Middle East" on the analogy of the autonomous committee for European Student Relief established by the World's Student Christian Federation. It would be an expensive committee, for it could work best by periodically taking a whole page in the national press to discuss the two sides; but it would be infinitely less expensive than the appalling Vietnam-like situation in the Jordan Valley which confronts the world at the moment of writing less than three months later. The history of warfare has alternated between periods when defence could repel attack, and when attack could overbear defence. In the guerrillas of today we have a new situation. For guerrillas cannot be defeated, and cannot win a military victory. All they can do is increase bitterness and double exhaustion. That is not a situation which will benefit the Arab world. But it will do a great deal more harm to Israel.

The stalemate on the military side has pushed into the background the problem of Jerusalem. If what is ultimately accepted is the protection of 'holy places' I confess not merely to a complete disinterest, but to an active dislike. None of the three religions can really claim that it has shown an attractive face to the world in the way it has gone about to sanctify earth and stones. But Jerusalem as the mother of holy men and women might still do something whose influence would spread beyond the Middle East itself. For the only justification for an 'interreligious' rule of the Old City of Jerusalem is that three religions can spread to the world from it. I would like to see a Moslem 'Regent' from Pakistan, a Jewish Regent from the U.S.A. and a Christian Regent from Europe—all laymen, and agreed between the U.N., Israel, and Jordan.

I do not believe it would be impossible to create a great wave of 'pro-middle-eastern' feeling. For much pro-Arab feeling rests on ignorance of the Jewish case, which inevitably requires more knowledge of the special facts than that of the Arabs. But it is not the fault of Jewry that its situation and its claims are so often difficult to understand. It is the fault of two millennia of a history which was not its choice, but which was imposed on it from outside. The same is true of the contemporary attempt to remake relations between Jews and Christians in terms of a dialogue between equals. And there one inevitable development is a great cause of sadness to me. With the ecumenical background coming to be universally taken

for granted in one's relations with other Churches, it has become acceptable that we can with courteous frankness express
our disagreement or regret at this or that quality of another
Church. We can say that its understanding or expression of
this or that element in the traditional faith seems to us inadequate or even distorted. Now it is inevitable that, with my conviction of the equality and indispensability of Judaism, I
should involve myself in a similar approach to the different
forms in which contemporary Jews express their religious
convictions. But Jews are not accustomed to such comments or
criticisms coming from outside, particularly coming from a
Christian source. On the whole the progressive synagogues
have come to accept my comments, but for the traditionalists,
caught like the continental Protestants in a rigid neo-ortho-
doxy, it is intolerable, or at least impertinent, that a Christian
should publicly criticise their practices or beliefs.

I mention the subject, because it will not be confined to my
personal idiosyncracies. It is inherent in the situation. A Christian who is a fundamentalist in relation to the New Testament
is not going to accept that Judaism is to be treated as an equal,
and that its survival of the coming of Christianity was right,
proper, and inevitable if it was to fulfil the purpose of God.
For such teaching is clean contrary to the reiterated statements
of Paul and other New Testament writers. Dialogue is, therefore a function of a more liberal attitude, whether among
Catholics, Anglicans or others. But it is, likewise, impossible
to be a liberal in relation to the New Testament and a fundamentalist in regard to the Old. One is therefore unable to
accept the premises on which the Jewish Neo-orthodox feel
themselves obliged to insist, and that makes real 'dialogue'
with them difficult. The Christian needs to be most humbly
sensitive about this. And yet it is very necessary, because the
traditional insistence that Judaism is a religion, not of general
principles, but of concrete situations and prescribed actions
in such concrete situations, is a most valuable corrective to the
general tendency of the religious to think that fine generalisations, eloquently expressed, are what the world needs of religion.

Some would say "Wait until the traditionalists are ready",
and it is true that after nearly two millennia of abuse, and its

appalling consequences, Jews are entitled to every courtesy.
If the purpose of dialogue was simply to increase goodwill,
then one might agree that one should wait. But there are two
arguments against it. The first is that Judaism has a contribution to make, which Christianity cannot make, to the world's
desperate need. For it is not personal relations which are the
world's most insoluble problem, but the complete failure of
man as social being to revise his conception of the relations
between states. Our national attitudes to each other would be
perfectly familiar to William the Conqueror, but our weapons
to express that attitude are rather more dangerous.

There is, however, another point which affects traditiona-
list Jews particularly, because of their isolation even within
the Jewish people. Being ordinary human beings, they are
influenced by awareness of the opinions of other people. They
react to approval as naturally as they resist condemnation. It
is good for them to know that non-Jews are full of respect for
some Jewish quality, that they desire to understand its reasons
and also to share its benefits.

When I.M.S. asked me how long I thought it would take to
tackle antisemitism, I replied "three hundred years". So I have
no reason to be surprised or impatient at the lack of Christian
response to my thesis that our whole attitude to Judaism needs
a radical reappraisal. It is, in fact, encouraging that there is a
general switch from the negative study of antisemitism to the
positive examination of the methods and means of dialogue,
from the condemnation of fascism to the positive study of
the psycho-pathology of politics. At the same time, so far as
dialogue is concerned, it needs a general change from the still
basically Barthian theology of today, in the form both of its
acceptance and its rejection, before a really satisfying ground-
work exists. For in the 'death of God' theology now emerging
in the United States, it is, of course, the Barthian godling who
has died. But the funeral orations still divert too much attention.

Nor is a new approach to Judaism helped by the present
veneration of Bonhoeffer. For it is not the genuine and profound Lutheran piety of Bonhoeffer which has caught the
imagination of the Anglo-saxon world, but a set of rather silly
clichés, of which the chief and silliest is that man is now adult

and needs no longer to depend on a god. It is difficult to realise how completely the Barthian deity must have been divorced from any responsibility for his creation before Bonhoeffer, in the midst of the horrors of Nazism and the massacre in cold blood of whole populations, could have associated the conception of man being adult with anything in his experience of life. Nor, while one tenth of the British population has at least some experience of mental illness, and while we hover on the brink of war and world starvation, can we possibly accept, a generation after his death, the statement that human beings have reached their full stature.

The absurdity of calling man as he is at present 'adult' by any standards has been accentuated while I am writing this in 1968 by the revolt among the students and the young which marks the capture of the first real peak in the mountain chain which separates one civilisation from another. Drug-taking, hippies, flower children, all emphasise the rejection of a world whose vista stretched before the young in mountain ranges of ever increasing and intolerable dehumanisation, a dehumanisation made terrifying or romantic in the prevailing science fiction. And the men in power have shown singularly little understanding of what the revolt is all about. Coming from the generation which witnessed the great divide between pre-1914 satisfaction and the worth-while but lost battle of the inter-war years, my sympathies are all with the young. The future this civilisation offers them is intolerable by any aesthetic, psychological or moral standard. My one regret is that there is no longer the academic world of the Student Christian Movement and International Student Service which I have described in earlier chapters. T. and Zoë would have understood the challenge and would have had behind them men like Temple and a hundred others in the universities and churches.

Of course there is confusion and lack of clarity; of course it is easy to trip the youngsters up—even with the best intentions; of course there is foolish and impatient violence. But that is inevitable when it is a complex totality of environment which they are rejecting, and when their experience actually touches only its fringes. It is probably also inevitable that the first reactions of those who have any measure of power and responsibility is to 'close the ranks', adopt measures for the support of 'authority' and so on. The success of de Gaulle in France, or the victories in national and local elections of the Conservative Party in Britain, show the trend in the summer of 1968. We may well see a world-wide wave of apparent 'conservative success' coupled with religious appeals to 'model our lives on Jesus'.

The attempt of the 'new Christians' to build a '*Jesus*-centricity' into a satisfying religion accentuates rather than diminishes the inadequacy of our previous *Christo*-centricity. It is even less able to bring into the common pool of experience and spiritual dynamic the insights and relevant experience of Judaism in our political and social, or Humanism in our scientific and technological, understanding.

I have in my various Hadhams said most of what I want to say on these themes. But lately my experience of Judaism has become relevant in yet another sphere. Judaism has very little systematized theology, but at least it has kept firmly to the conception of God as responsible Creator of this world in which we live. The Jewish God has singularly little 'otherness' about him. His ways are higher than our ways, not 'other'. The covenant relationship between man and God is basically different in the two religions, and the difference has had a profound effect on their development.

Where this is relevant to me in my present situation is that I am now a septuagenarian, living to some extent among others of my own age, retired like myself to this lovely corner of England. The end of our lives in this world is inevitably not far distant, and the question of survival is one which, however much we fear to speak of it, cannot be far from our thoughts. In fact, like many of my generation who lost friends and relatives in the first world war, it is not just today that the question has begun to interest me. But it is my deepening understanding of the traditional attitudes of Judaism that has come most to my assistance. It is God the Creator, not God 'the wholly other', whose reality overwhelms me with happiness and expectation.

Starting from the allegory in Genesis of God creating man 'in his own image', it is not unseemly to identify two particular characteristics of that image. The first is that the measure of our power is the measure of our responsibility; and the second is that a creator of anything is not satisfied until he sees his creation working to the full extent which he had planned for it. Why need I believe less of God? Why need I shame him with irresponsibility about his creation? Why need I attribute to him incompetence in what I believe he has made—or as perhaps we should put it, 'has caused to evolve'?

Man today is not adult, but we can imagine what a really adult humanity would be, and the vision is exciting. Many millions in this life have had no chance of fulfilling their possibilities even to the extent that I have had—choosing my own career, being able to follow it to retirement, with a wife wholly identified with our common concern. I might well be satisfied with what has already been given me. But those others? Is not God responsible for them, and for bringing them to their fulfilment? But it is not only that. When, after infinite preparation and experiment, the maker of a great machine sees it all complete and perfect, does he then send it to the scrap heap? It is then that the joy of creation is realised; for he sees it working harmoniously in all its parts. Why believe less of God as Creator? Surely the whole millennia upon millennia of evolution will then, in spite of all the suffering and frustration of its growth, reveal a beauty of perfection which will repay not God alone but every being which he has created. And for that eternity will not be too much.

INDEX

256 INDEX

Sand castles, 67
Sandmel, Prof., 200
Sargant, Tom, 182
Sark, 13, 215 f.
Schairer, Dr. R., 94
Schmal, F., 77
Schnaebeli, Dr., 109
Schneider, Rev. Peter, 237
Selbie, Dr., 65
Sharpe, Archdeacon, 76
Shaw, Sir John, 193
Shertok, Moshe, 195
Sieff, Israel (Lord Sieff), see I.M.S.
Sieff, Mrs., 173
Simon, Prof. Marcel, 216, 229
Simpson, W. W., 175, 209, 213
Singer, Dr. Charles, 115, 145 ff.,
  223 f., 229, 233
Singer's Prayer Book, 146
Sinkins, Sgt. C., 42
Smith, Dr. Everett, 94
Somerville, Mary, 160, 163
Southampton University, 203, 240
Spies, Nazi, 107
Spiller, W. E., 17
Stapel, Dr. W., 118
Stevens, Col. G., 229
Stiassny's, 193
Storrs, Sir Ronald, 179, 211
Strasbourg, 216 f.
Strathnaver, S.S., 189
Student Christian Movement, 58,
  59, 63, 77, 78, 83, 103, 104, 144,
  248. See Conferences
Student Movement House, 85, 89
Student Movement Press, 156
Student revolt, 248
Students, as guests in my flat, 96 f.;
  Jewish, 105, 115
Suicides, German and Austrian, 73
Surenhuis, W., 200
Sutton, Rev. Dr., 201

Talbot, E. K., 84
Talmon, Prof., 178
Talmud, The, 114, 141
Tatlow, Tissington, 70, 106, 141,
  144, 248
Tavener, Dr. E., 240
Teggart's Wall, 197
Teich, A., 114, 116
Temple, William, 58, 65, 75, 84,
  104, 127 f., 140, 141, 145, 159,
  163, 174, 209 f., 248

Theological Colleges, Lectures at,
  127
Thomas, Thomas, 129 ff., 138
Thurston, Leslie, 211
Tirat Zvi, 196
Toynbee, Arnold, 178
Trinity, Theology of, 84, 104, 223 f.,
  226
Trinity Manor, Jersey, 9
Turner, Col. Borden, 64
Tye, Keith, 174

United States, visits to, 93, 107, 117,
  199, 217 f., 218, 219, 220
University College, London, 239
Urdang, Bertha, 210
Usury, 140 f.

Vazon, 12
Visser t'Hooft, W. A., 104, 165

Wadsworth, Mrs., 172
Walberswick, 216
Waley-Cohen, Sir Robert, 143 f.
Walsh, Rev. Outram, 95
Warburg, Bettina, 86, 92
Waters, Miss, 167
Wauchope, Sir A., 179
Waugh, Evelyn, 65
Weizmann, Ch., 190, 195
Welch, Rev. J., 161
Wells, Rev. R., 241
Westmore, E. G., 208, 221
Wickings, D. See Parkes, Dorothy
Wickings, Mrs., 218, 221
Wiener, Dr. A., 228
Wiener Library, 233
Window-sills, yellow, 13
Wintringham, Tom, 182, 183
Wise, Rabbi Stephen, 177, 199, 201,
  203
Witchcraft, 11 f.
Witton-Davies, Ven. C., 190, 229
Wood-Legh, Dr. K., 206, 233
Woodward, Dr. C., 224
Woolwich, Bp. of, 162
World Jewish Congress, 199
World's Student Christian Federa-
  tion, 77, 101, 111
Wroczynski, Jan, 120

Young, Sir Hubert, 179, 198

Zagarowsky, M., 100 f.
Zander, Walter, 176, 198
Zionism, 150 f., 210, 211
Zoellner, Mr. and Mrs., 166